ML

The Project Manager's Guide to Handling Risk

The Project Manager's Guide to Handling Risk

ALAN WEBB

GOWER

Published by
Gower Publishing Limited
Gower House
Croft Road
Aldershot
Hants GU11 3HR
England

Gower Publishing Company
Suite 420
101 Cherry Street
Burlington, VT 05401–4405 USA

Alan Webb has asserted his right under the Copyright, Designs and Patents Act 1988 to be identified as the author of this work.

British Library Cataloguing in Publication Data

Webb, Alan
   The project manager's guide to handling risk
   1. Risk management 2. Project management
   I. Title
   658.1'55
ISBN 0 566 08571 2

Library of Congress Control Number: 2003109336

Typeset in Stone Serif by LaserScript Ltd, Mitcham, Surrey
Printed and bound in Great Britain by MPG Books Ltd, Bodmin, Cornwall

Contents

List of Examples

List of Figures

List of Tables

Foreword

A definition of insanity: *'doing the same thing over and over and expecting different results'*. This quote from Benjamin Franklin is why risk management is becoming a required process in projects and operations. The statistics of how many projects and operations are completed within the originally estimated time and cost with all required functionality are dismal, to say the least. The last numbers I saw from the Standish Group on software projects put the successful ones at less than 15% of the entire total of software development projects in the world. Various folk have stated time and again that we must start learning from our past actions and anticipating problems before they occur, otherwise we are doomed to continually repeat the past. Risk management is simply a formalized process to accomplish that: learning from our past actions and attempting to anticipate the future.

The *Project Manager's Guide to Handling Risk* brings together the skills, procedures and tools required to successfully accomplish risk management for your project or operation. It is aimed at the person who wants to start actually learning from past actions and attempting to change how things are done. Alan has gathered together much of the available information about risk management best practices in this one book, thereby enabling the novice and the expert to ponder the many and diverse factors that are at work in identifying, assessing and managing risk.

In my own risk management work, I have visited organizations and encountered many projects and operations in which failure seemed imminent and obvious, but no one was willing to acknowledge this reality. One of the best things about this book is that it encourages us to think about, confront and learn from past actions so that we can develop a better appreciation of what the future may hold. I highly recommend this book to my colleagues and to those in all fields of management endeavor who strive to successfully accomplish the goals their work entails. It is both a reference and a very useful guide to increasing those essential 'make a project successful' skills. Anything that helps us better understand the simplicity and the complexity of making projects and operations successful is a treat and should be read.

Dave Hall
Member, INCOSE Risk Management Working Group
Senior Risk Manager
Hall Associates – Upper Marlboro, MD, USA
25 May 2003

Preface

There cannot be many project managers who, at some time or another, have not been faced with an awkward decision that could have severe consequences for his or her project if it turns out to be the wrong one. That simply stated situation is the essence of the risk management problem: how do we make the best decisions when we face an uncertain future and there is the clear prospect that things could all go wrong? The higher you climb the project management tree the more likely it is that decisions like that will come to rest on your shoulders. It certainly came home to me when I was working as an assistant project manager in charge of manufacturing on a multimillion pound, multinational defence project which suddenly ran into a major problem. It was either keep producing or stop work; each could have serious consequences and the project manager said, 'Well Alan, what should we do?' Luckily, this was a problem that was subject to rational analysis and the right decisions were made, but back in the early 1980s, when this situation occurred, rational analysis was not the way in which decisions were necessarily taken and risk analysis was hardly known as a project management technique.

In the intervening twenty years, risk analysis and management has grown in stature and is now recognized as an important asset in the tool-kit of today's project manager. From a collection of assorted mathematical, data-gathering and cataloguing techniques it has grown into a recognizable discipline with a methodology of its own; a small cadre of 'project risk analysts' has emerged to give it professional respectability. Along with the growth in the profession there has, however, been a growth in the awareness of risk in a society that is increasingly less willing to accept that risks are a feature of our existence and that instances of bad luck can and will occur in an uncertain and changing world. This will undoubtedly place greater pressures on project managers, so understanding the nature of risk and how best to handle it is fundamental to survival in the new world in which projects are conducted.

Project management has certainly changed since it became a fashionable process in the mid-1960s in terms of both its application and the techniques that are employed. In the early period, project management was heavily focused on delivering the project in terms of cost, time and performance. If all the conventional techniques of project management had been as effective as some of the early advocates had claimed there would hardly be an instance of project failure today, but the plain fact is that failures and disappointments are still commonplace.

One thing has become very clear: seeing the process of project management as simply being one that concentrates on delivering the project in terms of cost, time and performance is too narrow a view. The external world has a part to play in the whole process and the higher the profile of the project or the more advanced the technology involved, the more significant will be the process of managing the external dimensions. Figure P.1 below shows a new model for the issues that project management must handle successfully. Three new items have been added: first, the technology itself and the opportunities it creates, second, the expectations that are not only the reasons for starting

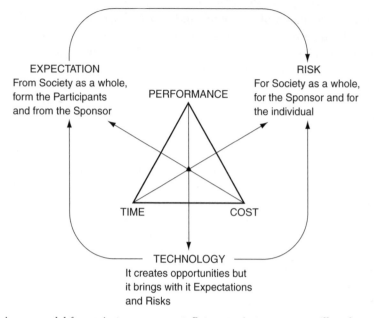

Figure P.1   A new model for project management. Future project managers will no longer be able to think in terms of the inward-looking Time/Cost/Performance triangle but increasingly he or she will have to manage the external dimensions. Advancing technology presents opportunities and projects will be created to exploit them but expectations are raised with each advance, not only from the technology itself but from a general rise in expectations on the part of society as a whole. Each advance in technology is a step into the unknown and brings with it risks that the expectations placed in the project on the part of society, the participants and the sponsor will not be fulfilled.

projects but the rising level of expectation in society as a whole, and third, the risks that exist with all new ventures.

The advance of technology throughout this century has been arguably the greatest factor both for social change on a global scale and the vast improvement in the standard of living for all but the poorest on this earth. Technology in its broadest sense embodies all the mechanisms and systems that have been created to serve mankind and our increasingly sophisticated society is becoming progressively more dependent upon advanced technological products for its very functioning. The 'millennium bug' that prompted visions of chaos at the end of the twentieth century shows just how technologically dependent society has become and how that dependency implies huge risks if the technology fails. The development of genetically modified crops which have been hailed in one section as a technological solution to world hunger is seen in another quarter as a threat to species of all kinds. The rapid and increasing pace of development in some areas, particularly electronics, computers and medicines, has led to increasing levels of expectation about what technology can deliver. In some cases those expectations are likely to be misplaced as all areas have not advanced at the same rate and, in some areas, clear barriers have been encountered. Neither technology, expectations or the risks that accompany them are so simply dealt with, as time, cost and performance and these issues cannot be easily reduced to a computer algorithm. Effective project managers must learn to be aware of all of them and adjust the project strategy to ensure that one or other of these external factors does not bring the whole project down. The new model can be seen as a general statement of the project management problem but, unfortunately, it does not contain the elements of an answer to it.

We can leave the issues of cost, time and performance to the established and often mechanistic techniques of project management, while issues of advancing technology and evolving expectations would fill books in their own right. Risk management is the subject of this book but it should never be forgotten that risk is just a part of the larger model and should always be set in its proper context. The chapters that follow provide a general description of the techniques and principles applied to the various aspects of a project in which issues of risk can make their presence felt. The principal audience for which it is written includes practising project managers, project workers and those interested in or studying project management. It is by no means an exhaustive treatment of this very complex subject, which can affect almost every aspect of a project, and practising risk analysts may feel that some issues have not been covered in perhaps the depth they might have deserved. This is deliberate as most project managers and many project workers are very busy people who do not require extensive in-depth descriptions but do need to understand the basic issues associated with any technique and be guided as to where and how they can be used. The more mathematical aspects are thus dealt with at a relatively elementary level as increased discussion using more complex examples does not always bring greater insight; furthermore much of the mathematical sophistication is now contained in software programs which would be the preferred approach in a real project situation. Issues associated with decision making are given a prominent place in the text as this is an area where risk management has its most direct impact and, from discussions with organizations involved with running projects, is an area where they often feel their performance is not as good as it should be.

The principles of risk analysis and management are now being adopted on many projects, either through the instigation of the project organization or through the insistence of the sponsor. This process will raise general awareness of what proper risk management can do but it can also create confusion and misunderstanding if the techniques are not understood and properly applied. It is my hope that this book will provide an insight into the more important aspects so that project managers need not fear risk but learn to handle it in a way that delivers most, if not all, that is expected from their projects.

Alan Webb
Horsham, May 2003

1 *Introduction*

Ask anyone in the street if they understand what risk is and the answer will be that risk is something he or she understands very well. If you ask them to define it the sort of answer you will get is that a risk is the chance that whatever you are doing could all go wrong, and no one has any doubt what that implies. Unless you happen to be a thrill-seeker, risk has a distinctly negative aspect that perhaps we would rather not think about. As friends are apt to say when we dismally contemplate some unpleasant prospect, 'Cheer up, it might never happen!' 'But', you might say, 'if I risk some money on the horses, it might all go right and I really could have a reason to be cheerful.' That is true as well, so perhaps we might feel more kindly disposed towards risks if we can see a bright side. Then, you might counter, 'But wouldn't life be even better if we had no risks at all?' That, unfortunately, is a matter of opinion and something that could be discussed forever without reaching a conclusion, except to say that most people, at some time in their lives, are forced to accept a risk they would rather not be exposed to.

Like it or not, risks surround us in our daily lives. In general, we accept these risks as part of life; we may choose to act in a way that minimizes some of them, particularly those we can clearly see, but for the majority we forget about them and get on with living. It would be a very restricted and unrewarding existence if we chose to assess all the risks that we encounter and sought to minimize them all.

Businesses face risks in the same way that we as individuals face them in that risks are accepted as a part of normal trading; to try to eliminate them all would be impractical and ultimately result in the demise of the organization. Risks cannot be avoided for the world is in a state of constant change; to survive, businesses must adapt to the changing world around them. There must always be a chance for every business that by choosing to make an adaptive change to something that is outside its control, that choice might turn out to be the wrong one.

The creation of a project is a visible expression of the desire for change; it is a response to a perceived need for something new and it creates an opportunity to be exploited. But meeting the challenge does not assure success; the need may disappear, unforeseen problems may dog the project or the opportunity may go to a competitor. A profitable outcome is the reward for taking risks in an uncertain world; it is not guaranteed and it may be negative. As businesses exist to make a satisfactory return for their investors, minimizing the risks to a satisfactory return must always be a business objective.

A project is a response to a stimulus to create something where nothing existed before. Some projects have little in them that is new; they may involve something that is well known and understood, only the unique nature of the undertaking makes it into a project. At the other extreme, a project may be an attempt to create something that has never been done before. The differences in the levels of uncertainty between the two extremes will be obvious and we all understand that the more uncertainty there is in the project the greater the chance it might all turn out badly. It is also true to say that with projects that are largely based on proven experience, the techniques soon become well known and the effect of competition drives down the profit potential. Risks and profits go hand in hand in a business situation and if we look for a risk-free world we are likely to be disappointed; either we are going to do nothing or ultimately we will become a sheltered servant to some more progressive organization. The potential for profit and the associated risk of failure with projects of all sizes has become the object of serious study over the last two decades. Industry has demanded it as both the pace of technological change and the associated costs have accelerated and it finds expression in the subject of 'project risk analysis and management'.

The history of major projects over the last half century is one of very mixed fortunes: there have been some significant successes such as the Jaguar and Tornado collaborative fighter-bomber projects and the Apollo moon shots, but there seem to have been an equal if not much greater number of projects that have either failed completely, for example the Nimrod AEW 3, or ended with an unsatisfactory outcome such as the Channel Tunnel. Even Concorde, which succeeded magnificently on the technical and national prestige fronts, was a failure in terms of sales. Some of these failures undoubtedly stemmed from inherent risks that were either not recognized at the outset or not managed properly during the course of the project. That is not to imply that in all cases the physical outcome would have been significantly different if the risks had been better managed, but some projects might never have been started while others would have progressed in an environment of more realistic expectations. Expectations matter; they embody what we hope to achieve from the project and are fundamental to the case for starting and continuing with it. But expectations can spread much further afield than those who are directly involved in it for all of society has a stake, even if it is a very small one, in the outcome of every project. Risks stem directly from the prospect that ours and society's expectations of the project will not be fulfilled. If we cannot say with certainty that all we expect from the project will be achieved then we have a risk situation. Whether those expectations are reasonable is another matter but where projects have failed, a clash of expectations or unrealistic expectations have often been at the root of the failure.

It would be easy to continue with a discussion of the reasons for project failure but this book is not about that; the process of risk analysis and management is all about project success. By a series of logical steps and some special techniques risks can be identified and managed in a way that should not allow them to harm the project to a significant degree if they should materialize. That does not imply that the process will create a generally risk-free project or that issues will not arise at any point that can seriously threaten it. Risks are placed firmly in the future and once a risk has materialized it is history; unfortunately, perfect knowledge of the future is something we might wish for but can never have. Nevertheless, a proper process of risk analysis and management throughout the life of the project can significantly influence its chances of success.

The subject of risk is perhaps the most difficult of all in the field of project management as it deals with those two most intangible of elements: the future and uncertainty. Furthermore, risk contains an emotional aspect which can never really be divorced from both our perception of it and the way in which we deal with it. We now have some of the most sophisticated methods for recognizing and handling risk and it has perhaps come to influence our business and our daily lives to a greater extent than ever before. It has not always been like that; our understanding of the concept of risk has evolved over 3000 years of human history; the way in which we view it today is quite different from our forefathers.

Developments in mathematics in the last 500 years have shaped our view of uncertainty as well as handing us some tools to make sense of it when we are forced to confront the risks in an uncertain world. The whole process of risk analysis is underpinned by these mathematical and logical techniques but they do need to be fully understood if they are to be used properly. The concepts involved with some of these methods are quite sophisticated but, luckily, they do not involve any particularly advanced mathematics in order to understand them. The very nature of some of the methods does, however, mean that computer systems are needed in order to use them; where the mathematics does get more complex it can be happily left to the software.

The early chapters in this book deal with the development of our understanding of risk and give an explanation of the mathematical techniques for analysing them. The later chapters deal with the process of risk management within the project framework; this order of presentation is quite deliberate as the management process is underpinned by the analytical techniques. Without understanding them and seeing what their inputs and outputs are, it will not be so easy to see how the management of risks uses these tools and where they fit into the overall cycle. Finally, there is a chapter on contemporary project risk analysis software; examples are given of some current products with brief explanations of how a few of them work. Software has become essential for some analytical techniques so anyone wishing to understand the subject as it is actually practised must eventually look at the tools. For some in positions of responsibility on projects, the issue of implementing risk analysis and management techniques will arise and the question of what software to choose will demand an answer. Whereas Chapter 11 'Software for risk analysis and management' is, in no sense, a definitive coverage of this constantly changing subject, it provides an analysis and grouping of the current tools that should act as a guide to any manager who might be required to decide on a software policy.

Projects cover an enormous spread of industrial activity and there are huge differences in scale, character and risks between individual projects. Some processes adopted by project managers, for example Earned Value management, can be described with precision because they are founded on a specific planning or accounting principle; the requirements and methods for implementing them can be set out in a reasonably prescribed manner. The same is not true for risk analysis and management; too much depends on the fundamental nature of the project, its inherent complexity and its aims and objectives for a prescribed implementation process to be appropriate. The reader will find the management processes are described in general terms in a way that should make it appropriate to industrial projects of any kind. Where examples of processes are given, they are inevitably industry specific and some might not find them appropriate to their situation; that has to be accepted and the reader is asked to try to see these examples as typical of a broader and generally applicable process.

We all understand that risks embody the concept of an adverse outcome and risk management might be assumed to deal only with the darker aspects. On the basis of the generally understood meaning of risk this should be the case but there is a current move to widen the meaning of risk analysis and management to include the management of 'opportunities'. Although this is understandable it is dangerous for two reasons. First, it creates a new meaning for the word risk that is different from the generally accepted view and thus has the potential to drive a wedge between the specialists in risk management and the wider community. Second, opportunities are actually quite different in character from risks; the community of risk analysts has spent the last twenty years developing a methodology for dealing with the negative aspects but has spent comparatively little time considering the management of opportunities and very little in the accepted methodology actually deals with it. So, if you really do want to know about creating, handling and exploiting opportunities, studying risk analysis and management is perhaps not the best approach as it could lead to a very distorted view.

The generally understood meaning of risk is taken throughout this text and it deals exclusively with the management of the darker aspects. Some might argue that such an approach is rather negative and does not cover the full spectrum of the tasks that risk analysts actually perform. This is a fair criticism as an important aspect of practical risk management is to recognize, capture and exploit the good luck when it comes along. Unfortunately, this is rather less of a science than risk management as Lady Luck is far too fickle in her attentions. It must, however, be recognized that too much attention to the risks at the expense of seeing the wider view that encompasses potential benefits that might be obtained can certainly lead to missed opportunities. It could even do worse as it could lead to an atmosphere of foreboding in which everything is viewed from the downside, which is clearly something to be avoided.

The book describes the generally used and accepted methods for identifying and analysing risk situations, making decisions under uncertain conditions, creating a management framework for the process and handling risk situations. It does not recommend any particular approach as being superior to others but it provides an explanation and guidance so that people engaged on projects can choose for themselves which aspects of the process are most suitable to their circumstances. For those who are actively engaged in project work it will, hopefully, provide enough information for a basic understanding of the various methods that will lead to actual application and further study. Risk analysis and management is ultimately a practical subject and it is left to the reader to take what is presented and put it into effect for the benefit of the projects in which he or she is engaged, without forgetting the personal benefits that can spring from understanding and knowing how to deal with some of the most difficult issues in the whole of project management.

2 *Origins and History*

Unlike many other aspects of management it is not possible to consider the origins and evolution of risk analysis and management without considering the development of our understanding of risk. Risk, as we have come to use and understand the term, is a comparatively modern development even though risks have existed throughout history. Everyone knows that in all the many activities we undertake in our daily lives there is always the chance that things might go wrong and if they go badly wrong we could be seriously harmed, either physically, in our reputation or our pocket. How we view this state of affairs is conditioned by our belief in our ability to control events when we make decisions about the activities we pursue. We might choose to believe that the events in the future are part of some grand plan in which we are merely players or we may see the future as something over which we can exert a measure of influence through our own direct actions.

In the lap of the gods

There is no doubt that among older civilizations, such as those of ancient Greece and Rome, it was accepted that the future was in the hands of the gods. In these societies, life was much harder than anything we can imagine today, death and injury were much more a part of everyday life and accepted as such; they were certainly not feared in the way that our contemporary society has come to fear them. That does not mean that everyone was inherently brave but if you were destined for an early grave then that was the will of the gods; nevertheless, it was just as well to have the gods on your side. The ancient Romans may not have perceived risk in the way that we do but they knew there was always an element of chance in what the future held and they certainly believed in luck. If one wanted to be a winner in some risky activity like chariot racing then it was necessary to invoke luck by making the appropriate offering to the gods and carrying the right charms and amulets. This was an important part of the pre-race ritual and woe betide any charioteer who did not do it properly: the gods might not be pleased.

Gambling was a highly popular activity in the ancient world and games of chance evolved as an entertainment with the potential for a cash reward. Ancient gamblers knew all about luck and some undoubtedly developed skills at playing some of the games which made them winners in the long term. What they did not understand was our modern concept of 'probability' and the fact that with games such as dice, the probabilities of particular outcomes are fixed. The ancient Egyptians, Greeks and Romans had a popular game called 'astragali', that used a type of die – astragalus – made from a sheep's ankle bone. The die was not a regular cube, like a modern die, so the chances of landing on a narrow or a wide face were different, but the scores attached to the numbers did not reflect this. The game was played by throwing four astragali at a time and computing a score; some combinations were worth more than others but they were not based on their likelihood of occurring. We would find it hard to make sense of this game today but as far as the ancients were concerned it was great fun and proof, if it was necessary, that luck governed everything.

Despite the highly sophisticated geometry and philosophy developed by renowned figures such as Archemides and Aristotle, neither the ancient Greeks nor the Romans developed any concept of probability as we would understand it, for three distinct reasons. First, the lack of a convenient system of numeration and computation made calculation difficult. Second, understanding was considered to be the preserve of the intellect; abstract thought brought enlightenment which in turn discouraged the idea of measurement through experimentation and observation. Finally, order and certainty were the preserve of the gods. In the heavens the ancients saw a familiar pattern of perfect order that repeated faultlessly with the passage of the seasons, it brought them rain and sun that made their crops grow and sustained life; this was something that was in complete contrast to the chaos and uncertainty of their own earthy lives. To attempt to put a degree of certainty where the gods had surely created uncertainty was to defy the gods – and everyone knew where that led.

If gambling was seen as essentially a recreation in which Lady Luck might choose to smile on some and frown on others, there was another group in the ancient world who were beginning to take risks a little more seriously. These were traders whose interest in the future might well involve sums of money greater than individual gambling stakes. Wise men began to see that even if the gods were angry and sent some misfortune their way there were things they could do to lessen the harmful effects that were rather more effective than simply making offerings. The first evidence of an understanding of risk as we would now recognize it came during the Babylonian Empire, established by Hammurabi (1792–50 BC) through a practical application in the area of merchant shipping. Shipwreck was a constant hazard that clearly spelt a significant loss for both the shipowner and the merchant that owned the cargo. The Hammurabi Code contains clauses that allowed a shipowner or merchant to obtain a loan to finance the voyage and the freight; however if the ship was wrecked the loan did not have to be repaid. It was the first form of risk-sharing insurance between financiers and traders.

The Greek and Roman Empires eventually fell (Rome in 476 AD), to be followed by one of the bleakest periods in human history, when the invasion of warrior tribes from central and northern Europe brought about the 'Dark Ages'. Through the medieval period that began around 1000 AD a gradual enlightenment started that finally came to fruition in the Renaissance beginning in Italy in the mid-1300s. Throughout the Middle Ages, scholars had continued to translate the mathematical texts of the ancient world, but by the mid-1400s mathematics had become a subject of serious study, as it clearly showed the potential to solve problems that were increasingly exercising mens' minds in all manner of activities. The practical aspects of an expanding world demanded solutions to problems in navigation, construction and the arts of warfare. But there was another group who also saw an application for mathematics: gamblers. However, it was a Franciscan monk, Luca Paccioli, who first proposed in 1494 the idea of the analysis of probability, in a work called *Summa de arithmetica, geometria et proporcionalita* (All about arithmetic, geometry and proportionality).

The measure of chance

A more analytical approach followed when Geronimo Cardano (1501–76), (also known as Jerome Cardan) wrote *Liber de ludo alaea* (Book on games of chance). Cardano was a philosopher, writing texts on many subjects including religion; he was also an original thinker in the field of mathematics. His book *Ars Magna* (the Great Art) introduced such concepts as complex numbers where his solutions to cubic equations demanded that square roots of negative numbers must exist. He was also a compulsive gambler, perhaps driven to it by the behaviour of his sons, one of whom was beheaded for poisoning his repeatedly unfaithful wife while the other was always in and out of jail. In *Liber de ludo aleae* (Book on games of chance), Cardano considers the problem of the chances of throwing single numbers with a regular die; he was the first person to calculate that the chance of throwing a single number was in fact 1 in 6, and from there to calculate the chances of throwing individual numbers or strings of numbers with a pair of dice.

He must have realized that he was founding a whole new branch of mathematics when he wrote in his autobiography that he considered *Liber de ludo alaea* to be among his greatest works, believing it contained the answers to 'a thousand problems'. However, it was not published in his lifetime; nearly 100 years after his death, in 1663, the book finally reached the wider world by which time others were working along similar lines. Cardano had, with hindsight, made a huge mental leap; prior to this time mathematics had dealt exclusively with issues of certainty, much of the work being concerned with the problems of geometry and the solution of equations. Despite this breakthrough, Cardano never saw how he could use his new knowledge to advantage, concluding with the words 'these facts contribute a great deal to our understanding but hardly anything to practical play.' Remarkably, given the great popularity of gambling in all societies, it was to be 400 years before anyone did consider how 'practical play' could be improved.

Independently of Cardano, two brilliant French mathematicians, Blaise Pascal (1623–52) and Pierre de Fermat (1601–65) started an academic correspondence on the nature of probability in simple, clearly defined cases. How much more their work might have advanced had they known of Cardano's theories we can only speculate but they confirmed his work and laid the foundations for what we now term 'probability theory' which gave the first theoretical insight into the true nature of uncertainty.

Social statistics

When Pascal computed the probabilities of single events in a sequence of similar events he noted that in simple cases they formed a regular pattern. He set these out in a pattern known as 'Pascal's triangle' as shown in Figure 2.1.

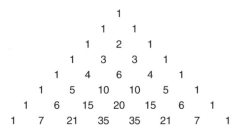

Each number in a row is formed by the sum of the corresponding two numbers in the row above.

Figure 2.1   Pascal's Triangle.

These numbers show the distribution of combinations of two mutually exclusive events, for example: something either happens or it does not, a newborn child is either a boy or a girl. The numbers form the coefficients in the expansion of the equation $(a + b)^n$ where a and b are the two exclusive events, viz.: $(a + b)^0 = 1$, $(a + b)^1 = a + b$, $(a + b)^2 = a^2 + 2ab + b^2$, $(a + b)^3 = a^3 + 3a^2b + 3ab^2 + b^3$, etc. This series means that if we were to consider event a to be the birth of a boy and event b to be the birth of a girl, on the assumption that it is just as likely to have a boy as to have a girl then, in the event of three births, $(a + b)^3$, it is three times more likely that there will be two boys and a girl, $3 \times (a^2b)$, than there will be three boys, a^3. This simple expansion leads directly to the idea of a distribution of possible events. In the particular example given we have the 'binomial distribution' as it consists of just two possibilities. It also shows that in simple cases the distribution can be found by calculation. Examination of the pattern in the triangle also tells us something about the nature of simple distributions: the greatest frequency tends to lie near the centre of the distribution and is a mixture of the two possibilities while the extremes, all of one or all of the other, get less and less likely the larger the number of events.

This was purely theoretical work on an elementary case but what neither Pascal or Fermat knew was that in parallel an Englishman, John Graunt (1620–74) was working on a real distribution. Graunt was a London merchant in buttons, needles and pins but his abiding interest was in the collection of mortality statistics. He gathered data on births and deaths, in particular: who died, how old they were and what they died of. His work was published in 1662 as *Natural and Political Observations upon the Bills of Mortality*. This single small book must have been one of the most revolutionary ever published – in it he introduced the idea of a sample of data that could be used to infer something about an entire population. Furthermore, he showed in tabular form the composition of an aspect of society that had never been seen before, revealing a society that was actually rather different from the common perception of the time. Scientists and philosophers of his time such as Isaac Newton spent much of their time devising laws that would describe the physics of the natural universe as they saw it, but Graunt's work showed that there were also laws that governed the man-made world of 'society' but these laws were different and contained far less certainty.

The importance of Graunt's work was recognized and he was made a member of the newly formed Royal Society in 1662. His remarkable book laid the foundations of modern statistics: the gathering of data, the ordering of data into a recognizable pattern, the use of samples to infer something about a whole which might be too large to measure and the use of historic data to make an inference about what the future may bring. His statistical measures also gave an objective view of a situation; in one simple statement he asserts that a society in which a greater number survive beyond 70 years must, in general, be more healthy than one where the number is lower. Graunt was careful in his title – by including the word 'political' he realized that publication of his data did not simply describe an aspect of society but raised issues about the functioning of that society that had political implications. To take just one point, he debates whether it is a good thing or a bad thing to provide hand-outs to beggars just to keep them off the streets and make life better for all, an issue we are still debating 300 years later! Graunt was the founder of 'social statistics'; something that was to have a growing impact on all aspects of life in the following centuries.

Inferring the future

Graunt's work was known to astronomer Edmund Halley (1656–1742) who also began to take an interest in social statistics as a diversion from his astronomical work. He was aware that Graunt's statistics were incomplete due to the poor state of record keeping at the time, however, Halley was presented by the mathematician Gottfried von Leibniz (1646–1714) with some very comprehensive mortality data for the German town of Breslau for the years 1687 to 1691. Using Graunt's approach he broke down the data, in particular noting ages at death. In doing so he discovered the distribution of life expectancy. His data formed the basis of the 'mortality table' which for the first time allowed a person to calculate his or her chances of surviving to any particular age. The invention of the mortality table led to the prospect of taking a reasoned bet on how long a person might live and what return you might get if they survived longer or died earlier. In his paper published in the Transactions of the Royal Society in 1693, Halley computes the odds of a person surviving for a given number of years from any year in his life and from there the annuity rates for life insurance purposes. Here we see the beginnings of the life insurance industry and the start of 'risk management' as we now know it.

Risk taking has always been the preserve of gamblers and they do it with an aim to make a profit if the future coincides with the bet. The expansion of trade between London and the New World meant there were fortunes to be made exporting and importing goods. But seventeenth-century shipping was a hazardous business, ships could be lost due to navigation errors, bad weather, unseaworthy vessels and pirates. However, there were sufficient merchants of wealth with a gambler's instinct to start a fashion for insuring each other's cargoes as both a sport and a profitable venture. The favourite meeting place was Edward Lloyd's coffee house which he opened by the River Thames in 1687. He moved to larger premises in 1691 and, more importantly, he set up a network of correspondents in each of the major ports on the trade routes to provide intelligence about trading conditions, markets and hazards. This, along with details of shipping movements, he published in *Lloyd's List*, essential information for anyone in the newly created marine insurance business.

Just when the term 'risk' came into use as a term for a specific aspect of endeavour is not clear. Insurers certainly recognized it as that was the business in which they dealt; but learned papers started to appear in the early eighteenth century on the specific matter of risk as a mathematical probability, from persons such as members of the Bernoulli family and Abraham de Moivre (1667–1754) whose work was inspired by the actuarial demands of the growing insurance industry. In 1733 de Moivre made a discovery about the nature of the spread of an effect in a population subject to that effect; he noted that it often followed a regular, bell-shaped pattern centred about the average and he devised a measure of the spread: the standard deviation. From a consideration of the binomial distribution, he devised the curve we now call the Normal Distribution, although his paper describing it was not published until 1924.

With the growth in the availability of statistical data and the growing reliance that was placed on it by both businessmen and academics, it was an English clergyman who was to challenge the view that the future was just a simple extension of the past, even if the past could be measured with precision. Thomas Bayes (1702–1762) was a non-conformist minister whose position was the Presbyterian Chapel in Tunbridge Wells, Kent. He was also an amateur philosopher and mathematician elected to the Royal Society. His great contribution to our understanding of the nature of probability came in a paper entitled 'Essay towards solving a problem in the doctrine of chances'. In it he considered how past knowledge of the behaviour of a system subject to chance might be used to make a prediction of how it will actually behave in a particular instance. It would seem that he never made any use of the theorem that derives from his work in his lifetime, as the essay was found after his death in papers which he bequeathed to his friend Richard Price. Price recognized the significance of the paper and sent it to the Royal Society who published it in 1764. Bayes' essay came to the attention of the great French mathematician Pierre-Simon Laplace (1749–1827) who agreed with Bayes' findings, publishing them in the second edition of *Theorie analytique des probabilities* in 1814. These went unchallenged until English mathematician George Boole (1815–64) questioned the basis of Bayes' ideas in a treatise entitled *An investigation into the Laws of Thought on Which are founded the Mathematical Theories of Logic and Probabilities*, published in 1854. Since then Bayes' Theorem (or Rule) has remained controversial and divided the statistical community. However, Bayes' Theorem laid the foundations for 'predictive statistics' (or 'inferential statistics'); it allows a decision maker to take a view of the past and revise it in a logical way in the light of more recent information. Although popular in the nineteenth century, Bayes' Theorem went out of fashion as a new method gained scientific acceptance in the early twentieth century. Recently, however, it has returned as it fits well with our current approach to making decisions about future actions. For example, it allows predictions to be made based on historic data, (such as, the pattern of sales over the last ten years) combined with the latest information (such as, a recent market survey).

The eighteenth century ends with the work of Laplace on the probability of errors in repeated observations and of Carl Gauss (1777–1855), both of whom made use of the Normal distribution. Both published papers in the early nineteenth century involving its use, hence it is sometimes known as the 'Gaussian distribution' although neither may have known of de Moivre's work of eighty years earlier. The Normal distribution is one of the most important concepts in any understanding of how variations in some effect exist in a population, be it man-made or natural. It describes how random variations affect individuals and thus how an effect spreads at random through a group. It was first noticed when graphs were drawn of the errors in repeated estimates of a given parameter and was originally known as 'the law of errors', it was later realized that the Normal distribution applied to many other randomly scattered phenomena. Its well-known bell-shape is familiar to all who have studied clusters of related data. Although many phenomena do not actually fit the Normal distribution precisely, the approximation is often so close that its use for prediction is entirely justified, hence its supreme place in statistical analysis. The occurrence of a few events at random in a large population is the basis of the risk assessment that insurance companies make; without the Normal distribution they would be unable to calculate the premiums that we take for granted when we insure the house or the car.

In the two hundred years since Paccioli first considered the analysis of chance we can see the development of all of our modern notions of probability, statistical data, sampling, distributions and inference, and we have the mathematical tools to make reasoned calculations about situations in the future which contain significant uncertainty.

Understanding reality

The nineteenth century was to see a revolution in technology and a transformation in society that has never been equalled. With the exceptions of electronic computing, nuclear energy and powered flight, practically all the trappings of modern society evolved in a hundred hectic years. With so much change going on around them it was not surprising that men of intellect, having sorted out the mathematics, turned their attention to the practical matters of measuring that change. With an understanding of probability, statistics and the Normal distribution (which seemed to hold the key to understanding so many natural phenomena), they had the tools to predict how societies would evolve; or they supposed that they did. Belgian statistician Adolphe Quetelet (1796–1874), a founder of the Royal Statistical Society of London, set out to gather statistics on every characteristic of the persons in society. In 1835 he published *A Treatise on Man and the Development of His Faculties* in which he first identified that hero of the modern world – 'the average man'. But Quetelet's 'average man' was the sum of the average of all his characteristics, and some contemporary mathematicians began to question, perhaps for the first time, the veracity of such statistics: who exactly is this 'average man', can anybody find an example of him or is he some kind of monstrosity that does not exist in any form other than in tabulations? To put it in modern terms, does anybody know anyone with 2.4 children? In short, what some began to realize was that whatever we might be able to say with some confidence about a group we can have much less confidence in when we apply it to any individual.

Francis Galton (1822–1911) was, like John Graunt before him, a great collector of data; having started upon a medical career he turned towards mathematics and became fascinated by social statistics of any kind – he even attempted to deduce the distribution of beauty in Britain by assessing the attractiveness of girls he saw in the streets on his travels! His collections of data led to a further development: that statistics gathered about one aspect could be used to show a relationship with another aspect. With this he introduced the idea of correlation, an idea that has many applications in the field of research. However, his gathering of social statistics and the characteristics of people led to the idea of manipulating society through selective breeding and development; he founded the science of eugenics, a subject that has remained controversial ever since. Despite the controversies, the desire for statistics, particularly social statistics, continued and the Normal distribution seemed to describe all the attributes; even if it didn't quite fit then, with suitable selection of the data, the differences could be explained away. A sense of suspicion undoubtedly lay behind Prime Minister Benjamin Disraeli's remark 'There are three kinds of lies: lies, damn lies and statistics.'

The Victorian era was one of materialism on a grand scale: new inventions proliferated, age-old problems such as disease epidemics were being steadily cured and life was improving for all but those at the very bottom of society. Behind much of this lay rational thought, understanding, inventiveness and the entrepreneurial spirit. Against this background mathematicians and statisticians sought greater insights through a belief that the deeper and more rational the understanding, the greater was the certainty with which any proposition could be viewed. But one person, American economist Frank H. Knight (1885–1972), took a different view; he had seen the convulsions through which societies had gone during and after the First World War. The order and certainty of the Victorian era had been replaced by a new world of upheaval and change and it was a world in which one could be certain of very little.

Knight published a seminal work in 1921 entitled *Risk, Uncertainty and Profit* in which he explored these three aspects in terms of both business and society. Risk was a well-understood term in the insurance industry: it was what you took when you wrote an insurance contract and profit was the objective of all business ventures. Using classical probability theory, risks and profits could be mathematically related; even if there was random variation the rules were fixed, so it would all work out in the long run. Uncertainty, however, was a property that was quite different: it was something that lay outside all the equations yet it had an influence on the result. Uncertainty, by its existence, undermines all the old certainties; we can no longer view the past as a reliable guide to the future, in fact it may be completely misleading. In his book he outlined the true nature of risk management, that is, how to make the best decision in the face of an uncertain future.

In *Risk, Uncertainty and Profit*, Knight defined a popularly held view of 'risk' and one which has come to bedevil the subject. In it he sought to distinguish between a situation where there was some objective measure of the variability – 'risk', and a situation where there was no objective knowledge – 'uncertainty'. In this view he was clearly influenced by the insurance industry's use of the term risk to mean a chance that a loss might be incurred. He also noted that the insurance industry only took on 'risks' when they had some objective information on which to base the premium and the degree of cover. However, it is not difficult to reason that where there is random variation, even with a known past, there must also be a degree of uncertainty, thus all risky situations are a subset of all uncertain situations. This semantic use of the word 'risk' has led to a degree of confusion; even though it is a purely artificial distinction this idea has been taught without much consideration in business schools for many years. K.R. MacCrimmon argued that this distinction was untenable on both logical and empirical grounds and concluded from a survey of industrial managers in 1974 that 'Few executives made this risk-uncertainty distinction at any time and none made the distinction in all the situations presented, and, on reflection, very few thought that such a distinction was reasonable.'

Risk had been the subject of study before Knight's book was published. In 1901 A.H. Willet wrote *The Economic Theory of Risk and Insurance* in which he gave a rather more meaningful definition of risk, albeit in the context of insurance, namely, the objectified uncertainty regarding the occurrence of an undesirable event. In this definition he sees that risk is an aspect of uncertainty that is concerned with the undesirability of the outcome if the risk materializes. Opportunities for profit in an uncertain world have no place in this definition of risk. In Willet's view, risks always involve the chance of bad outcome and in this respect he was in tune with the popular usage of the term.

Risk was a term that was increasingly used by economists; it has no particular place in the world of pure mathematics and probability as the theories are indifferent as to whether or not the result of some event is good or bad. Economists such as John Maynard Keynes (1883–1946) writing in the 1930s saw uncertainty as much the biggest problem as the future always contained new situations about which the past was no reliable guide, for example, the stock market crash of 1929, which seemed to come out of the blue, and the depression that followed. Economic history was one of unstable cycles and, if you suddenly found yourself at the bottom of the cycle you were in for trouble. It was Keynes's great idea to propose that cycles of boom and bust created as much misery as they did happiness and the answer was therefore to damp them out. The question was how to do it and the answer he proposed was state intervention. In doing so he started to change the popular view of risk in our personal lives and with it our expectations of the state.

Modern times

With many of the basic mathematical issues associated with probability theory resolved by the early nineteenth century, the practical applications occupied statisticians over the next 130 years. The questions raised by Knight and Keynes prompted one of the twentieth century's most gifted mathematicians, John von Neumann (1903–57), to consider decision making in the case of games of chance. Perhaps he had remembered Cardano's remark of 400 years earlier that his study of games of chance had taught him nothing about how to play the game better. Von Neumann was also prompted by mathematical economist Oskar Morgenstern; their collaboration resulted in one of the most important books of the twentieth century: *The Theory of Games and Economic Behaviour*, published in 1954. In it von Neumann explores the range of outcomes that can arise when two or more players in a game interact with opposed or mixed motives. This is a competitive situation and has parallels to many that can occur in business in a market economy. It leads to the idea of developing a strategy that will bring the best long-term result; that strategy might include cooperating with the opponent rather than tackling him head on. Von Neumann notes an important result for risk management, that a strategy aimed at not losing may generate a better result in the long run than a strategy aimed at winning the maximum. It was the first time anyone had considered this approach. Compared to earlier attempts at devising rules for rational betting in game situations, von Neumann's was a radical breakthrough as he considers a situation in which both players are attempting to find strategies to defeat the other. In doing so he goes to the very heart of uncertainty in any form of competitive situation; uncertainty lies in the intentions of the opponents which, for the most part, we are not privileged to know. Despite this, both von Neumann and Morgenstern were committed to the idea of rational analysis leading to rational decisions; in essence they were harking back to a nineteenth-century view.

Since it was first derived, the term 'game' has come to be used by mathematicians to mean any situation whose outcome is determined by the interaction of opposing parties. It has been used to study many phenomena involving not simply games, as we would commonly use the term, but social and political situations as well. It leads further to a study of how people actually make decisions in uncertain situations; if they are not the optimal decisions how do they rationalize them? Contemporary techniques such as probability trees and decision-making theory all stem from von Neumann's work, yet this was not his greatest achievement. From an early start in pure mathematics he gradually transferred his attention to practical applications, first his work on nuclear bombs through the Second World War and later into development of electronic computing. Von Neumann was well aware that high-speed computing would offer solutions to mathematical problems that were intractable by analytical means due to the enormous effort involved. In simple terms, they could be used not merely to calculate strings of values but they could be used to simulate dynamic situations.

Project management as a distinct activity goes back to a time during the Second World War when engineering managers charged with high-priority projects became frustrated with the inherent slowness created by functionally organized companies that were common at that time. Foremost among them was aeronautical designer Clarence 'Kelly' Johnson (1910–90) who persuaded the Lockheed board to let him set up a dedicated team away from the mainstream organization to develop a new jet fighter. He created the famous 'Skunk Works' and showed how a tightly knit team of high-calibre staff could accomplish a great deal in a short time. With the war over, the Lockheed board saw no reason to continue with that arrangement until more high-priority jet projects came along in the 1950s, when the Skunk Works was reconstituted and has remained in being ever since. The lessons of the Skunk Works were not lost on US Department of Defense civil servants: in the early 1950s they started to demand that defence contractors nominate one individual, who was not a departmental manager, to have overall responsibility for delivering the project to the requirements of the government who, for the most part, were paying for it. This was the 'project manager' and with him came the process of 'project management'.

Project management took on a new significance in the mid-1950s when the advent of high-speed computers for commercial applications meant that new mathematical techniques could be used to calculate the future of projects. This was the era of 'scientific management', when much faith was placed in the newly developed method of critical path analysis. For the first time project managers would be able to see with clarity the path to successful project completion on time and on cost. That was the hope but, from the very beginning, defence civil servants knew that uncertainty in terms of estimating was a fundamental feature of all project plans and they sought to incorporate this feature with the three-estimate method of the PERT (Project Evaluation and Review Technique) system. By using three estimates it was hoped to establish some statistical measure of how likely the project was to end on a given date. In fact, PERT was a failure from the start, as it was attacked on theoretical grounds and the software available was just not up to the job. Despite this problem, critical path methods gained general acceptance and the role of the project manager became more clearly defined. During the 1960s many companies started to adopt project management principles to handle their projects and new contracting practices such as the appointment of 'prime contractors' added to the momentum.

By the late 1960s, belief in the process of project management that had spurred its development in the first 15 years began to subside for a number of reasons. First, project failures and disappointments continued in the same way as before despite the new methods and, second, a societal change had come about. Improvements in almost all areas of life had been fuelled by advancements in technology that had been exploited in a host of projects throughout the 25 years since the end of the Second World War. These projects had met with general public approval but by the end of the 1960s this attitude was beginning to change. Fears over damage to the environment started to raise protests over high-profile public projects such as Concorde, the Trans-Alaska Pipeline and the US Supersonic Transport. The latter project was cancelled; it was the first time in history that a major advancement in technology had been halted by public opinion and more examples were to follow. By the mid-1970s the old optimism had gone. Projects, and the approach to managing them, were now viewed in a completely different light: they were seen as risks, not opportunities. There were risks for the sponsors – they might not get what they wanted at a price they could afford; there were risks for the contractors – they might end up making a loss. Finally, there were risks for project managers – they could, if it went wrong, lose their reputations and their jobs. It was in this environment that 'Risk analysis and management' became a new gospel for project managers and the movement to promote this approach has grown in strength ever since.

Although risks have always existed for both societies and individuals, the perception of risk and our attitude towards it has changed markedly in 3000 years of human development. For much of that time risk was accepted as part of the perils of life; ultimately one's fate was in the hands of the gods. An interest in mathematics and the growth in world trade that followed the Renaissance brought an understanding of the rules of probability and a realization among businessmen that matters in the future were not solely the preserve of God – there were practical things one could do to improve the chances of a good outcome. A belief that controlled observation and rational theories could explain the mysteries of nature governed nineteenth-century thinking but experiences in the twentieth century completely altered that view. Risk came to be seen as something separate from pure mathematics and moved instead into the arena of the economists, who saw risk taking as a rational approach to opportunities that presented themselves in a rapidly changing society. But that change itself was cause for concern, it brought with it the notion of uncertainty; the past, however well measured, might still be no guide to the evolving future and the chances that things might go wrong might be even harder to assess. Social changes have also heightened an awareness of risk in our daily lives: risk is increasingly seen as something to fear or, better still, something to be eliminated. Accident statistics, murder rates and food scares have all prompted people to see dangers all around them that before they might just have taken for granted and accepted as normal. Changes in risk perception have prompted behavioural changes, for example, risk-reducing measures such as driving the children to school rather than letting them walk, blaming others when misfortunes occur resulting in court actions for damages for minor injuries, and demanding that the state play a more active role in reducing risk in our daily lives through such acts as health and safety legislation.

Risk has taken a position in business that has never been so prominent; scandals involving corporate collapses such as that involved in the Enron affair and perceived fiascos such as London's Millennium Dome have shaken public confidence in the management of companies and major projects. Well before this, the proper handling of risks in the management of public companies had been seen as a sufficiently significant issue for the UKs Institute of Chartered Accountants to prepare, under the chairmanship of Nigel Turnbull, a set of guidance notes for the internal control of businesses.[1] The Turnbull Report accepts that the generation of profits in business is the reward for successfully taking risks and thus risks should not be eliminated, but it lays considerable stress on the organization having suitable systems that continuously monitor risks in its business and report the situation to those with decision-making authority. Responsibility for both instituting and maintaining the systems and the decision-making process rests squarely on the shoulders of the Board.

History shows that our notions of risk and our understanding of it have evolved as society has evolved and perceptions have been coloured by the expectations of society about the world in which that society exists. Today our understanding may be greater than ever before and we may have the most sophisticated tools to peer into an uncertain future, but we may also be becoming more fearful of a future that contains more uncertainties than we experienced in the previous fifty years. Risk is an enduring part of life itself, be it personal or business, we cannot remove it as it is inherent in the uncertainty that always exists in the future. It needs to be understood and above all respected, but it should not be feared; to fear risk might lead us into areas of irrationality and there we might find the biggest risks of all, but we may not recognize them until it is too late.[2]

Notes

1 The Institute of Chartered Surveyors (1996) 'Internal Control – Guidance for Directors on the Combined Code', ISBN 1 84152 010 1 (The Turnbull Report).
2 A tragic shooting of some school children took place at a school in Dunblane, Scotland. Following a wave of public hysteria encouraged by certain politicians, a ban on legally held hand-guns was introduced which effectively outlawed the sport of pistol shooting. Illegally held hand-guns, which accounted for 90% of all gun crime, were not affected. The result was the controls that did exist over the possession of hand-guns effectively disappeared. It is now generally recognized by the police that there is no difficulty in obtaining a hand-gun illegally and gun crime is significantly higher than before the ban was introduced.

3 *Understanding the Nature of Risk*

As we have seen in Chapter 2, the term 'risk' has attracted different definitions at various points in history. The basic understanding of a 'risk' being an opportunity for something bad to happen has been well accepted as a feature of our everyday existence and our common parlance, but during this century this broad concept began to take on rather more specific meanings in the context of business activities. A.H. Willet, in 1901, defined risk as 'the objectified uncertainty regarding the occurrence of an undesirable event'. This definition contains four elements:

1) that the risk event is 'objectified' that is, not merely of the mind (subjective) but a *de facto* reality
2) that uncertainty about it exists
3) that it can occur
4) that the result is undesirable.

The significant elements in this definition are the objectified nature and the undesirable outcome. Both these elements were to change in emphasis with later definitions and these changes have lead to much confusion about just what a risk is in business terms. In particular, F.H. Knight used the term 'risk' to define a difference between a situation in which a decision maker is faced with an outcome about which he can have no knowledge, and one in which he possesses some objective information about what the outcome might be. In the former case, the decision maker faces 'uncertainty' whereas in the latter he or she faces a 'risk'. Knight further defined a risk situation as being one in which:

- the problem can be structured,
- the range of outcomes are known, and
- some measure of likelihood can be attached to them.

The essential feature of this definition is the emphasis it places on knowledge about the possible outcomes and, more particularly, the ability to provide some objective measure of both the outcomes and their likelihoods. With hindsight, this can be seen as an impractical definition as it considers objectivity and measurability to be the defining features of risk rather than undesirability of the outcome. Furthermore, it acknowledges that uncertainty about the outcome must exist in any risk situation whilst at the same time attempting to define risk as being something distinct from uncertainty, with the principal distinction being one of measurability. This attempt to draw a distinction between risk and uncertainty has been widely accepted and is still regularly taught even though few people outside of the insurance industry, if asked to define the term risk, would consider measurability in the definition. Risk in common parlance means quite simply the chance that something undesirable can happen.

We all feel comfortable with things or situations that we can describe with a reasonable degree of precision, but the more uncertain things become the less comfortable we also become. This degree of discomfort and the resulting lack of precision can cause real problems for those who are attempting to analyse risks, particularly in their dealings with those who have to take decisions in risk situations. The analytical fraternity have tended to promote a new definition of risk and one that contains the quantitative elements implicit in the earlier Knight definition but disguised in a mathematical formula. The 1994 publication *Introducing RISKMAN Methodology*[1] gives a definition of risk exposure in the equation:

$$Risk\ exposure = impact\ value \times probability\ of\ occurrence$$

RISKMAN goes on to state: 'This theory seems, and indeed is, simplistic in approach but it is completely valid.' However, as risk contains the concept of exposure within itself, it can be argued from this definition that risk itself is the product of an impact and a probability; in other words, in order to define a risk we must have objective descriptions or measures of both quantities. By using the word 'impact' it conveniently side-steps the defining feature of risk in that the impact should be a negative one. The reasons for this seem to lie in a new view of risk in projects which differs somewhat from the popular understanding of risk and is the source of more confusion about the nature of risk.

Objective measurement?

The idea of objective, that is, quantitative, assessment of both impact and probability is implicit in both the Knight definition and the RISKMAN formula but are either really necessary for a risk to exist? The answer of course is 'No'; a risk can exist if we can conceive of it existing. It is the basis of all our irrational fears, some of which we might consider far from irrational and choose to act on them; not making any major decisions on Friday the 13th being just one example. Irrational risks and the preventative steps that one might take to avoid them are the basis of all superstitions, if someone will not make an important decision on Friday the 13th their reason is likely to be 'I don't want to risk it.' So the impact can be imagined as something unspecified that is bad – we don't have to know anybody that actually took a bad decision on Friday the 13th to believe in this superstition; we can simply choose to believe it even though we have no objective information about either the harmful effect or the probability of it occurring.

Superstitions are easy to identify and one can consider them as a luxury, they can be believed in if one wishes to, leading to behaviour such as carrying a lucky charm and providing a degree of comfort that would not otherwise be there in an uncertain world. There are, of course, much more serious situations where superstition clearly has no part but the risk is very real. The fallacy of the quantitative argument based on objective data is clearly demonstrated by the situation that developed when bovine spongiform encephalopathy (BSE) was first discovered in cattle in the mid-1980s in the UK. When first diagnosed it was a complete surprise to vets, but it soon became apparent that it bore a resemblance to sheep scrapie with the resultant inference that a disease endemic to sheep had crossed a species barrier in a way previously unknown. What *was* known was that humans had eaten scrapie-infected sheep for over two hundred years with no known case of it transferring to humans (in a disease similar to Cruetzfeldt-Jakob Disease, CJD) but suddenly it appeared to have evolved into a form that could infect cattle. What no one knew was if humans would still be safe when eating beef from an animal that was sick with the cattle equivalent of scrapie. In this case a risk was perceived at the very outset simply because it appeared that the disease had found a mechanism for transference between mammalian food animals. There were no probability statistics for transference to humans because no one had seen any instance of it, no one knew if a transference was at all possible and, if it could occur, how likely it might be. It was soon discovered that the agent occurred only in the brain and spinal cord of affected cattle. Whereas it was not difficult to conceive what the impact of having the disease on a human would be, the lack of any objective likelihood data did not make the perception of a risk any less real. If anything, the lack of any objective data and the expected long gestation period only added to the growing worries about the disease. The assumption was made that the BSE agent existed in cattle food made with infected sheep offal and the bans on putting sheep offal in cattle rations and putting cattle offal in the human food chain came into effect well before any CJD cases in humans that might be related to eating beef emerged. Thus a risk was both perceived and acted upon without any objective likelihood data or even positive proof of the mechanism; the mere suspicion was sufficient to indicate a risk.

The risk paradox

The BSE example also serves to illustrate another feature of risk that is not necessarily contained within the definition given in Chapter 1: that risk is a matter of perception rather than an absolute fact. In other words, a risk can exist if we can perceive of it existing, that is, if we can conceive of an undesirable outcome and cannot state absolutely that there is no possibility of it occurring. Of course, it could be that a risk might be perceived that on further investigation turns out to have no possibility of occurring; in this case it was a perceived risk but not, in the event, a real risk. In the case of BSE, when the action to ban offal was taken, a perceived risk had to be treated as a real risk even if it was not known with certainty that this was the mechanism for the disease.

Unfortunately, risk is not simply a matter of perception as a real risk can exist even if we cannot perceive it. Our ignorance of the effects of actions taken at the present time on things that may happen in the future is the source of many of the risks we currently face. Whatever mechanism created the high incidence of BSE in cattle – and a number are possible – the undesirable outcome, in the form of BSE-infected cattle, only became apparent after the event. When the mechanism was created, a real risk was introduced but no one saw the opportunity for an undesirable outcome had also been created.

So risk remains something of a paradox in that all risks we can perceive must be treated as real risks, unless we can prove a) that they do not exist, or b) for all practical purposes either the effect is inconsequential or the likelihood is infinitesimal. However, the total of all perceived risks is not necessarily the total of all real risks. Furthermore, if a risk is perceived but does not, in the event, materialize, that does not necessarily mean that it was not a real risk. It might simply mean that the conditions were not right on this occasion for it occur; the source of the risk may have arisen in the first place from uncertainty regarding what conditions are required for the risk to materialize. The paradoxical nature of risk is further compounded by the fact that if a risk is perceived, the less we can say about it with confidence, the greater we might have to assume it is in order to deal with it.

Are risks desirable?

Throughout the foregoing, risk has been described in terms of the undesirable outcome that will arise if the risk materializes. However, some writers have chosen to describe or define risk in projects in a more ambiguous way, stressing only the uncertainty of the outcome without necessarily including the unwelcome aspect, thereby implying that there can also be a benefit contained within the concept of risk. *Introducing RISKMAN Methodology* goes on to state that 'risk exposure can be valued either positively or negatively', positively implying that a benefit could arise. Sadgrove, 1996, endorses this view by stating that 'risk applies to any management decision that could have a good or bad outcome'.[2] Some people have even used the term 'upside risk' to imply a positive return rather than a negative one.

To say that risk can have a positive aspect is misleading, as the following example illustrates. Suppose you are invited to play a game of tossing a coin in which you pay the opponent £1 each time a head is thrown and gain £1 each time a tail appears. In the long run, the result would be likely to be neither a loss nor a gain but in the short term, say seven tosses, you could, if fate is unkind, stand to lose a pound or two. Now suppose the rules are changed to a game in which you gain £1 from your opponent each time a head is thrown and gain £2 when a tail appears; this is a much more favourable situation for you, as now there is no possibility of a loss even though there is uncertainty about what you might win. Would anyone consider themselves in a risk situation if invited to play this game? The answer is clearly 'no', for although there is uncertainty, there is no possibility of a unfavourable outcome; anyone in this situation is bound to come away a winner. When compared to the earlier pay/gain situation, the all-gain situation has no risks for the player as the only possible outcome is a benefit. Thus it is the unwelcome or unfavourable aspect of a situation rather than the uncertainty that creates the risk, remove that element and all that is left is a neutral or beneficial outcome. It is therefore important to understand that **risks stem solely from the possibility of an unwelcome outcome and are not, in themselves, either desirable or beneficial** in a purely rational world. This fact has led to the attractiveness of the 'risk-free' stock-market bond; if you hold it for five years its value will rise in line with the rise in the total value of the stock market at the maturity date, but if the stock market falls you still get your premium back. This is a 'might win, can't lose' situation for the investor; anyone who purchased one in the late 1990s will be glad of the risk-free aspect given the falls in the stock market in the years following 2000.

Taken in its simplest form, the idea that risk only has a negative side might seem an endorsement of a totally risk-averse approach to every situation, yet most of us recognize that there are also gains associated with some risks. However the gain is not a part of the risk but it stems from the act of **taking a risk if a situation arises that has the opportunity for both a loss and a gain.** This implies that placing oneself in a risk situation may be a necessary act in order to give oneself the opportunity for a gain. A good example of this is taking part in games such as the National Lottery. Here the decision maker has a simple choice: does he or she spend some money on buying a ticket in the uncertain knowledge of gaining anything but with the very small chance of winning a very large prize? The risk is that the stake money will be lost, in which case the player is worse off than if he had not bought a ticket. In this case the player has taken a risk in order to create the chance of a large gain; the opportunity for both a loss or a gain is the product of this particular situation, not of the risk *per se*.

The same situation applies to betting on horses at the races, as precisely the same choice is involved, with the added complication of picking a particular horse. However, anyone who has done this may feel there really is no loss involved. Providing the stake is affordable, if the stake money is lost, the added interest and excitement associated with having a bet on a horse and watching it race precisely compensates for being out of pocket. For many who attend horse-races, this is an essential element of the enjoyment; remove it and there would be little point in going. In this case the risk is balanced with a positive *quality* rather than a necessarily positive *quantity*; the stake money need not be looked upon as money at risk but as the price of entertainment with the gains from any winnings as a bonus: a win-win or zero-risk situation if the punter chooses to view it that way. Although it has been stated that risks are not desirable in themselves, risk in its purest sense can be attractive but this is a personal thing; ultimately it tends to come from the positive *quality* aspects and people that find risks desirable are thrill seekers.

In the lottery and betting examples, both the choice and the potential loss are clear-cut; the decision maker has the opportunity to either place himself at risk of losing an amount of money in the hope of a win or he has the option to avoid the risk by not taking part. Given the relative rarity of big winnings on the National Lottery and the fact that a sizeable proportion of the stake money is taken out of the 'pot' to go to good causes, the totally rational decision maker would conclude that the opportunity for losing the stake money is greater than the long-term opportunity for making an overall gain and hence avoid betting. No doubt Dr Samuel Johnson had this in mind when he referred to lotteries as 'a tax on all the fools in Christendom'. Taking a risk in this case is essentially a voluntary process and it can be very profitable as the whole insurance industry is based on the voluntary acceptance of clearly perceived risks as a route to profits. But in many project or business situations the voluntary element may be absent; the option to side-step the decision by simply opting out may not be open. Here a risk situation has been thrust upon the decision maker and whatever decision is made one or more possible outcomes could prove to be unwelcome; there may not even be a gain to be made, it may be a choice between evils.

Perceptions and emphases

In the discussion throughout the rest of this book, we shall confine ourselves to risks as they are perceived in situations familiar to managers of industrial projects but they are not the only people in industry involved in risk situations. Other managers such as those concerned with finance or health and safety also see risks but in their particular context; they may look at risk in a different way and confine the concept of risk to a narrower definition. Current financial theory uses the term risk in a precise way that defines the probabilistic distributions of market returns. The insurance industry also tends to view risk in a precisely defined form as the issues involved can all be reduced to sums of money paid in (premiums) against sums of money paid out (claims or settlements); generally there is some statistical history on which to base the calculation of what premium to charge for a given level of cover.

In the case of the finance director making investment decisions or the insurer calculating premiums, the risks, in the first instance, are to the organizations for which they work: a bad decision could create a loss-making situation. These people are, however, in a position to manage their risk exposure as they always have the option not to make the investment or not to grant insurance cover if they do not feel the risks are justified. Whether or not these turn out to be the right decisions only time will tell. There are other people in the business world who see risks that exist for third parties who are quite separate from the decision makers and these are not people who are necessarily in position to manage the risks to which they are exposed. Health and safety personnel are concerned with the possibility of injury to persons who work on the company's premises or use the company's products. For these people, risk is associated with malfunctions, accidents and the physical harm that can be done due to a physical and functional situation. Such risks, if they materialize in a sufficiently severe way, will ultimately result in financial losses for the person who suffered, the company whose plant or product was involved, or the insurer if insurance cover had been bought.

Yet another group of people view risks as the direct threats that are posed by the actions of individuals; these people are concerned with issues of security. Here a risk is viewed as an opportunity for someone with ill intent to penetrate and harm some aspect of an organization, perhaps to steal its property, wealth or knowledge, to disrupt or destroy its information systems, to threaten its staff or any other way in which an organization can be harmed. If a breach of security is involved, it tends ultimately to have a financial impact.

So the term risk is widely used by various sectors of the business community and each has tended to place a special emphasis on the use of the word 'risk' within their own particular context. The only thing on which they all generally agree is that where a risk is perceived, something unwelcome could happen to someone.

Uncertainty

So far we have considered only the concept of risk and its various interpretations but contained within this is the idea of uncertainty, but what do we mean by this? Uncertainty may be defined as: **a state of incomplete knowledge about some proposition.** If we know all the relevant facts about the behaviour of a system and the system always behaves in exactly the same way we have a situation of certainty, we can always predict its behaviour with absolute confidence. Remove just one aspect of that knowledge and we now have an uncertain situation.

Chance effects can also generate uncertainty, not through lack of knowledge but because of the behaviour of the system. For example, there are six numbers on a regular die and, assuming it is unbiased, each has an equal chance of appearing on top when it is thrown; what cannot be known is what number will actually occur in a single throw. This element of uncertainty in the behaviour of a system with fixed parameters is the basis of games of chance such as roulette or the National Lottery.

Two basic types of uncertainty have been identified. The first type is associated with a situation in which only pure chance plays a part; for example, a person may decide to bet at roulette on a particular number but the number that emerges is a matter of pure chance, quite unaffected by the betting decision. The second type is associated with a situation in which the decision maker's own judgements and actions contribute to the uncertainty. For example, if an investment manager decides to sell large numbers of shares in a company it will predictably lead to a fall in the share price but it might also start a general slide in share prices in a particular sector. The action of selling the shares has set in motion a train of events that are not entirely due to chance but cannot be predicted in advance, as the total market position is made up of a series of individual decisions and reactions by all the market traders.

Further distinctions can be drawn between uncertainty that can be measured in some precise and unbiased way (objective uncertainty) and the uncertainty that exists in the mind without any precise measure (subjective uncertainty). The regular six-sided die is an example of a system that shows objective uncertainty as all the outcomes and their respective probabilities can be stated precisely; the judgement of the individual is not a factor in determining these values. However, few if any issues of uncertainty in business are ever as mechanistic as the throw of a die; for the most part an element of judgement is required about what the outcomes and their likelihoods might be. An element of subjective uncertainty exists in all practical risk analysis; it can never be removed as no two business situations ever repeat in exactly the same form and each new form must contain, even in a small way, a situation that has no previous history on which to base a totally objective assessment.

Hazards

Hazard is another term that has come into use in the context of risk assessment and it is worth considering for it can be used to define a condition that presents a risk but within specific limits. Hazards are **risks to the person (or system), mental or physical, that form a part of life** – they have to be accepted though action can be taken to minimize their effects. The term risk analysis has tended to become synonymous with risks in business situations, if only because the concept was born in the insurance industry; but some safety experts have also used the term to describe the analysis of safety or accident conditions in systems, factories, products, etc. In many cases, people that are placed at risk under these circumstances do so in an involuntary way, most probably because they are not aware that a risk exists. For example, if a person bought a new electrical appliance such as a toaster and, when first switched on, received a severe electric shock, that person would be right to be angry as it would be reasonable not to expect to be placed at personal risk from a new domestic appliance. The chance of receiving an electric shock could be regarded as a hazard, something unwelcome or dangerous we encounter from time to time. We tend to expect safety from the goods we purchase and the conditions under which we work and don't make a conscious decision about the risks involved unless we are specifically warned about them. If particular dangers are known to exist with certain jobs they are commonly referred to as 'hazardous occupations'. There may be a fine distinction between risks in a business sense and hazards that may result from the way the business operates or the products generated, but it is a useful distinction nevertheless. Much of the work of health and safety engineers would be better described as hazard analysis as it tends to identify the opportunity and mechanism for loss, injury or death to third parties involved with a particular system or procedure if that system malfunctions or the procedure is not carried out correctly. One may talk of 'taking a risk' but not of 'taking a hazard' – taking a risk contains within it the idea of looking for a trade-off or making a provision associated with the risk. Hazard analysis looks only at the negative outcomes. The term hazard can be extended to cover risks to objects and systems, usually by stating what the object or system is, for example, 'the pilot's actions were a hazard to the aircraft'.

Opportunity, possibility, probability, likelihood, chance and fate

It is not possible to discuss risks and the management of them without a clear understanding of the terms opportunity, possibility, probability, likelihood, chance and fate. All six terms are frequently used in discussions of risk but each has a specific meaning even though the distinction may be subtle. Unfortunately there has been a lack of precision in their use which has perhaps added to the confusion about the real nature of risk. In this text the meanings that are given to these terms are described below; for the most part they follow accepted dictionary definitions to avoid any misunderstandings over semantics.

Opportunity may be defined as **a combination of circumstances that favour a particular outcome**. This definition contains within it the idea that when certain circumstances arise in a particular combination then one outcome is more likely than any other. It says nothing about the actual likelihood of occurrence of the particular outcome but does imply that the circumstances have to be right for it to happen; opportunities, when they arise, have to be taken in order to reap any potential reward.

Possibility contains the idea of **something that has the potential for turning into a reality**. It bears a relationship to the concept of opportunity but without implying anything about the need for the circumstances to contribute to the reality, even though they may be an important factor. Thus the concept inherent in the word 'possibility' is weaker in the context of risk than the concept inherent in 'opportunity'.

Probability is perhaps the most frequently used of all the words in the context of risk assessment because it has been given a very specific meaning by statisticians. The term probability contains **an implied expectation that something will occur** given sufficient opportunities. The concept of expectation suggests that there is more than a possibility as either a proof or an objectified belief exists that something particular can happen. This idea has been taken up by mathematicians, in particular, the 'proof' aspect indicates something objective that can be measured. In the context of statistics, probability has been given the special meaning of **the ratio of the number of the particular case to the total number of possible cases**. Thus if a phenomenon happens on ten occasions out of fifty, it has an observed probability of occurrence of 0.2 or 20%. One must always remember that statistics deal only with phenomena that are repeatable in a similar way; the ideas of similarity or repeatability are not in themselves contained within the idea of risk. Some risk situations will have aspects of similarity and repeatability and the insurance industry deals in this field. But risks occur just as easily with the new and untried, the difference being that the objective quantification of probability may not be possible.

Likelihood is the noun derived from the adjective 'likely' which means 'may well happen'. Likelihood is the term that indicates **the scale of opportunity for something to happen.** It is similar in meaning to 'probability'; if anything, the idea of a measure is rather stronger in its definition but it has never acquired the strict quantification associated with 'probability' because it has not been used as such by statisticians. Likelihood can thus be used to describe situations where something has the chance of occurring, and we might like to attach some measure to that chance, but without implying that any measure is known. Once we have some objective measure of the chance of occurrence of some event, or choose to assume a value for the purposes of calculation, we can use probability in the special sense it has acquired.

Chance means **the state of being undesigned or unplanned.** It usually refers to some event or to the concept of events occurring in an undesigned way. By removing the idea of a design or a plan, 'chance' contains within it the concept of randomness; events due to chance occur in a totally unpredictable way.

Fate is the last of the terms commonly used in the discussion of risk that will be given special consideration here; it means **that which is destined to happen**. Fate implies there is something in the future over which we can have no control, despite our best efforts.

More terms are used in the general discussion of risk and its management and brief explanations of them are given in Appendix 1.

Project risk management

All of the foregoing has stressed the negative side of risk, the reason being that popular usage of the term has always concentrated on that aspect. When we are told something is risk-free, we do not expect to be harmed or to lose something. The expression 'risk-free' does not, in normal usage, imply that there is any gain or benefit to be had, it simply implies there is no loss involved. By considering risk to only have a negative aspect we have also shown that it has some special properties that help us to understand a situation which contains the potential for loss or harm. In the last few years however, it has become popular to divorce the negative aspect from the term risk as is seen in the RISKMAN definition. Instead, a more ambiguous view is taken that risk is associated with situations that have either positive, negative or both aspects. The recently published standard ISO/IEC Guide 73:2002, 'Risk management – Vocabulary – Guidelines for use in standards', defines risk as a 'combination of the probability of an event and its consequences'.[3] As a note to this definition it states 'the term "risk" is generally used when there is at least the possibility of negative consequences' and adds 'in some situations risk arises from the possibility of deviation from the expected outcome or event'. This is clearly a very weak definition of risk but it could be considered as a good definition of uncertainty. Things are made more confusing by the annex to the standard which gives a definition of terms for safety-related risks; in this case risk is defined as a 'combination of probability of the occurrence of harm and the severity of harm'. This latter definition is perfectly reasonable and fits the popular understanding of the term; in the context of safety-related issues or technological systems in general, the concept of risk having a positive side makes no sense at all.

Why should this confusion over the meaning of a well understood and generally accepted concept have come about? The answer must come from a number of reasons. First, businesses exist to create profits for their owners and projects are undertaken to create some benefit for the parties involved be it sponsor, contractor or user. This is the opposite of a risk but we have no commonly used single word to define this chance of a gain in the future.[4] The opposite of a risk is a 'potential benefit', it is not an 'opportunity', it is not 'luck' nor is it 'fortune'; all three terms are neutral about the outcome as opportunity, luck and fortune could turn out to be good or bad. This lack of a single word to mean precisely the opposite of risk is one reason why, in situations where there are chances for both good and bad outcomes, risk has come to be the term used to describe that uncertainty as we generally wish to ensure that good outcomes are achieved and, more importantly, bad outcomes are avoided. The second point is that situations that have the potential for both good and bad outcomes contain uncertainty, but the term 'uncertainty management' has never been used even though it might be a better description of the process. The reason for this is that the term 'uncertainty management' could too easily be construed as meaning weak, indecisive or uninformed management. There are simply too many negative connotations with a term like uncertainty management. The third reason, perhaps, stems from a view held by some managers that too much emphasis on avoiding the bad outcome might lead to a failure to recognize and exploit the good luck when it arises. They have argued that risk management should include the idea of exploiting what luck or opportunities arise and should not simply be concerned with limiting the negative effects of risks. This is a perfectly reasonable view and one which this author would fully support; the danger comes from altering the definition of risk in order to accommodate this process.

It seems that some managers, and project managers in particular, are creating a danger through an attempt to change a well-understood and widely accepted concept in a way that suits themselves and applies solely to their world. Risks and potential benefits might be seen by some as the opposite sides of the same coin and can thus be treated as one; this, however, is a mistake. How we perceive risks can be quite different from how we perceive potential benefits and our responses to them, both emotional and rational, can also be very different. The danger is that by bringing the two into a single definition that distinction will be lost. It could lead to more confusion about the real nature of risk and open up a communication gap between those managers charged with handling project risk and the wider community, and that represents a big risk for the profession.

Notes

1 Carter, B., Hancock, T., Morin, J.-M. and Robins, N. (1994) *Introducing RISKMAN Methodology*, Oxford: NCC Blackwell Ltd
2 Sadgrove, K. (1996) *The Complete Guide to Business Risk Management*, Aldershot: Gower
3 ISO/IEC Guide 73: 2002, 'Risk management – Vocabulary – Guidelines for use in standards', available from British Standards Institution, 389 Chiswick High Road, London W4 4AL <www.bsi-global.com>
4 The only word this author could find to describe the opposite of risk is the ancient word 'fortunacy' first recorded in the English language in 1580; it means being blessed with good luck. Perhaps because the business and insurance community became preoccupied with avoiding bad luck, risk became the dominant issue and fortunacy was forgotten. The 1966 musical *The Happiest Millionaire* written by Richard and Robert Sherman features the word 'fortuosity' in a song of that title which contains the line 'fortuosity means lucky chances'. This is the precise opposite of risk which can be taken to mean unlucky chances; it is interesting to note that the writers had to coin a new word to describe this concept. Fortuosity does not appear in the Shorter Oxford English dictionary or any other dictionary the author could find.

4 *Risks in Projects*

All projects involve casting the mind forward into the future and devising ways to bring about an end result that we require. The future always contains uncertainties and things about which we can have no knowledge until they occur; some of these uncertainties will include an element of risk. Just how much it is possible to manage these risks and uncertainties in the context of industrial projects must be open to debate. If risk could be managed perfectly then uncertainties would largely be removed, all decisions would be correct and by and large projects would be completed to everyone's satisfaction. Of course, we all know that often it does not happen that way and stories of project disappointments and failures continuously fill the news bulletins.

The concept of managing risks implies the ability to control what risks arise and to decide on which risks are acceptable and which risks can be rejected. It would be nice to think that this could be done but in the real world of industrial projects this may not be possible. The only industry to which this is truly applicable is the insurance business, as insurers are able to decide how much risk they are prepared to take and what the charges will be. If they don't like a risk they can simply refuse to grant cover. They are thus able to balance, on a probabilistic basis, their risk liabilities against their assets and, hopefully, make a profit. Even so, insurers can still get caught as the problems for some syndicates at Lloyd's showed after the great storm of 1987 in Britain. Industrial projects are rather different; they can start in an air of optimism with a well-thought out business case and a clear plan, but during the project unforeseen difficulties can arise and the environment in which the project is being conducted can change to the extent that what was initially a bright prospect now has a decidedly cloudy future. Risks which nobody would have wished for can suddenly materialize, they cannot be rejected or side-stepped, they have to be confronted and dealt with. They can demand that tough decisions are made with less than perfect information. Even if these decisions are right, it can still lead to a level of dissatisfaction and disappointment with some aspect of the project. Sometimes these decisions turn out to be wrong but that may not be seen until much later when the full effects become apparent.

How do risks arise?

Risks stem directly from our inability to accurately perceive how the future will turn out. This might sound like a serious problem and that life would be much better if we could have perfect knowledge of what was going to happen, but that is not the case. For a start, all gambling would disappear; not just gaming, but activities such as gambling on the stock market would cease and with it all speculative investment in industry and commerce. An imperfect knowledge of the future creates the space for that uniquely human quality – hope, and it is a quality that has fuelled all human endeavour.

All projects are started in an atmosphere of hope or expectation that benefits will arise and the costs will not be so great as to eliminate the benefits. Simple though this may seem industrial projects are rarely simple affairs. They are frequently a mix of personal, technological, social and commercial aspects and this mix has the potential to create risks and uncertainties in all areas. It must be said that some projects are inherently more risky than others; anything involving novel technology, grand schemes, environmental impact, social impact and untested markets has considerable inherent risk as each of these areas must contain major uncertainties about what will happen in the course of the project. In fact, any aspect of a project where we do not have perfect knowledge is a source of potential risk.

Risks stem from the nature of the project itself and some projects have more inherent risks than others. They could stem from:

- The *project objectives* may be unrealistic or poorly perceived.
- The *technology employed* may turn out to be a poor choice or be only partially developed.
- The *true nature of the work to be done* may not be recognized until the project is well under way.
- The *project organization* may not be the best for the work being undertaken.
- The *socio-political environment* in which the project is being undertaken could become hostile.
- The *physical environment* in which the project is being performed may contain hazards.
- The *commercial/economic environment* could be under threat from competitors, or the required support might not be available.
- The *market for the output of the project* might be poorly perceived or change its character.
- The *project sponsor* could frustrate the project.
- The *contracting organizations* may lack expertise and capability or may lack the required resources and commitment.
- The *contract conditions* may be unsuitable to the degree of uncertainty in the work.
- The *project manager* may lack the required competence to manage the project.
- The *project staff* may lack key skills and motivation or give poor advice.

Risks in projects stem from every aspect, some of which will be much more easily handled than others. The more of these issues that can be considered as factors in the performance of the project the more risky it is.

What sort of risks are there?

The above list of sources of risks gives a good indication of the types of risks that arise. Risks can, however, be categorized in other ways that perhaps give a better insight into their origins, areas of activity and ways in which the problems will be seen.

FUNDAMENTAL RISKS – THOSE THAT THREATEN THE REASON FOR THE PROJECT

Risks to the objectives

These are the most important of all, they are associated with failure to achieve the basic objectives for which the project was started. Such a failure generally results in a failure of the project overall, it is often signalled by premature ending of the project and a significant loss to the sponsor. The overall objectives need to be held firmly in view at all times, anything that directly threatens them is a serious potential risk and needs to be dealt with. However, it may become apparent during the course of the project that not all the objectives can or should be met, perhaps because some were unrealistic at the outset or circumstances have changed to the extent that the original objectives no longer have the importance they had at the start. In this situation it becomes a question of whether the project is worth pursuing.

Investment risks

These are risks that the project will not produce the required return on the investment; in the case of commercially inspired projects, this will also be one of the fundamental objectives. With some public sector projects, undertaken on behalf of the nation, the investment return in pure financial terms may be absent but the government does not have a bottomless pocket and will still expect value for money spent. The value of the investment and the expected return needs to be kept under constant review. If the payback starts to look unacceptably low or negative, it becomes a question of whether to continue making further investments in something that is unlikely to make a worthwhile return.

RISKS FROM THE INTERNAL ENVIRONMENT – RISKS IN AREAS NORMALLY UNDER THE CONTROL OF THE PROJECT

Technical risks

These stem from the chosen technology not performing as required. They can show themselves in extended development timescales, cost overruns, test failures, redesigns and rework, poor product performance, missed market opportunities and liquidated damages claims. Technical risks can never be eliminated where novel technology is employed but it can be reduced by a proper consideration of the technology and the creation of a technical development programme that addresses the areas of uncertainty in a logical way and deals with them.

Planning risks

These stem from our inability to conceive a plan that can be adhered to and addresses all the pertinent issues. Risks can show themselves in schedule overruns, frequent replanning, budget increases, crisis meetings, 'who shouts loudest wins', people doing their own thing and lack of sponsor confidence. Planning risks are inherent in all projects as they involve looking into an uncertain future and there are always likely to be some surprises. However, planning risks can be reduced by giving proper consideration to all the issues that are likely to arise which result in work that must be done or expenditure that must be made and incorporating them into the plan along with a realistic assessment of the timescales and the level of resources that are likely to be available.

Organizational risks

These stem from the organization that is created to handle the project and how well suited it is to the task it has to perform. Risks can show themselves in lack of project direction, lack of information on progress, uncoordinated activities, contractual disputes, wasted effort, overruns and poor morale. The type of organization that is created can vary greatly from relatively simple structures for small projects to complex arrangements involving many companies where large projects are involved. Choosing the right organization structure to suit the task can be a vital component of project success; it is important that the structure provides a framework in which each element, individual or contractor, receives the direction and information it needs and reports back in an appropriate way; furthermore it must allow each to make a contribution to the project in a way that is appropriate to what is asked of it. The latter point is particularly applicable to the contractual arrangements and there are a number to choose from; it could, at one end, be simple cost-plus-fee working while at the other end of the spectrum it could be a risk-sharing partnership. Each will produce a different type of organization and a different contractual relationship between the sponsor and those doing the work. It is important to choose the right one according to the type of project and the risks and rewards.

Personnel risks

These stem from the people chosen to work on the project, they might not be the most suitable. Risks can show themselves in poor quality of work, poor advice and decision making, squabbles between individuals, lack of personal drive and commitment, lack of cooperation and generally slow progress. There is no doubt that the quality of staff employed on a project can make a huge difference to both the conduct of the project and its outcome. In many cases the personnel employed will be drawn from the ranks of the existing staff rather than recruited specially for the project. Although internal staff may have a great deal of local product knowledge they may also have all the local cultural traits which may not always be helpful, particularly if departmental loyalties and practices are uppermost rather than project loyalties. Some of the problems associated with personnel can be corrected with the appropriate leadership but sometimes that alone is not enough. If the quality of the staff is not good enough then efforts should be made to bring in staff of the right calibre from wherever they can be recruited.

Legal risks

These should be comparatively infrequent but they can arise from falling foul of the law in some way; they should not be confused with contractual disputes. Risks can show themselves in claims and prosecutions. Breaches of statutory requirements regarding working conditions such as the Factories Acts or health and safety laws can result in prosecutions. Furthermore, there is a growing body of legislation covering the design of products and services such as the Disability Discrimination Act which must be complied with. In an increasingly litigious society, more claims can be expected where there are issues of negligence involving some form of loss or injury; this can be expected from all sections of society from employees to bystanders. Finally, there is always the very low but real possibility of deliberately criminal acts usually involving fraud; mostly these are the actions of individuals, but as has been shown in some recent cases in the United States, corporate fraud is possible, and on a grand scale. Legal risks should always be kept at the back of the mind and, if there is any doubt, specialist advice should be obtained.

RISKS FROM THE EXTERNAL ENVIRONMENT – RISKS THAT ARE NOT NORMALLY UNDER THE DIRECT CONTROL OF THE PROJECT

Market risks

These stem from the perceived market for the product or service not behaving in the way that is expected. These risks can show themselves in poor sales figures, unsold stock, price cutting, high advertising expenditure and generally reduced profits. This type of risk only applies to projects which are concerned with the creation of products or services to be sold to the world at large. In many cases the principal activities of the project phase will be completed when the product finally goes into production and general sale. However, with privately funded development projects this is the only way in which the costs of the project can be recouped and a profit generated. This type of entrepreneurial project is among the most risky of all ventures hence understanding the market is vital at every stage from initial project concept to market launch and beyond. Project managers must ensure that the developing product meets the market needs at every stage of the development project. A business-based culture must dominate all decision making, innovation for its own sake should not be allowed, where significantly innovative proposals are put forward they should be thoroughly examined and only proceeded with if the business case is proven. (Radically innovative projects should not necessarily be discouraged but they need to be managed in a different way from the conventional project.)

Sponsor risks

These stem from the acts of the sponsor, who may want the project yet act in a way that frustrates its progress. (In this instance the sponsor is treated as being external to the project, but could also be considered as internal.) Such risks can show themselves in repeated changes of direction, stop-start funding, lack of timely decision making, endless reviews and paralysis by analysis. Sponsors could range from internal people such as a company board member to large external corporate or ministry clients. The fact is that many organizations that sponsor projects for products or systems to meet their requirements sponsor many projects at the same time; these projects may all be at different stages in their lives and make different demands on the sponsoring organization. It is therefore not surprising that conflicts of priorities do arise and that can leave the sponsor in a quandary over where best to apply scarce resources. It can also cause the sponsor to change his view of the project as time goes on; this might help the project or hinder it. Organizations in the position of a contractor should be aware of this aspect of risk and ensure that they establish the right working relationship with the sponsor, including a contractual arrangement that ensures they are fully recompensed for what work they do and that costs associated with delays and changes of direction are fully covered.

Socio-political risks

These stem from the expectations of society, or the part of society, in which the project is performed; they could be hostile and have a political element. These risks can show themselves in protest marches, site occupations, boycotts, newspaper and hate-mail campaigns. There is no doubt that among some sections of the community there is growing resistance to projects of a certain type; these tend to be when the project is perceived as being as damaging to the environment in some way, for example, new roads or airport runways or research projects like those involving genetically modified crops. In some cases the critics can be defeated or won over by reasoned explanation from an early stage of the project's life, but there will be other critics who, through deeply held convictions, are opposed to the project and not susceptible to any arguments. They should be recognized for who they are and their likely methods to frustrate the project anticipated. The effect of a small number of people to hold up a large project should not be underestimated. The forces of law and order might have to be used as a last resort and the media should be fully briefed to avoid adverse publicity which can be damaging. Another form of societal risk is that of crime, usually break-ins and theft; such risks can be dealt with through suitable security arrangements.

Environmental risks

These stem from adverse behaviour of the physical environment. They can show themselves in delays and cost overruns due to bad weather, flooding and earthquakes. These types of risk are specific to certain types of project, most frequently large-scale construction projects and marine projects such as building and positioning oil-drilling rigs. Global warming appears to be a growing phenomena and with it comes the prospect of changed weather patterns which may include more severe conditions. The full extent of this may take decades, if not centuries, to establish; in the meantime insurance against natural disasters and the inclusion of *force majeur* clauses in contracts may be the most obvious courses of action.

RISKS FOR THE INDIVIDUAL – EVERYONE INVOLVED IN THE PROJECT EITHER ON THE INSIDE OR OUT COULD STAND TO GAIN OR LOSE SOMETHING

Employment risks

These are associated with continued employment if the project should fail. It is a fact of life that few people can now expect to remain with one organization over a whole working lifetime as there are simply too many changes taking place. Those working specifically on projects, which tend to be temporary affairs, are perhaps at greater risk of discontinuous employment than those in other sectors of the economy.

Reputation risks

These are associated with loss or damage to the personal reputation if the project should fail. Project failures do occur from time to time and one of the biggest losers could be the project manager. Even if the project was doomed for a variety of reasons, none of which might be attributable directly to the manager, it can still leave a stigma that can take years to shake off particularly if he or she remains in the same organization.

Physical risks

These are risks of harm to the individual. These risks can apply to persons both inside and outside the project so the effect can be widespread. Compared to the way in which people worked in the first half of the twentieth century, we now demand much greater safety awareness from both the workplace and the individual. Deaths and accidents on large construction sites were once accepted as commonplace and a hazard of the job but attitudes have changed and work is now much safer than it used to be. Nevertheless, some types of work do contain more hazards than others, for example tunnelling, but it is often a matter of choice for the individual if he or she wants to do this type of work. Physical hazards can also be created for those persons who are external to the project but might be affected by it in some way; an example of this is the fear over genetically modified crops finding their way into the food chain and affecting the population at large.

Lifestyle risks

These are associated with the expectation about lifestyle or living conditions being affected by the project. As a society we tend to expect more from our lifestyle than our forebears and are perhaps more prepared to defend it if we see it threatened. Projects such as new airport runways involving increased aircraft noise might be seen to directly threaten the lifestyle of some members of the public and who is to say they are wrong to complain about it? The existence of a project does not necessarily mean it is good for everybody, even if the majority might benefit.

It will be seen from this categorization that risks can exist in all aspects of the project including the people involved on both the inside and the outside and they can manifest themselves in a wide variety of forms. Few, if any, projects contain all the risks indicated above but the larger and more complex the project the more likely it is that a good proportion of them will appear.

5 *Project Selection*

The first big decision, which some may feel carries the greatest of all risks, is whether or not to start the project in the first place. To start means to commit resources, both financial and physical, but with no guarantee of a return, while not to start could imply a loss of something in the future that might be of great benefit. With commercially motivated projects the benefit will generally be continuing profitability, while public sector projects generally involve something of value to the state. If commercial projects are not started it will lead to an eventual loss of profitability as new products and services will not be created leaving the field open to the competition. In the public sector, the issue of simple profitability may not be a matter that is directly measurable. For example, if road building is not undertaken traffic congestion will ensue with a loss to society in wasted time and fuel; if defence projects are not carried out in the home country then the equipment will have to be purchased from abroad, with a straight outflow of capital, loss of jobs and possible voter reaction.

Commercial projects normally must satisfy two basic criteria in order to be selected: **wealth creation**, and **business merit**. Wealth creation means quite simply that overall it should generate a worthwhile return for the expenditure incurred. Business merit implies that the project fits in with the organization's business strategy, either through retaining existing markets, developing new markets or making good use of the organization's assets. With public sector projects, the basic criteria are rather different as neither wealth creation nor business merit need be a factor. Matters relating to government policy and the national interest will be the principal criteria and they cannot be expressed so simply as issues relating to wealth and merit, as such they will not be considered further in this text.

Wealth creation

All projects are started in the expectation that something of value will be created and, overall, the value is greater than the cost. This direct measure of value is not always easy to calculate when the project is carried out in the public sector, as the benefits may be for society as a whole. Such projects are usually justified on political grounds and politicians cannot, in a democracy, ignore the demands of society. Even if the benefits may be difficult to quantify, the costs are always assessed when the public purse is involved.

Projects may have a speculative element or they may not. Projects that are started with a capital outlay and which aim to generate a return through exploiting the resulting products contain an element of speculation. The costs of the project or the product may be greater than assumed or the market may not perform as expected, in either case the project is likely to generate a loss. Of course, many organizations that take on projects do not do them on a speculative basis either because the project is an internal affair and the results are not accounted for in a conventional way, or they are contractors to another organization that may be carrying the risks associated with the overall venture. However, organizations in the position of a contractor may not be able to eliminate a speculative element completely if they undertake the work on a fixed-price basis where the costs of any overruns are borne by the contractor.

With speculative commercial projects the selection criteria is that the expected benefits should be greater than the expected costs, but what are the benefits and the costs? A number of different methods have been devised to answer this question, unfortunately they are not guaranteed to all give the same answer when put to the same problem. For the most part, the methods are most applicable to questions of choice between projects, whether to accept one and reject the other, or for setting some hurdle criteria if projects are considered singly. In terms of the costs and revenues, the methods used for evaluating the worth of projects fall into three broad types: payback, return-on-capital-employed and discounted cash flow.

The **payback** method is the simplest and has the longest history. If the project cost curve in Figure 5.1 is taken, the break-even point is easily identified and can be calculated directly from the figures for cash outflows at the start and inflows once sales begin; working capital tied up in the project is not considered. All the cash figures are taken at present-day values and the time at which the inflows exactly cancel the initial investment is found – this is termed the 'payback period'. In general, projects with shorter payback periods are to be preferred to those with a longer period; when given a choice between two projects that are equal in all other respects. Companies may also set a maximum payback period as a decision criteria.

The simplicity of the payback calculation makes it popular where only elementary comparisons are required, perhaps where the projects are of low value and short duration. What it does not take into account is the relative size in money terms of the project or the size of the expected benefit. To counter the objection of ignoring the size of the benefit, the

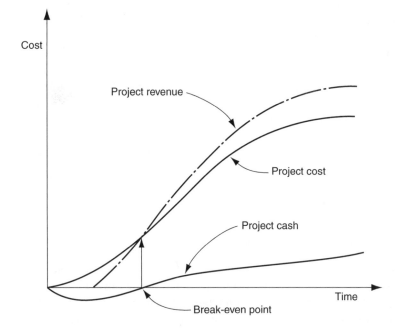

Figure 5.1 Typical project cash flow curves.

return-on-capital-employed method has been used. Several variations have been devised for this technique both for calculating the capital employed and the return. In essence, the average annual profit is divided by the average capital employed to produce the return figure. The average capital employed is calculated from the initial outlay (written down on an annual basis over the life of the project) plus the annual operating capital. By taking the average amount of capital tied up in plant, stocks and wage bills and dividing that figure into the annual profit, the annual return-on-capital-employed is obtained. Firms that are able to turn their stock and wages into profitable sales very rapidly will have a better return-on-capital-employed, for the same amount of profit, than firms where lead times are long and the amount of capital tied up in stocks and work in progress is large. This method is perhaps the least useful in the context of project selection but is useful for measuring the efficiency of production processes where profit on costs does not show how efficiently the conversion of capital into profit takes place.

THE TIME VALUE OF MONEY

A simple analysis to find the break-even point and expected profits may be all that is necessary if the undertaking is a very short-term one, perhaps over two or three years, and either of the above methods can be used to make a decision. However, where longer-term projects are involved the time at which profits arise can also become a concern that neither method takes into account. Where such projects are contemplated, it has become the normal practice to consider 'the time value of money' by applying a **discount rate** to future cash flows. In effect, it says that money earned now is worth more than money earned at some time in the future because of a) the additional return that could have been obtained if the money had been invested in the intervening period and b) the reduced purchasing power that accompanies inflation. The high interest rates of the 1970s and '80s has focused the minds of accountants on this point. Applying discounting rates tends to show that projects that generate a profit early in their life-cycle are to be preferred to projects where profits are obtained further downstream. Besides the purely financial appeal of this argument, there is merit in it as the further forward one looks in time, the less one can be certain of. Profits to be obtained many years away are thus more vulnerable to changed circumstances than profits to be generated in the near future. The technique of **discounted cash flow** (**DCF**) has become common in the financial evaluation of both capital and developmental projects as it takes into account the timing at which expenditure and profits arise. It shows the effective rate of return on the total investment over the whole life of the project. When evaluating the worth of the project this rate of return can be set at some boundary level which, if not met at the initial evaluation, will indicate that the returns are likely to be too low for the project to be worth pursuing, this may be 4 or 5% above the long-term view of interest rates.

EXAMPLE 5.1: PROJECT INVESTMENT DECISION

A project is divided into two phases, a development phase lasting four years and a production phase lasting eight years but overlapping the development programme by three years. This is a common situation where consideration is given to the production phase whilst development is proceeding but the cost accounts for the two activities are kept separate. Table 5.1 shows the annual cost figures at current rates. Also shown is the

Table 5.1   Project expenditure, revenue and cash flow at current rates.

Year	Expenditure £m			Revenue	Cum.	Cash flow	Cum. cash flow
	Development	Production	Cum.				
1	0.5	0	0.5	0	0	−0.5	−0.5
2	1.5	0.1	2.1	0	0	−1.6	−2.1
3	2.0	0.2	4.3	0	0	−2.2	−4.3
4	0.7	2.5	7.5	0	0	−3.2	−7.5
5	0	5.2	12.7	3.8	3.8	−1.4	−8.9
6	0	7.1	19.8	10.6	14.4	3.5	−5.4
7	0	6.8	26.6	12.2	26.6	5.4	0
8	0	6.4	33.0	11.6	38.2	5.2	5.2
9	0	3.6	36.6	6.6	44.8	3.0	8.8
10	0	1.4	38.0	3.2	48.0	1.8	10.0

expected revenue from sales (after tax). The total cost of the project over the ten years is £38m, made up of £4.7m for development and £33.3m for the production phase. The total revenue over the expected life of the project is £48m, there is thus a net benefit of £10m on an expenditure of £38m giving a benefit-to-cost ratio of 26.3% at current rates.

If, for example, a rate of return on investment of 10% could be expected over the life of the project, a discount rate of 10% can be applied to the cash flow figures to determine the net worth of the project under these conditions; the resulting figure is termed the **net present value** (**NPV**). The formula for calculating the discounted value of any sum of money at some time in the future is:

$$D = \frac{1}{(1+r)^n}$$

Where:
D = The discount factor
r = The discount rate as a decimal value
n = The number of years from start

Thus, for a discount rate of 10% at the end of year 1 the factor is:

$$D = \frac{1}{(1+0.1)^1} = 0.9091$$

Discount factors can be calculated directly from the formula or it is sometimes more convenient to use a published table. Table 5.2 shows the calculation of the net present values for the whole project at the 10% rate.

It will be seen that the £10m profit figure that resulted from the undiscounted calculation is now reduced to £2.602m. It will also be realized that if a sufficiently high discount rate is chosen, the net worth of the project will be reduced to zero. The figure that produces this zero return is termed the **internal rate of return** (IRR) and the

Table 5.2 Cash flow discounted at the rate of 10%.

Year	Cash Flow	Discount Factor	Net Present Value	Cum. NPV
1	−0.5	0.9091	−0.455	−0.455
2	−1.6	0.8264	−1.322	−1.777
3	−2.2	0.7513	−1.653	−3.430
4	−3.2	0.6830	−2.186	−5.616
5	−1.4	0.6209	−0.869	−6.485
6	3.5	0.5645	1.976	−4.509
7	5.4	0.5132	2.771	−1.738
8	5.2	0.4565	2.374	0.636
9	3.0	0.4241	1.272	1.908
10	1.8	0.3855	0.694	2.602

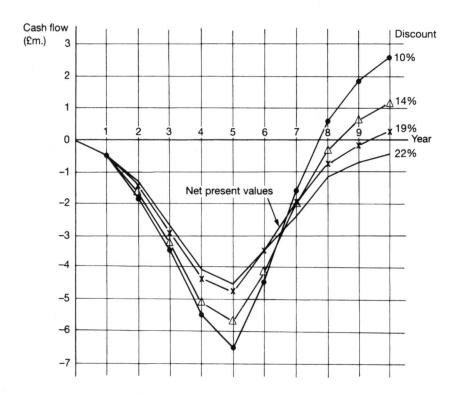

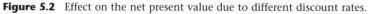

Figure 5.2 Effect on the net present value due to different discount rates.

discounted cash flow method aims to find this figure. Figure 5.2 has been drawn showing the effect on this example of discounting at different rates. A discount rate of about 19.15% will produce a zero result and is, thus, the internal rate of return in this case.

The above example has been somewhat simplified when compared to many real situations where the additional effects of borrowed capital, investment grants, if available, and the effect of corporation tax including deferred payments would have to be taken into account. When evaluating the worth of projects, there are some arguments against using the internal rate of return as a suitable measure, in particular, its difficulty of calculation and also the possibility, depending on the shape of the cash flow curve, that two different IRRs can exist. The argument is, therefore, that projects should be evaluated by calculating the Net Present Value using a predetermined hurdle rate as it is both simpler and avoids the problem of dual rates. Any project that yields a positive NPV at the set rate is potentially worth pursuing as, overall, it is seen to be wealth creating.

Although there is no fundamental flaw in the DCF or NPV methods, they have attracted some criticism as to their appropriateness. A statement sometimes heard is 'any project can be DCFed to death', implying that setting the discount rate sufficiently high will make any project look unattractive. This is certainly true where projects with a return in the longer term are involved and, as Example 5.1 shows, a discount rate of around 20% can reduce the benefit-to-cost ratio to zero. However, in applying high hurdle rates to DCF or NPV calculations, firms should note that investment in new projects may ultimately be necessary for the firm's survival. To fail to invest could leave the company without anything to compete with products and services developed by rivals who have taken a less cautious view.

It must be remembered that Discounted Cash Flows calculated to justify the initial investment decision represent only a snapshot of how a project is viewed at the start. As the project proceeds events could cause the planned expenditure to vary considerably from that on which the original investment may have been based. If the situation is serious enough it can lead the project into a trap. This can happen when costs rise and timescales extend to the point that the project can no longer be viewed as potentially profitable at a time when a large proportion of the money has been spent. The dilemma is that without further expenditure and project completion there can be no prospect of recovery of any of the costs. This situation occurred on the Channel Tunnel project, which rose in cost from an initial estimate of around £4bn to a final cost in excess of £8bn, all paid for by shareholders' investments plus loans from a group of 225 banks and financial institutions. Potential interest payments on the accumulated debt grew to the point where they were likely to be substantially greater than any revenues, after basic expenditure, from operating the tunnel commercially. In this situation its debts could only grow; the tunnel could neither be sold nor operated to recover all its costs. The position of the tunnel was saved by a 'debt-for-equity' swap, leaving 44% of the ownership of the tunnel in the hands of the banks rather than the project's original sponsor and shareholders; the banks could then set interest rates and write off any loans to suit themselves. As operating revenues began to rise, the tunnel's owner, Eurotunnel, began buying back its own equity from the banks at a time when interest rates were falling. This is a fortuitous situation; falling interest rates meant the profitability of the tunnel looked rather better at the end of the 1990s than it did at the start due to a change in an external factor.

Business merit

Commercially inspired projects often tend to involve the creation of a new product or service; to be a success any product or service must satisfy three criteria:

- It must be attractive to customers, that is, it must satisfy a market need.
- It must be technically feasible, that is, it must be capable of being made to work or being performed satisfactorily.
- It must be capable of being supplied for a cost that will allow a satisfactory profit when offered at an acceptable selling price, that is, it must be cheap enough to produce or deliver to be competitive.

Each of these represents an area of risk; a product that fails in any of these areas fails overall. A careful examination of each of these criteria is necessary if a realistic assessment of the risks are to be made. Herein lies the first difficulty; it is one that will always bedevil the concept of risk analysis and it is that of subjectivity. Although risk analysis can adopt strictly logical mathematical disciplines, the factors to which the maths are applied are, in many cases, subjective assessments. Any assessment of the outcome of events that will take place in the future contains an element of guesswork and that element can never be removed. However, the more detailed the study of the above criteria and the more evidence of past performance that can be taken into account, the more likely it is that the subjective assessments will be of the right order of magnitude. The term 'order of magnitude' is used here to indicate that precision is not expected; too much experience exists to indicate that forecasts of the outcome of projects, and particularly novel projects, are often wildly inaccurate and almost always optimistic. Given that inaccuracy is a built-in feature of project assessment, senior management still demand, and rightly so, that thorough assessment is done as the expenditure on projects must be justified on some grounds. Normally this is done on the basis of benefit-to-cost but that alone does not allow for the risk element. One way of identifying those projects that are worth pursuing is to set some boundary criteria which any new project must meet in order for it to gain approval.

A simple formula that can be used product or service development projects is:

$$M = \frac{G}{(C_d + C_p)} \times P_t \times P_m$$

Where:
M = A figure-of-merit
G = The gross profit from sales over the life of the project
C_d = The total cost of development
C_p = The total cost of the assumed production run or delivery of the service
P_t = The probability of a technical success, (functionality and cost)
P_m = The probability of achieving the anticipated sales at the assumed prices

It will be realized that this formula takes into account the three basic criteria for a successful product or service. It generates a dimensionless number (M) of value less than one and a minimum value such as 0.125 can be set as the boundary condition; any project that falls below this is automatically rejected. There are, however, a number of obvious criticisms:

1) The magnitude of the costs relative to the organization as a whole is not taken into account; the same answer would arise if the costs and profits are in the same ratio for a £100k project as for a £100m one.
2) The disparity in time between the expenditure and the accrual of profit is not included.

3) The eventual effect on the business of not having the new product in the market when there is a reasonable expectation that a competitor will have one is not taken into account.

When these three additional considerations are assessed, the boundary condition may become an issue that is far from simple. In the end, corporate culture (risk averse or the opposite) or long-term corporate strategy may become the final arbiter in the decision to go ahead.

Various formulae have been suggested that take into account the additional factors and they are of the general form:

$$M = \frac{G}{(Cd + Cp)} \times P_t \times P_m \times (M_t + M_b) \times S \times T$$

Where:
M_t = Technological merit
M_b = Business merit
S   = Strategic fit with other projects, products and markets
T   = Timing or discounting factor based on the time at which profits accrue

Formulae such as these have their place but they should also be treated with caution. Factors such as technological merit or business merit are complex issues yet this formula demands that each is reduced to just a single number between 1 and 0. With so many factors that are gross simplifications or probabilistic estimates, the single figure that results from such a formula cannot be considered as definitive. It would be better to assume that it is merely a guide (and subject to wide error), as to how the project is viewed at one point in time. If formulae have a real merit, it may be at the extremities where they can clearly demonstrate either very desirable or very undesirable projects. However, one would expect normal business acumen within the organization to identify these possibilities without too much formal analysis. There is one other danger and it is that formulae which contain so many subjective elements can be used to justify anything. All project managers associated with development know that the greatest obstacle to be overcome is that of initial selection. There may be a natural temptation to use formulae to justify the starting of projects in a wholly undeserved way as part of the infighting that goes on in some companies when it comes to development expenditure.

An extension of the figure-of-merit concept can be found in a class of techniques known generally as 'Multiple-Criteria Decision Making' (MCDM) methods. These techniques deal with a common problem: how to make the best choice in a situation which involves a series of essential, but not necessarily compatible, attributes. This is particularly true of the initial project selection process where issues beyond pure profitability come into the decision. The methods aim to generate either a numerical score or a ranking order by which proposals for projects can be judged; they use a four-stage process which involves:

1) identifying a series of attributes of the project that are important to the decision,
2) applying a weighting that determines the importance of the attribute,
3) applying an assessment of how each attribute will perform, and
4) summing the parts of the analysis to generate an overall result.

NEW PRODUCT EVALUATION SHEET

Application no. P-171	Product description *SYNTHETIC STEAK FOR ARMY USE*	Recommendation *SECOND STAGE FEASIBILITY STUDY*
Date 20/3/93	Project reference	

Positive factors		Weighting (W)	Scoring guide			Assessed score (S)	Result W x S
			High (Good) 1.0	Medium 0.5	Low (Poor) 0.1		
A	Profit over ten year period	60		X		0.5	30
B	Contribution to corporate image	5		X		0.5	2.5
C	Strategic fit in overall programme	20		X		0.5	10.0
D	Technology benefits	15	X			1.0	15.0
E	Total score of positive factors: A+B+C+D						57.5

Negative factors		Weighting (W)	Scoring Guide			Assessed score (S)	Result W x S
			High (Poor) 1.0	Medium 0.65	Low (Poor) 0.2		
F	Development cost as a % of budget	100	X			0.85	85
G	Risk of technical failure	25	X			1.0	25
H	Development risk					$\frac{F \times G}{100}$	21.25
J	Capital for production as a % of budget	100		X		0.65	65
K	Risk of failure in market	50			X	0.2	10
L	Production risk					$\frac{J \times K}{100}$	6.5
M	Discount due to time at which profits accrue	25		X		0.65	16.25
N	Total score of negative factors: H+L+M						44.0
	Overall total score: E−N						13.5

Figure 5.3   Example of a new product evaluation sheet.

Figure 5.3 shows an example of a new product evaluation sheet. It will be seen that it identifies a series of project attributes, listed at the left-hand side that are important to the decision. It is further divided into an upper half containing the positive attributes and a lower half detailing the costs which are considered to be negative attributes. The relative importance given to each attribute is shown by the weighting column. The expected outcome for each attribute is given in the grid at the centre which allows scores to be assigned, indicating if things are likely to be good, bad or somewhere in between. Multiplying the score by the weighting gives an overall score for each attribute; adding them all together gives an overall score for both the positive and the negative aspects. Subtracting the scores for the negative aspects from the positive aspects gives an overall score for the project. Any overall score which is positive indicates the project has the potential to be worth pursuing. This simple approach can be used in situations where the attributes are relatively few in number and it is easy to assign weightings that reflect the real worth to the organization.

Sometimes there can be a large number of attributes, some of which have conflicts and to which it is not easy to assign any clear pattern of weightings. With sufficiently sophisticated mathematics this can be resolved; much of the theory concerns itself with how choices can be evaluated given the decision maker's preferences for one attribute over another. Using the mathematical approach involves looking at each of the attributes in turn, considering each one against all the others and deciding for each pair and in the light of some higher objective, which is the more important and by how much. To take this further, each choice has to be given a numerical score, for example, 10 = very important, 1 = no difference, with the values in between representing shades of feeling. This alone will not tell us much until we can see how each decision appears in the light of all the other decisions. This can be done by taking the geometric average (nth root of n items multiplied together) of all the scores against each attribute. It must always be remembered that when making the comparison that the score given to attribute A with respect to B must be the reciprocal of the score given to B with respect to A. After computing the overall weightings, the result will be a reasoned ranking of the importance attached to each attribute.

Having arrived at a ranking, one still has to take the decision about what choice to make and for this each attribute must be considered and a view taken about how it is likely to turn out. Again, a scoring system is needed, for example, 10 = very favourable to 1 = very unfavourable. Multiplying these scores by the weightings and totalling the results gives an overall score for the project. A final step could be to multiply this score by some overriding value such as the expected return on the investment in the project to get the final result. This result could either be used to see if it meets some hurdle criteria for a decision or to choose between a variety of possible schemes, the highest score indicating the most valuable option.

This, or some very similar process, is the mathematical basis of MCDM methods. The mathematical method of defining the attribute weightings is a modern refinement of a well-understood process. It will be realized that the MCDM approach can accommodate many more factors in the decision-making process than those associated with wealth creation and business merit. For this reason it is suitable for use with projects of a non-commercial nature, such as those in the public sector and it was in the context of such projects that a particular variant of it emerged. The 'Analytic Hierarchy Process' developed by mathematician Thomas L. Saaty of the University of Pennsylvania is a version of the MCDM process that makes extensive use of pairwise comparison. It started in 1971 with his work on contingency planning for the US Department of Defense and continued to mature until a fully developed method was defined in 1978. A principal feature of the method is the ability to deconstruct

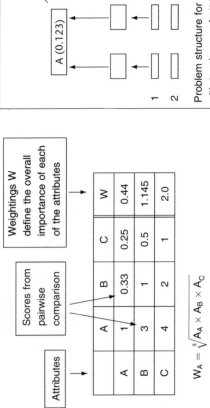

Attributes

Scores from pairwise comparison

Weightings W define the overall importance of each of the attributes

	A	B	C	W
A	1	0.33	0.25	0.44
B	3	1	0.5	1.145
C	4	2	1	2.0

$$W_A = \sqrt[3]{A_A \times A_B \times A_C}$$

$$A_B = \frac{1}{B_A}$$

The score in the box B_A indicates that with respect to the goal, B is 3 times more preferable than A

Using pairwise comparison to assess the relative importance of a variety of attributes

Goal

A (0.123)   B (0.319)   C (0.557)

Attributes (or criteria)
With normalized relative importance

Sub-attributes

1 Alternatives
2

Problem structure for the Analytical Hierarchy Process to make a choice between two alternatives with two layers of attributes or criteria

The normalized weighting for A is

$$\frac{W_A}{W_A + W_B + W_C} = \frac{0.44}{0.44 + 1.145 + 2.0} = 0.123$$

Figure 5.4 Mathematical basis of evaluating pairwise comparisons in the analytic hierarchy process.

the decision problem into progressively lower levels of attributes or criteria; this is the reason for the 'analytic hierarchy' part of the title. Since its inception it has attracted some criticism on theoretical and practical grounds but it also has firm advocates and it has been widely used for many complex decision-making problems such as the siting of power stations, choices between product development projects and social policy issues. Software is now available to aid the decision-making process using the Analytic Hierarchy Process and is described in Chapter 11. Where complex decision-making problems are involved, this is an approach that should certainly be considered.

Figure 5.4 shows the computational process used for arriving at the relative importance of a series of attributes or criteria by making pairwise comparisons and calculating the geometric average. It also shows how this can be used in a hierarchical decision problem as formulated using the Analytic Hierarchy Process.

Before leaving this subject, the question of risk trade-off should be considered. It is sometimes said that there is a balance between low-risk and low-profit projects and high-risk and high-profit projects. Whereas it is clear that low-risk and low-profit projects do exist, the question is whether or not there really are high-risk and high-profit projects? The answer depends on how risk is defined and where the risks lay. A truly high-risk project is one in which there is both a high technical risk and a high risk of it failing in the market. If both these factors are known it would be difficult to conceive of how its chances of making a high return could be seen as good because the odds are firmly against it. A project that has a high technical risk but a low market risk is far more likely to achieve a high return but such a project could not be said to be a high-risk project overall as one significant aspect of risk is low. Using the weightings of Figure 5.3 and considering the positive factors to represent the benefits and the negative factors to represent the risks, Figure 5.5 can be drawn. The null

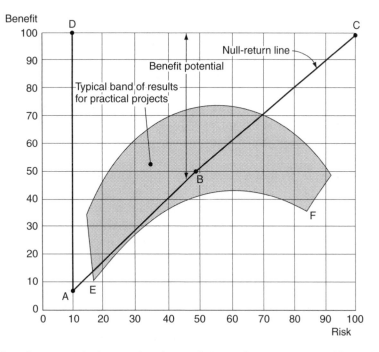

Figure 5.5   Benefit versus risk, drawn using the weighting and scoring system of Figure 5.3.

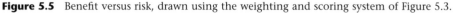

benefit line, A,B,C, which joins points of equal high, medium and low scores represents the line above which any project must score in order to show a benefit that outweighs the risk. The boundary of this area is given by the figure A,B,C,D and it is clear from this that the greater the risk the lower is the potential for high profits, as the gap between the null-benefit line and the upper benefit boundary decreases with increasing risk.

In practical cases the actual profit from low-risk industrial projects tends to be well below the upper boundary because of the effects of competition; however, the ideal project is one that combines low risks with high earnings. High risks do not automatically carry the potential for high profits, it is far more likely that they will result in low or negative rewards particularly if there is a large market risk. The Sinclair C-5 tricycle exemplifies a product with low technical risk but very high market risk; predictably it was a financial disaster. However, attempts to reduce market risk or capitalize on a market opportunity can also backfire:

- The Ford Edsel car of the 1950s was a product closely tailored to the perceived market requirement containing all the features that, from extensive research, it was felt motorists would love. Its launch in 1957 was preceded by huge marketing hype but the resulting car was a complete failure; big and ugly, the whole design approach lacked character and reliability was abysmal. By 1959, when it finally died, 80% of dealers were losing money and Ford was forced to buy back stocks of unsaleable cars.

- Facing a threat from Proctor and Gamble's Ariel Future washing powder in 1994, Lever Brothers (Unilever) decided to improve on their popular Persil brand with a new version called Persil Power. This contained a manganese 'accelerator' designed to shorten washing time; despite millions spent on research, the accelerator's damaging effect on clothes was not discovered until it hit the market. Following a public outcry, the product was withdrawn despite Lever Brothers insistence that its technology was 'first class' and 'well ahead of the market'.

- Coca Cola had successfully marketed its famous drink for 99 years without ever changing the closely guarded recipe. For decades it had been locked in a head-to-head battle with its rival Pepsi Cola, when in 1985 it decided to change the drink to a sweeter, more Pepsi-like, flavour. With huge publicity, Chairman Roberto C. Goizueto launched the new Coca Cola with the line 'the best has been made even better'. The customers did not agree, two-thirds preferring the original flavour, and Coca Cola were forced to reintroduce the old drink as 'Coca Cola Classic' three months later.

The band E,F represents a far more typical characteristic for practical projects and it indicates that the best profit potential lies in the low- to medium-risk category. Projects with potentially high risks may still have an appeal in certain circumstances; for example, where a failure to instigate a new-product project in the knowledge that a competitor is working on one would signal to the world a withdrawal from an important market sector; some aerospace defence projects have been undertaken on that basis. Where risks are seen to be high but there is a belief in the potential for high earnings, the approach should be one of moving the project into the medium-risk category, either through further technical evaluation and market testing or the adoption of a defensive market strategy, letting competitors take the initial risks.

One suggestion that is sometimes put forward to counter this problem is a portfolio approach to projects in which a balanced mix of low-risk, low-profit and high-risk, high-profit projects is maintained. As has been pointed out, few high-risk, high-profit projects exist. In the pharmaceutical industry it has been said that 15 out of 16 drug development projects that are started do not result in a profitable product. Many will fail at the clinical trials stage and of those that reach the market less than a third will recover their development costs. However, for a few products the profits can be enormous. The anti-impotence drug Viagra developed by Pfizer Corp. is likely to be one of the most profitable drugs but it actually started as a drug to combat angina. It was a side-effect, unsuspected at the start but noticed during clinical trials, that led to its development as a cure for male impotence and opened up a market in which no previous product existed.

Where high risks are concerned it might be better to contain them to pure research projects, expecting most of them to be failures but, when one does look to be a potential success, the research will have already removed much of the risk before it goes to the development stage.

6 *Making Decisions in Uncertain Situations*

Once the initial decision to go ahead has been made, many more decisions will be required concerning the multitude of issues that confront the project. Some will be routine matters that can be simply incorporated into the project plan while others can be fundamental to the entire conduct of the project. Fundamental issues that might have to be resolved at the start could include such things as:

- whether to seek risk-sharing partners or go it alone
- whether to appoint a prime contractor or manage the overall project oneself
- whether to use subcontractors or do the work oneself

Whatever decisions are made they will influence all that follows.

The concept of strategy

It is a fundamental feature of all projects that they have a unique goal and that goal lies somewhere in the future. Furthermore, projects imply that the goal is something new and not merely the continuation of an established process. But whenever we contemplate the future we can usually see two things: the opportunities the future presents, and the uncertainties about what may happen. These issues confront us daily and, for the most part, we make simple decisions about what we are going to do in the short term without giving each decision too much consideration; often the issues involved are trivial and, if things do not turn out as expected, changes can easily be accommodated. From time to time, however, much more significant issues arise and the question of what to do and how to go about it needs much more careful thought. Choosing the family holiday is a typical example; here considerable expense may be incurred, the interests of several different parties, such as Mum, Dad and the children, are involved and there is the host of possible holiday venues to choose from. It would normally be expected that such a decision would only be taken after a search of what is on offer, at what time in the year, at what cost, and a comparison with how well all the different interests can be satisfied. Choosing the family holiday is the first step in the execution of a personal project that most of us do each year. But the holiday itself is not the goal of the project, the real goal is a happy and memorable time for all the family and the holiday away from home is our strategy for achieving it. The things that might be done on the holiday, visits to beaches or other attractions, are the tactics of ensuring the expected enjoyment comes about.

The term 'strategy' has acquired several meanings but they all imply one thing: how do we go about influencing the future in a way that suits our interests? Until recently, strategy had a specific military meaning: the art of deploying one's troops, ships or aircraft so as to force the enemy into fighting on terms favourable to oneself. What actually happens when the fighting takes place is covered by the tactics employed on the field. During the Second World War the term 'strategic' acquired a special meaning in that it referred to the long-term or overarching plan to defeat the enemy. Thus strategic bombing involved striking at the enemy's factories, working population and infrastructure that supported his army and navy; it was a long-term approach aimed at reducing the will and ability to continue the fight. Tactical bombing involved attacks on troops or supplies in the field to ensure victory in battle.

The term 'strategy' acquired a somewhat different meaning following its use by John von Neumann in his book *Theory of Games and Economic Behaviour.*[1] Here strategy refers to the rule used to decide between alternatives when there is uncertainty about the outcome. In a game of chance the best strategy would be the one that is most likely to win. In a project situation, a manager may be faced with a choice between alternatives, each of which could result in a loss or gain to the project. Faced with this situation the strategy adopted could depend on the manager's own situation; if he feels that perceived losses would be severely penalized he may adopt a **cautious strategy** by choosing the course of action that **minimizes the perceived maximum loss**, ignoring the potential gains if the future turns out well. A more confident manager may adopt an **entrepreneurial strategy** by choosing the course that **maximizes the perceived maximum gain**, ignoring the potential losses if things go badly.

Both these meanings have come together in the context of project management, as the concept of a project strategy contains the idea of an overall approach that embodies the principal decisions about the project, its objectives and its method of execution. The tactics of the project are contained in the detailed plans that define all the activities that will take place. Thus strategy is placed at a higher level than the project plan and tactics are always subordinate to strategy.

Alternative strategies

All projects at the outset are subject to a simple go/no-go decision. However, a 'go' decision may not be straightforward as there may be alternative paths that can be followed. The paths that are open are termed 'courses of action' and the decision maker has the choice of which one to pursue. Choices that can exist concern: the product specification: simple or sophisticated, the project timescale – extended or compressed, the size of the budget – extensive or shoestring. These choices are not necessarily independent; it is difficult to develop a sophisticated product in a short timescale on a shoestring budget although some firms persist in thinking this can be done. There are always choices to be made but some may be dictated by practical considerations such as the availability of staff, facilities and cash flow. It is important to note that whichever course of action is chosen it will have a bearing on the eventual outcome of the project. A choice thus represents a risk that the selected strategy may turn out to be the wrong one for the conditions that arise in the future.

John von Neumann devised his classic work on decision strategy during the Second World War, so he was well aware of the issues that can be at stake. All competitive decision makers can be said to be analogous to players in a game, each has a choice of courses of action with different outcomes but neither can be sure what strategy the other will choose.

Von Neumann showed that whenever one is faced with a decision in a game there is always a best strategy that a player can adopt. However, the analogy with a business situation cannot be taken too far as the rules of business may not be defined with the precision of a game and each player may have different objectives. However, the concept of a best strategy is valuable to the decision maker.

In any project there are always variable factors that are either internal to the project and generally controllable or external and outside of control; it is this interaction between the controllable and the uncontrollable factors that combine to determine the eventual outcome of any decision. The best strategy is the one which gives the best result over a range of possible outcomes. To evaluate the strategies that are open it is necessary to define outcome descriptors that are meaningful and can be used to gauge the success or failure of each decision. Usually these descriptors are given in economic terms such as profits or overall value to the organization, but they could include such other factors as corporate image and prestige.

EXAMPLE 6.1: CHOOSING A DEVELOPMENT STRATEGY

Consider the following situation involving the choice of a development strategy. After a successful prototype testing phase of a new product, a company decides to start a full-scale development and production project but there are three alternative approaches to the way the development programme is undertaken. Once a course of action has been adopted it will be difficult and expensive to change to an alternative; the problem is which course to choose.

The alternative courses of action are:

1) Perform a minimum change development and productionizing programme based on the existing prototype and launch the product on the market in one year.
2) Perform further market research, refine the product definition, value engineer the design and launch the product in two years.
3) Invest more in development technology and launch a more sophisticated product in two and a half to three years.

The Marketing department have assessed the potential for future sales but find their estimates to be subject to wide margins; the best that they can do is to classify demand as high, medium or low. Six factors are deemed to be relevant to the sales potential and the eventual profitability:

a) the cost of development including production tooling
b) the unit production cost
c) the unit selling price
d) the cost of promotiont
e) the effect of competition
f) the shape of the market.

Factors *a* to *d* can be expressed in purely numerical terms but *e* and *f* are qualitative judgements that have a bearing on the size of the market. For each of the alternatives the assessments are as follows:

Option 1, Existing Technology
a) Cost of development: £2.5m
b) Unit production cost: £125
c) Unit selling price: £150
d) Cost of promotion: £0.7m
e) Effect of competition: Relatively little over the first year of sales
f) Shape of market: Peak demand at end of first two years

Option 2, Further product refinement
a) Cost of development: £3.0m
b) Unit production cost: £110
c) Unit selling price: £135
d) Cost of promotion: £1.0m
e) Effect of competition: Competition fierce after first year of sales
f) Shape of market: Peak demand at end of first year

Option 3, More advanced product
a) Cost of development: £4.0m
b) Unit production cost: £130
c) Unit selling price: £150
d) Cost of promotion: £1.5m
e) Effect of competition: Competition fierce at product launch
f) Shape of market: Anticipated high demand for the advanced product

The market forecasts based on the above assessments are shown in Table 6.1.

Table 6.1   Alternative sales estimates for various courses of action.

Course of action	Total sales		
	High	Medium	Low
Option 1	500,000	400,000	200,000
Option 2	600,000	500,000	200,000
Option 3	750,000	550,000	150,000

For each case, the outcome, in terms of eventual profits, can be calculated (ignoring the effects of discounting). Taking Option 1, for high total sales, the total cost of the programme is made up from the development cost plus the promotion cost plus the cost of making 500,000 units:

$$£2.5m + £0.7m + £125 \times 500,000 = £65,700,000$$

The total revenue from 1 with high sales is:

$$£150 \times 500,000 = £75,000,000$$

The total profit in this situation is thus;

$$£75,000,000 - £65,700,000 = £9,300,000$$

The outcomes in terms of profit for all the courses of action and levels of sales are given in Table 6.2.

Table 6.2   Profit forecasts for alternative courses of action.

Course of action	Profit from sales		
	High	Medium	Low
Option 1	9,300,000	6,800,000	1,800,000
Option 2	11,000,000	8,500,000	1,000,000
Option 3	9,500,000	5,500,000	-2,500,000

Table 6.2 is termed an *outcome array* and the alternative circumstances that may arise, in this case 'high', 'medium' or 'low' sales, are termed *states of nature*. Here 'nature' means the world in which the project exists – it contains uncontrollable and uncertain elements but it does not necessarily act in the same way as a competitive player in a game.

Examination of the outcome array shows that there is no single course of action that is superior to the others in all cases, although Option 2 is always superior to Option 3. If one course exhibits superiority over the others in all cases it is said to exhibit *dominance* and would be the best course to choose. As this example does not show a dominant route it is necessary to consider other ways of making a choice.

The first strategy could be to take the cautious view and assume that things always turn out for the worst and therefore only the worst possible outcomes, that is, those associated with low sales, should be considered. Under these conditions the course to choose is that which gives the best outcome from the worst conditions; in this case it is Option 1 as this has an expected profit of £1.8m whereas Option 2 has a profit of £1.0m while Option 3 shows a loss. The advantage of this strategy is that the lowest level of profit is reasonably assured; with any other state of nature higher profits can be expected. This decision rule is termed a *maximin* strategy as it aims to *maxi*mize the *min*imum return. The weakness of this approach is that it ignores the chances of much higher profits that may be returned with the other options if things turn out better than the worst case. In this case Option 2 shows a better profit by £1.7m if high or medium sales arise. One could choose a strategy of picking the course which offers the best profit opportunity, in this case it is Option 2. This is a strategy based on a *maximax* decision rule, but for all states of nature other than the best, the return will be lower. There is a further strategy available; it is to ask for more information, in particular, how likely are any of these forecast sales to be attained?

Expected values

The idea of an expected or anticipated outcome has already been introduced in Chapter 5; the concept is embodied in the figure-of-merit formulae and the product evaluation sheet shown in Figure 5.3. It incorporates the idea of a value attached to some attribute multiplied by a figure which indicates our belief in the likelihood of the value being achieved. The **expected value** (**EV**) is a specifically defined parameter that comes directly from probability theory and is very useful in the process of evaluating outcomes of uncertain situations. It is given by the simple formula:

$$E = V \times p$$

Where:

E = the expected value
V = the value associated with a particular event or outcome
p = the probability of the event or outcome occurring on any occasion.

It gives the value that one would expect to generate in the long term or over an extended number of occasions on the assumption that the particular event occurs at random with probability p. The value p can be a guess based on a view of the future or it can be a measured quantity based on the observed frequency of the event occurring on previous occasions. Thus an event with value £100 that has been observed to happen 3 times in 10 occasions has a value of p = 0.3 and an expected value of £100 × .3 = £30 for a single occasion. This figure is neither the value of the event if it occurs (£100) nor the value if it does not (£0); it is an average value that we would expect to see over a large number of occasions on which the event might or might not occur. Unfortunately it does not tell us what will happen on any particular occasion in the future. Despite this obvious weakness when it comes to making a decision about a single event in the future, it is still useful when we wish to compare alternatives.

EXAMPLE 6.2: ADDING THE EXPECTED VALUES

The Marketing departments of all companies should be able, with sufficient research, to attach some level of probability to any sales figure they derive. Suppose, in the case of example 6.1, that the Marketing department argues that because Option 1 gets the product to the market quickly and it has already established its appeal, a probability of 0.7 should be attached to medium sales, a probability of 0.2 should be given to high sales while low sales should only be given a 0.1 probability. Option 2 involves better tailoring of the product to market needs and a more competitively priced item but it arrives later in the market and may face more intense competition. In this case Marketing attaches a probability of 0.7 to medium sales but high sales now get a probability of 0.1 and low sales go up to 0.2. Option 3 is much less clear as it involves new technology and is even further away in terms of product launch into a market which will be well supplied; in this case Marketing attaches equal probabilities of 0.333 to high, medium and low sales. Given this additional view of the likely state of nature one can make a choice between the options on the basis of the one that should give the best result in the long run. By multiplying the probability figures by the outcome values and adding the results, the *expected value* from each strategy can be derived:

Option 1

Expected profit = £9.3m × 0.2 + £6.8m × 0.7 + £1.8m × 0.1 = £6.8m

Option 2

Expected profit = £11.0m × 0.1 + £8.5m × 0.7 + £1.0m × 0.2 = £7.25m

Option 3

Expected profit = £9.5m × 0.33 + £5.5m × 0.33 − £2.5m × 0.33 = £2.78m

On the basis of this calculation one could conclude that Option 2 is superior and thus the best course of action; in this case the strategy is to make the choice on the basis of the best expected outcome. However, had the Marketing department taken a slightly more cautious view by saying that the probability of medium sales is 0.6 and that of low sales is 0.3 then the expected gain is reduced to £6.5m and Option 1 now looks more attractive. Calculations of this type are termed *sensitivity analyses*, they serve to show if small changes in assumptions can cause significant changes in the indicated outcomes. Sensitivity tests should always be carried out; where uncertainty is concerned it is unwise to rely on a single figure estimate. Looking again at the example it is clear that there is little to choose between Options 1 and 2 but Option 3, being late into the market and with heavy development expenditure, comes out the worst in this analysis by any of the decision strategies. It tends to emphasize the point, made previously, that formalized analyses tend to point out the obviously best or worst extremes. In the middle region, choices are not so clear-cut and the risks of making the wrong decision still remain. In a case such as this, the choice between options would be made using additional considerations that have not been included in this analysis, such as:

• The timing and need to fill the production shops with new work: if work is needed earlier rather than later, Option 1 is preferable
• The cash position in respect of development funding
• Longer-term corporate objectives.

Once the project has started, further choices between courses of action will present themselves and decisions will be required on a regular basis. Some will be so trivial as to need little more than cursory consideration but from time to time situations will arise where decisions could, if they are wrong, have serious consequences for the project. They may not be quite as critical as the initial decision to go ahead but the momentum of the project may mean that decisions have to be made in a relatively short time frame and with less-than-perfect information. A similar procedure to that already described can be used as an aid to finding the best way forward.

Decision trees

An extension of the ideas contained in the problem given above is the **decision tree**. Whenever a decision has to be made there are always two or more courses of action that can be taken. This can be represented diagrammatically by two or more branches springing from a single node that represents the initial decision. If the value to the decision maker of adopting each course of action can be established, it is a relatively simple matter to choose whichever course offers the best value.

However, the identified courses of action often lead either to further decisions or to uncertain outcomes. When this happens, further branches can be drawn from the outcome of each of the original branches and the whole diagram develops a tree-like appearance. If all the branches have potential outcomes that can be stated with a high degree of certainty then it is a straightforward matter to evaluate the overall outcome at the end of each branch, choose the most favourable one, then work backwards through the tree to find the series of decisions that leads to the chosen result.

Where outcomes cannot be stated with certainty there is a risk that whatever decision is made it could turn out to be the wrong one. Decision trees can reflect this situation but in this case some of the branches will represent the decision options (the 'decision-maker's tree') and other branches will represent the outcomes determined by fate or the state of nature ('nature's tree'). In this situation, probability theory can be applied to determine the best decision.

Decision trees are a structured way of breaking down any decision problem and then evaluating the outcomes so that the best course of action can be chosen. The construction and evaluation of decision trees is a five-stage process:

1) The manager must set down the options that are open to him when a decision has to be made (the decision-maker's tree).
2) The range of outcomes from each option must be identified (nature's tree).
3) Each outcome must be evaluated in quantitative terms.
4) The probabilities of each outcome arising must be established.
5) The complete decision tree must be evaluated to find the expected values of the outcomes resulting from each decision.

Consider the problem of the project manager who has to decide whether to continue with an existing contractor who has been continuously falling behind schedule or switch to a new contractor who is promising to recover or better the schedule. The decision-maker's tree consists of the options open and on which a decision has to be made; in this case it is between sticking with the existing contractor or switching to another. Nature's tree consists of the possible outcomes and for this problem let us assume that there is a range that covers a best, a worst and a middle outcome, all of which are possible. Both the decision-maker's tree and nature's tree are shown in Figure 6.1 Whatever decision is made, nature's tree will result in an outcome and this can be attached to the node at the end of each decision option to create the complete tree. Steps 3 and 4 in the process require an assessment of the likely outcomes of nature's tree and the probability of each outcome arising; some data about this situation is given in Table 6.3, showing the costs associated with each outcome and also the assessed probability associated with each branch on nature's tree. When this data is added, the complete tree can be evaluated. In this case a fairly conservative view has been taken

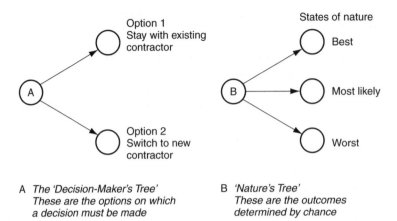

A *The 'Decision-Maker's Tree'*
   These are the options on which
   a decision must be made

B *'Nature's Tree'*
   These are the outcomes
   determined by chance

Figure 6.1 The 'decision-maker's tree' and 'nature's tree' for the project manager's problem.

Table 6.3 Courses of action and possible outcomes.

Courses of action		States of nature		
		Best (10% chance)	Most likely (70% chance)	Worst (20% chance)
Option 1 Stay with existing contractor	Outcome Cost	No slip £0	2-month slip £40k	4-month slip £80k
Option 2 Change to new contractor	Outcome Cost	1-month gain £20k	No slip £30k	1-month slip £50k

with the greatest probability (70%) being attached to the middle outcome with only a 10% chance of the best outcome arising. The decision tree resulting from the data in Table 6.3 is shown in Figure 6.2. And it has been evaluated in terms of expected costs using the rules of probability. The analysis shows that Option 2, looks to be the better decision as it shows the lower overall expected cost: £33k, as opposed to £44k for Option 1. Before making a final choice, it would be wise to assess the outcome under a variety of different assumed levels of probability. In this case, with the assumed outcomes and costs, only with a very optimistic view does sticking with the existing contractor look the better decision. Nevertheless, switching contractors is a big gamble; if one has completely lost faith in the existing contractor it might still be the best decision but only time will tell.

Figure 6.2 illustrates the use of the decision tree for the straightforward analysis of options. However, there can be situations where the decision paths and the events due to chance that spring from them can lead to increasingly divergent scenarios. In this case finding the end conditions on which to base a valid comparison can be difficult. The following Case example 6.3 shows one such decision situation that arose on a project and the course that was adopted.

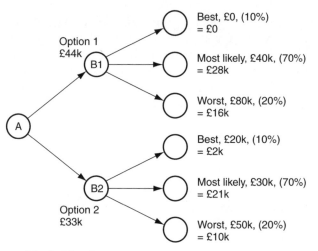

Figure 6.2 The complete decision tree.

EXAMPLE 6.3: CASE EXAMPLE: THE STABILIZER FIN DECISION

With air-launched free-fall weapons, it is common practice to use folding stabilizer fins to ensure the weapon strikes the target at the appropriate speed and altitude. During the development of an air-launched device a problem arose with a stabilizer used on a weapon that was part of a larger system being managed by a prime contractor. The stabilizer fins were released by a timing device operating on a spring that opened the fins; a large number of these weapons were needed in the test programme. Due to the quantities involved, the weapon contractor had built a special assembly line and staffed it to meet the delivery rate demanded by the prime contractor's programme. Just when assembly work was due to start, some wind tunnel work using small models revealed that, under certain circumstances, the stabilizer might not open in sufficient time because the spring had insufficient energy; however, the amount of energy needed was difficult to establish. Furthermore, there was very little space for the spring and any increase in space could involve significant changes to the rear of the weapon. Concern grew and eventually a spring was designed with double the energy of the existing one that would still fit in the available space without extensive changes. Doubts, however, still remained; what was needed was a flight test.

Considerable urgency was attached to the test as the weapon manufacturer was aware of the problems that would follow if the new design proved unsatisfactory but, at the same time, he had a labour force ready to start production. One trials aircraft fitted with the special weapon release unit was available and preparation for a test with a prototype modified unit was put in hand. Shortly before the test was due, a sister aircraft to the trials plane suffered a fatal accident; investigation revealed a serious fatigue problem with the whole fleet and all were grounded including the trials machine. Repairs to the trials aircraft were expected to take six months; a suitably modified alternative aircraft was not available. The weapon contractor asked the prime contractor for a decision on how to proceed given that the labour force was in place; to stop would involve a lay-off of staff and a lengthy period of run-up once production resumed. However, if the spring did not work, a major redesign would be necessary.

This is a classic project manager's dilemma: is it better to go ahead knowing that if hardware is produced and the system has a problem it will result in expensive scrap, or would it be preferable to wait for a test knowing that a delay will affect the overall project cost significantly? With either decision there is a risk that if fate is unkind both the cost and timescale of the project will be adversely affected.

Before this problem can be analysed some basic facts need to be assembled:

- availability of other aircraft – none that were not of the same type and affected by the same problem
- ongoing cost of the project – $0.75m/month
- existing committed cost of weapons – $0.5m
- cost of 5000 test weapons to be supplied over 6 months – $1.5m
- salvage value of committed items – $0.25m
- slip if the new spring fails – 12 months.

Two courses of action are open to the project manager: wait for possibly 6 months and conduct the flight test, then give the go-ahead for weapon output, or go ahead immediately with the batch of 5000 units and maintain the programme. Only two outcomes are possible: either the new spring works properly, or it does not.

It becomes clear however that finding the end conditions for evaluation is not a simple matter as the course of the project will be rather different depending upon what decision is made and what actually transpires on the flight test. It then becomes something of a matter of opinion as to how far one looks into the future to determine a set of equivalent conditions on which to make a comparison and what costs are assigned to each outcome. The array of outcomes that was used to evaluate this problem is given in Table 6.4 which assumes the costs incurred plus those foreseen at the time the result of the flight test is known. This is a logical if still somewhat arbitrary choice.

Table 6.4 Stabilizer decision, outcome array.

Decision	Outcomes			
	Stabilizer works		Stabilizer does not work	
STOP FOR 6 MONTHS	H/WARE COMMITMENT	$0.5m	H/WARE COMMITMENT	$0.5m
WAIT FOR TRIAL	SLIP 6 MONTHS	$4.5m	SLIP 12 MONTHS	$9.0m
	AT $0.75m/MONTH		AT $0.75/MONTH	
			SALVAGE	−$0.25m
		$5.0m	RE-MANUFACTURE	$0.5m
				$9.75m
GO AHEAD WITH 5000	PROJECT ON COURSE	$0m	H/WARE COST	$1.5m
	H/WARE COST	$1.5m	SLIP 12 MONTHS	$9.0m
			SALVAGE	−$0.25m
		$1.5m	RE-MANUFACTURE	$1.5m
				$11.75m

If there was no knowledge of the likelihood of either a pass or a fail on the flight test then a probability of 0.5 could be assigned to each outcome and a decision tree drawn and evaluated. In this case nature's tree consists of two branches, either the stabilizer works on test or it does not. The decision tree has been drawn and evaluated for its expected values at equal probabilities and is shown in Figure 6.3. It shows that going ahead with production has the lower expected costs and is therefore the preferred option.

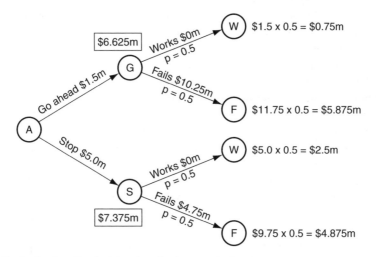

Figure 6.3   Evaluating the decision tree for its expected outcomes.

It was assumed in this evaluation that there was no knowledge about the likelihood of a failure or a success and this was the justification of the 50% probability assigned to each outcome. However it is possible to find out what level of probability of the new spring working is necessary for the expected costs from both options to be equally likely. If the actual probability of it working is greater than this value then going ahead will be the better course of action, if it is less it will pay to wait.

Let x = The probability that the new spring works.

Then the minimum probability for success occurs when the outcomes of both strategies have equal expected costs:

The expected cost of waiting for 6 months is: $5x + 9.75(1 - x)$
and the expected cost of going ahead is; $1.5x + 11.75(1 - x)$

$$5x + 9.75(1 - x) = 1.5x + 11.75(1 - x)$$

Therefore $x = \dfrac{2}{5.5} = 0.36$

With any probability of the spring working that is higher than 0.36 there would be a benefit in going ahead with production of the weapons. In this case, after consultation with the weapon manufacturer, it was judged that the likelihood of the stabilizer fins working with the new spring was above 0.9, the most sensible decision was to instruct the weapon maker to go ahead with production in the absence of the flight test.

What happened when this recommendation was put to the prime contractor's project manager? The reaction was not as one might have expected, or was it? He said, 'I don't think that we'll tell them anything; give them enough time and they'll decide to do something on their own accord. If they go ahead and it works: that's fine. If it turns out the other way and they're wrong, we can blame them.' This decision could be viewed as avoiding the issue but the progress of the project is not the only issue involved. Clearly, there is a risk but in this instance the manager viewed the greatest risk as a personal one, that of being seen to make a wrong decision where large sums of money were involved. Such a perception of risk may lie in the corporate culture, if it is one that tends to penalize wrong decisions; even if they are taken in the most rational of ways, this is the kind of decision making that may result. Under these circumstances a project manager may not act in a way that is rational in minimizing the risk to the project.

As to what happened; the weapon contractor decided, unilaterally, to go ahead with production in the absence of a test. After about two months of further investigation, the prime contractor found that an alternative rig fitted to an aircraft of a different type could be modified to test the weapon. The rig was duly modified and the test carried out about a month later; it showed that the new system worked perfectly.

The decision-tree method is a formalized way of assessing complex decision problems and it can aid the decision maker by:

- showing clearly good or bad options
- showing marginal differences between options that can help in deciding how much it is worth paying for more information (for example, through research or testing) in order to improve the decision.

Before making a final decision, a sensitivity analysis should be performed. Small changes are made on the input assumptions and the final result is noted. Where small changes in assumptions cause the decision to alter then the problem is sensitive and more work needs to be done to validate the assumptions if that is possible. If large changes in assumptions do not cause the result to change then the problem is insensitive and the decision maker can be much more confident. Finally, all decisions have to be seen in terms of the wider context and this aspect should always be considered before the decision is ultimately made.

Decision trees need care in their construction and evaluation, a logical and disciplined train of thought is essential. However, evaluation can become difficult if the train of events leads to increasingly divergent scenarios; it then becomes difficult to find a valid point of comparison to determine which is the better option. Formalized decision trees are thus better suited to the simpler situations in which a reasonable comparison can be made of the end conditions. After the evaluation has been done, one thing should be noted: managers that follow a logical and reasoned decision-making process can be said to be making good decisions and that is all that can be expected of them. There is, however, a difference between a good decision and a good outcome. In an uncertain situation the outcome is in the hands of fate and if fate chooses to be perverse a good decision can still lead to a bad outcome.

Making use of further information

From time to time a decision may be required on an assumed set of probabilities but perhaps the option exists to obtain more objective information that could alter our view. For example, if, in the case of the stabilizer decision, there was an option to perform a quick test on the ground that would give some hard evidence of how well the system was likely to perform in the air, is it worth doing a test and if it is, how should we revise the probabilities of success and failure in the light of the results of the ground test? As related in Chapter 2, problems of this type were of interest to an eighteenth-century English Presbyterian minister, Thomas Bayes, who formulated an approach that bears his name.

Suppose a decision has been made to start a venture on an assumed probability of success based on previous experience but there is a key element of that venture that is the cause for doubt, let us say, for example, the market take-up of a new product. Suppose further there is an option to test that key element by a market survey. We might wish to know by how much our estimate of the success of the venture will be altered depending on the outcome of the test.

For this proof we shall use the convention that X|Y means event X given that event Y has occurred. This is an important concept as in a great deal of statistical work it is assumed that events are independent; this was the justification for the use of the expected value. However, we can also have a situation where a subsequent event is not independent of but conditional upon another event having occurred. This is a *conditional probability*; with this idea Bayes made his contribution to our understanding of probability theory.

Let X = the venture being a success
X' = the venture not being a success
Y = the test indicating a success
Y' = the test not indicating a success
$P(X)$ = the probability associated with event X

Then $P(X + Y) = P(X) \times P(Y|X)$
and $P(Y + X) = P(Y) \times P(X|Y)$

As these must be equal $P(X) \times P(Y|X) = P(Y) \times P(X|Y)$

and $P(X|Y) = \dfrac{P(X) \times P(Y|X)}{P(Y)}$ (1)

If we remember that $P(X) = 1 - P(X')$

It can be shown that $P(Y) = P(Y|X) \times P(X) + P(Y|X') \times P(X')$ (2)

By substituting 1 in 2 we get:

$P(X|Y) = \dfrac{P(X) \times P(Y|X)}{(P(Y|X) \times P(X) + (P(Y|X') \times P(X')}$ (3)

This is the formula that will give us the new probability of success with this venture in the real market following a success being indicated by the market survey. This is Bayes' theorem (or rule) in its simplest form and it can be expanded to cover more than just two cases. The value P(X), our initial view of the probability of event X, is known as the *prior probability* and the conditional probability that results from event Y, that is, P(X|Y), is known as the *posterior probability*. The easiest way in which the simple situation can be visualized is with a *probability square* and this is shown in Figure 6.4.

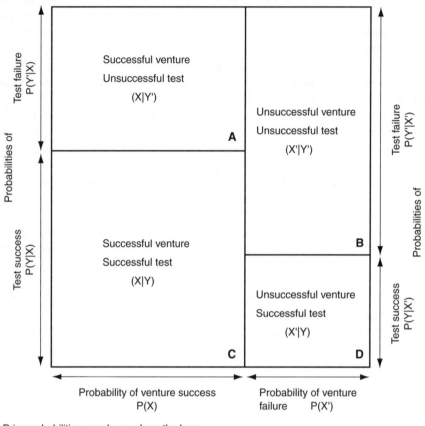

Prior probabilities are shown along the base
Posterior probabilities are shown inside the square

Figure 6.4   Probability square for the venture and the test. The original assumed probabilities for the venture being a success are the prior probabilities and are given on the base. When the probabilities associated with the test are applied, it results in the areas that show the posterior probabilities of each of the pairs of outcomes. The probability of a successful venture following an unsuccessful test is the area A divided by the total area associated with an unsuccessful test: A + B.

EXAMPLE 6.4: INCLUDING FURTHER INFORMATION IN THE DECISION-MAKING PROCESS

Suppose in Case example 6.3 the project manager was not forced to make an immediate decision but had an option to perform a test on some dummy munitions incorporating the new spring in a wind tunnel and this test could be arranged in a matter of two weeks. Suppose further that the manager decides to wait until the wind tunnel test is complete before making a decision; we can ask how we might view the chances of the air test succeeding after the wind tunnel test has been concluded. Here Bayes' Theorem can help the project manager revise his view of whether or not to order production following the wind tunnel test but before the air test has been carried out.

We need to make an assumption about the confidence we can place in the wind tunnel test being a good predictor of the outcome of the air test. Let us assume that confidence is high that what is seen in the tunnel will be representative of what is seen in flight but always remembering that the dynamic conditions of a wind tunnel are not truly representative of the real system. For this reason we might assign a probability of 0.9 (90%) that what occurs in the wind tunnel will occur in flight.

In the problem as initially stated, Bayes' Theorem would not have proved any more useful than the original 90% confidence that we have in the wind tunnel test being an accurate predictor because the 50/50 probability associated with the success of the stabilizer indicates there is no preference for one outcome over the other. Let us therefore assume that after discussion with the stabilizer manufacturer the probability of the stabilizer being successful is revised to a figure of (0.75) 75%. Bayes' Theorem will help decide what new level of confidence can be placed in a successful air test.

Let the probability of the stabilizer being successful in the air = X = 0.75
Let the probability of the stabilizer being unsuccessful in the air = X' = 0.25
Let the probability of the wind tunnel test correctly indicating the air test result as
    Y = 0.9
Let the probability of the wind tunnel test incorrectly indicating the air test result as
    Y' = 0.1

Consider the situation where the wind tunnel test indicates a success, what confidence can now be placed in the air test being a success?

From Bayes' Theorem:

$$P(X|Y) = \frac{P(X) \times P(Y|X)}{(P(Y|X) \times P(X) + (P(Y|X') \times P(X')}$$

Substituting:

$$P(X|Y) = \frac{0.9 \times 0.75}{(.75 \times 0.9) + (0.1 \times 0.25)} = 0.9265 = 92.7\%$$

Thus success in the wind tunnel would raise the project manager's confidence in the air test from 75% to 93% and be a good reason to initiate production.

In the event of a test failure in the wind tunnel what figure would be given for confidence in the air test indicating a success?

From Bayes' Theorem:

$$P(X|Y') = \frac{P(X) \times P(Y'|X)}{(P(Y'|X) \times P(X) + (P(Y'|X') \times P(X')}$$

Substituting:

$$= \frac{.75 \times .1}{(.1 \times .75) + (.9 \times .25)} = .25 = 25\%$$

Thus if the wind tunnel test is a failure the project manager might now feel there is only a 25% chance that the air test will be successful, perhaps too low to order the items into production until the air test has been completed.

It was stated in Case example 6.3 that the confidence level in the stabilizer working was in fact 90%; substituting this figure in Bayes' Theorem gives the probability of success in the air following a test success of 98.7% while for a success in the air following a test failure we still have a probability of 50%. With a degree of confidence in the stabilizer working that is as high as 90%, Bayes' Theorem has indicated that there is very little value in authorizing the wind tunnel test as even with a test failure there is still a 50% chance of a success in the air; the project manager would be wise to go ahead immediately and order manufacture. However, had the confidence in the stabilizer working been as low as 75% then clearly there would be value in holding off the decision and conducting the wind tunnel test, as a failure in this case indicates a rather more serious condition and is a reason for delaying manufacture as well as looking at alternative designs.

Bayes' Theorem has shown not only the revised probabilities associated with the expected outcome following a test but it can also indicate whether performing a test is likely to have a significant impact on the choice of what to do next and thus what value we might place on gathering more information to improve both our knowledge and the decision.

Bayes' Theorem combines an initial belief about the outcome of a situation with a belief about the value that can be attached to an experiment or some other objective data; in this respect it is a more sophisticated concept than the straightforward approaches of such methods as decision trees or MCDM (multiple-criteria decision-making) methods. However, it has attracted controversy since the mid-1800s because of its heavy dependence on the prior probabilities. The example above shows how sensitive the result can be to the assumed prior probabilities; in some real cases they may be based on objective evidence but in others they may be no more than guesswork. It can be argued that if one has a particular view of the likelihood of success associated with an experiment why should one revise one's view of the situation on the basis of a prior perception which might easily be wrong? For these reasons the world of statistics has become divided into those who accept Bayes' Theorem (the Bayesians) and those who do not believe in placing any reliance on it (the frequentists).

From the 1920s, classical statistics has always considered objective probability, that can be measured through observed frequency, as being the best guide in a decision-making situation. This has led to the standard statistical test being the 'null hypothesis' in which any proposition, based on a calculated statistic, is assumed to be false unless it can be shown through objective measurement that the probability of this being the case is very low: typically less than 5%. For any probability higher than this, the null hypothesis is accepted and the proposition is assumed to be untrue. This rather rigid, though intellectually defensible, view fails to take account of subjective data that may also be available and, according to Bayesian advocates, can lead to a wrong view being taken. Although Bayesian inference was popular until the 1920s, accepted practice in the later twentieth century meant that few practitioners in the field of decision making have taken much time to understand the Bayesian approach until recently. However, it has always had its advocates and new uses are being found for it. Market researchers are making use of it to predict behaviour patterns where information exists about previous behaviour and it is wished to know what can be expected with new situations; this has been used to identify potential customers for new financial products. It has also been used in drug development projects for the assessment of results from clinical trials and the analysis of military situations involving the prediction of enemy movements. In a world of mass communication, the Bayesian approach is being used as a method of screening information transactions to see if communication in one area might be relevant to developments in another; by assessing key words and phrases, an inference can be drawn about what a communication in one field is about and, by measurement, the probability that it could be relevant to something seen elsewhere.

The ability to combine an educated guess with some objective data is a concept that has obvious attractions when it comes to assessing how to deal with future situations and is clearly relevant to the type of decisions that sometimes face project managers. With new applications being found, the Bayesian approach to decision making is likely to become a technique of growing importance.

The influence diagram

It has already been said that using logical processes such as decision trees to express a complex problem can sometimes be difficult as absolutely clear thinking is essential. One method of formulating the decision problem that was created to aid and simplify the process is the construction of an **influence diagram**. This method was devised in the late 1970s, principally by mathematicians R.A. Howard and J.E. Matheson, as a way of expressing decision problems. A simple example is given in Figure 6.5 which shows how the influence diagram can be used to express a problem concerning the choice of product pricing and its effect, in an uncertain market, on overall profitability. It will be seen that it consists of arcs and nodes: the nodes represent events, conditions or decisions, and the arcs indicate the path and direction by which one node influences another. In this diagram three types of node have been used: a decision node, a node that contains an element of chance and a node that combines the values from nodes that influence it. These are the three most basic nodes but some practical software tools make distinctions regarding the types of functions that are contained in the combined effects nodes.

The concept of the influence diagram derived from the decision-making process and all influence diagrams of the type shown in Figure 6.5 can be converted into a probability and event tree, which is often conveniently, though incorrectly, referred to as a 'decision tree'. An example of an equivalent tree is given in the lower part of Figure 6.5. Attempting to reverse the process by creating an influence diagram from a probability tree can lead to ambiguities and thus it is never done. There are certain limitations as to what can be depicted and analysed with a conventional influence diagram; processes that involve a repetitive cycle cannot be solved and situations where the values of the variables alter with time could also prove difficult to evaluate. These limitations tend to show that, in its original form, the influence diagram is most suitable for evaluating decision situations that are essentially static at a point in time.

To analyse the influence diagram and draw some conclusions about the relationship between the start and finish nodes, it is first necessary to define the nature of the influences and their effect on each node. In practical terms, with current software, these influence effects must be specified in strict mathematical terms. Before the influence diagram can be

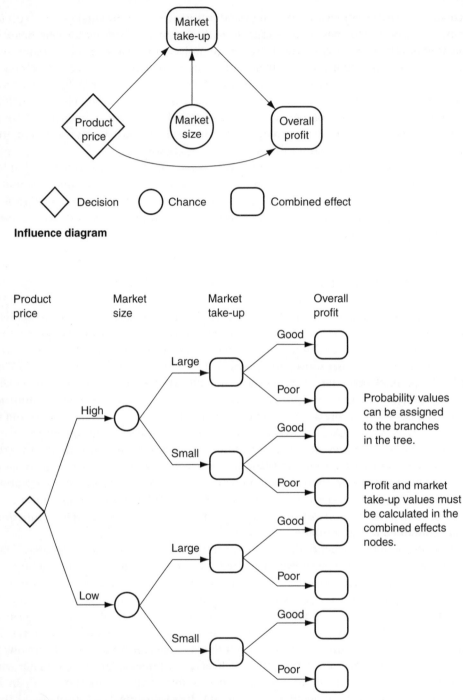

Figure 6.5 Example of an influence diagram and its equivalent event and probability tree. In this case the problem is one of choosing between a high or low product cost in order to achieve the best profit. To evaluate this problem the combined effects nodes must incorporate the rule that determines their value; for example, the overall profit is a function of the numbers of items resulting from the market take-up and the actual product price.

evaluated, all the nodes must be considered and the influences and their output effects established. If there are many inputs to a node, the analysis of influences and probable outcomes can become complex, hence the need to express the problem in its simplest and most logical form. It will be realized that as influence diagrams can be made analogous to probability trees they can be solved using the rules of probability. They can also be evaluated using the more sophisticated Monte Carlo simulation method. To evaluate the diagram, the influence effects generated at one node are transferred to the next, where they are combined with all other influences before being transferred to the next node, and so on until the final node is reached and an end result produced.

The compact and simple relationship between the variables is easy to understand in the influence diagram when compared to the tree representation. Even with such a simple problem as that in Figure 6.5, the tree is beginning to grow large and will do so exponentially as more nodes are added to the influence diagram to refine the problem definition or expand the issues involved. The ease of problem definition associated with the influence diagram has led some to claim that its simple and intuitive nature means that experts in risk analysis are not required as anyone can be taught to construct them. This may be true at one level but there is a big difference between being able to draw an influence diagram and being able analyse it. To do so one may have to determine probabilistic values associated with the outputs from some nodes and the equations that govern how quantities such as product prices are transformed into overall profits. These relationships may be complex if a variety of factors are involved and it may take an experienced analyst to determine them.

The influence diagram shown in Figure 6.5 can be evaluated to determine the best strategy for product pricing in the same way that a decision tree is solved with the added complication of incorporating the functions in the chance and combined effects nodes. This can show either the best pricing strategy or the range of profit values for a range of prices. Attempting to evaluate influence diagrams by hand calculation for anything other than the simplest problem is not recommended for anyone but the most mathematically inclined but help is at hand. Influence diagrams have been embodied in some software products as the principal method for formulating the problem under study and examples of two such systems are given Chapter 11. The approaches are rather different as one system, *DPL*, is aimed directly at decision making and follows the original approach while the other, *(I) Decide,* is derived from a system that started as a method for dynamically simulating the behaviour of projects, rather than decision analysis, and for which the influence diagram was selected as a suitable way of depicting the dynamic interactions.

Sensitivity analysis

Sensitivity analysis is an important aspect of risk assessment; it throws into highlight those factors that have the greatest effect on the predicted outcome. Before any major decision is made, a check should be made on all the major variables and assumptions used in the analysis to see just what the effect on the decision will be if any are changed by a small amount. At its simplest, sensitivity analysis can be performed by changing each significant variable independently in small increments and measuring the effect on the overall outcome. The results of the analysis are usually presented in a sensitivity diagram which is sometimes referred to as a 'spider diagram'; it shows the magnitude of the effect of each variable on the measured outcome and an example is shown in Figure 6.6.

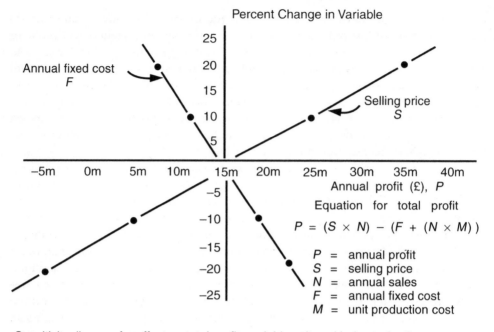

Sensitivity diagram for effect on total profit, variables altered independently.

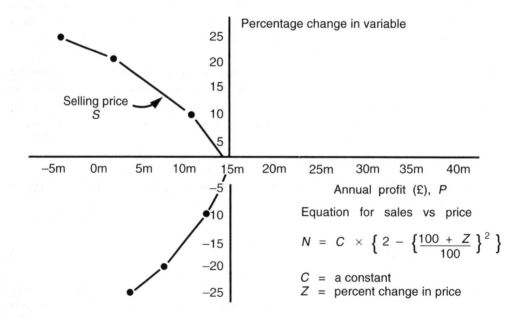

Sensitivity diagram for the effect of selling price on annual profit taking into account the effect of selling price on annual sales.

Figure 6.6 Examples of sensitivity diagrams showing results, in the upper half, where variables are treated independently and, in the lower half, where a dependency between variables has been included in the calculation.

The general principle employed with sensitivity assessments is to treat each variable independently, but sometimes this can be misleading. Care should thus be taken in interpreting sensitivity diagrams – they can give a false picture if they do not take into account the interrelationships that may exist between variables. Where significant variables do interrelate a sensitivity diagram exploring this relationship should be drawn as it can provide an insight that is not apparent from the simple unrelated diagram. Examples of both types of diagram are shown in Figure 6.6; it can be seen that the effect on total profits due to altering the selling price looks very different from the simple independent case when the effect that the selling price has on annual sales is taken into account.

The decision-making process

The management of all projects consists of making decisions on a daily basis, some can be made with little in the way of a formal analysis and with high confidence that the decision is the right one. However, situations can arise when the decision is of great importance; sometimes they can be seen well in advance and plans can be created to ensure that when the decision has to be made there is sufficient knowledge and understanding to assist in making the right choice. On other occasions, such as in Case example 6.3 (the stabilizer fin), important decisions with potentially serious consequences might have to be made at short notice and with incomplete information. These situations can present themselves at any time and without warning; they can represent significant risks for the project if the decision turns out to be the wrong one.

As an aide-memoir, the steps in the decision-making process are

1) **Understand what the decision is that must be made** – take time to understand developing situation and identify the key decisions, separating them from side issues that may be obscuring the problem.

2) **Assemble as much information as is available** – find out as much as possible about the issues that are contributing to the decision situation, separate the objective information from the subjective.

3) **Identify the courses of action that are open** – consider what options are open; some free thinking might help.

4) **Consider the range of possible outcomes that could spring from each course** – identify the outcomes and consequences that could stem from any chosen course of action.

5) **Evaluate the end conditions associated with each outcome** – make an objective assessment of where the project might find itself as a result of the chosen course of action, ideally expressing the result in quantitative terms.

6) **Make a rational choice that is most likely to preserve the project's objectives** – use one or other of the analytical approaches to choose the course of action that appears most likely to ensure the project remains on course to meet its goals.

7) **Perform a sensitivity analysis on the results of the decision against the basic assumptions** – see if the decision is sensitive to small changes in assumptions; if it is, consider the assumptions in more depth and if necessary, do more research.

8) **Consider the implications of the chosen course of action in the wider context** – before any decision is finally made consider how it could affect the overall project, its environment and its stakeholders; be certain there could be no adverse consequences that have not been considered which could create a new set of risks.

Following this approach should ensure that sound decisions are made when they are required, but sadly it does not ensure that all decisions will necessarily turn out to be the right ones as fate can occasionally be perverse. Making good decisions in the face of uncertainty is the key to effective risk management and every project manager should be aware of how to do it.

Note

1 Von Neumann, J. and Morgenstern, O. (1954) *Theory of Games and Economic Behavior*, Princeton, NJ: Princeton University Press

7 *Changing Conditions*

In previous chapters we have considered situations where there was uncertainty about the result that would flow from a decision because any decision could lead to a range of possible outcomes and we cannot be sure which one will arise. There are other occasions where the course of action is already determined but the risks lie in the project not going according to plan. This is a very common situation and one that could, if the deviations from plan are serious enough, lead to some tough decisions that the project manager might be forced to take. Typical examples of deviations from plan are:

- Planned activities may take longer than estimated.
- Failures may occur on test.
- Resources may not be available when needed.
- Costs may rise above the amount in the budget.
- The external environment might change.

Effects such as these can and will combine to cause the outcome of the project to be different from that in the plan and, for the most part, they will make the position of the project worse. If it is known that some of these effects are likely to happen they can be allowed for in the plan by adding suitable time and cost contingencies. The question becomes one of how much contingency to add and what faith can be had in the result.

The PERT (Project Evaluation and Review Technique) concept was devised in the late 1950s and dealt with project durations; it recognized that uncertainty is a feature of all estimating and it sought to quantify this by allowing estimates of the shortest, longest and most likely task durations to be entered into the analysis. PERT was rather more advanced in concept than the contemporary Critical Path Method as it was concerned with variability of the project end-date and the confidence to be attached to any estimate of when the project might end. The PERT technique fell into disuse in the late 1960s for both technical and practical reasons but the fundamental problem of uncertainty has not gone away and a revival of the idea has come about in some of the more recent software systems which are now being marketed either as risk analysis tools in their own right or as risk analysis modules that can interface with standard project planning software.

Combined probabilities

The concept of the expected value has already been introduced in the context of simple situations with one, two or just a few more outcomes. Using the rules of probability theory, the expected value can be extended to cover a situation where a parameter with one range of possible outcomes can interact with another parameter with a different range of outcomes to produce a resulting third range of outcomes.

The method by which probabilities for any range of values can be combined is shown in Figure 7.1. In this case it has been applied to the durations of project activities and it will be seen that Activity 1 has a range of possible durations and it is followed by Activity 2 which also has its own range of durations. The question is what will be the range of durations when Activity 1 is combined with Activity 2? Using the expected value concept plus the rules of probability allows us to work this out but before it can be done the distributions of the durations of the activities have to be expressed in terms of equal time intervals. Any two distributions can be combined to produce a resulting distribution by direct calculation as indicated in the Figure and thus a string of activities of any length. This approach is known as the 'controlled interval and memory' method; as a hand calculation method it is very tedious for anything other than the simplest problems. Nevertheless, it contains most of the elements that allow us to deal with some complex and uncertain situations.

Conditional uncertainty

The three basic parameters in which the expectations of a project is often expressed are cost, time, and the performance of the product or system. In general, we expect a project to deliver the required functional performance from whatever the end product is for a cost that is not greater than we are willing to pay and in a time that meets our needs. A project may not fail overall if it exceeds the cost or time aspects as many ultimately successful projects have

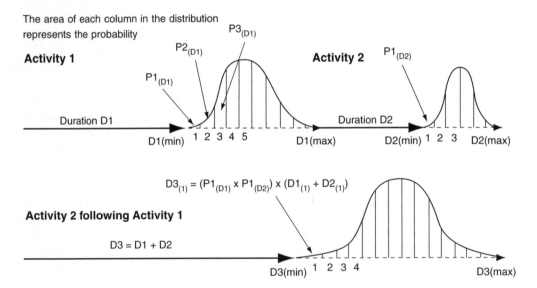

The principle of combined probabilities allows the distribution of the activity D3, which is the result of activities D1 and D2, to be calculated. This is the same principle used by random number simulation, it relies on the fundamental precept that all activities are independent i.e. what happens during activity D2 is not influenced in any way by the result of activity D1.

Figure 7.1 How probabilities and durations of two activities are combined to generate a third distribution relies on the expected value concept and the principle of independence.

shown, but a significant failure in functional performance generally results in a failure overall, unless some compromises are acceptable. It is often the requirement to achieve the desired performance that causes projects to overrun both their costs and schedules as more work is done and more time is consumed pursuing the ultimate goal. All instigators of projects know that stopping the project when the original budget has been spent and the planned duration exceeded but before the performance has been achieved would be likely to result in something worthless but in which they have made a significant investment. Unless there are clear indications that the performance is never likely to be achieved within an acceptable cost and time, most instigators would carry on working until something useful has been created.

The issue of technical performance is always one of the most significant areas of risk in any project and that risk increases with the degree of innovation involved. Projects which have a heavy dependence on novel technologies or aim to take existing technologies into new areas have shown themselves to be highly risky; they might succeed brilliantly but equally and far more likely they will experience significant difficulties at some point leading to escalation or, at worst, cancellation. Figure 7.2 shows this author's assessment of the potential for overruns on projects in the light of the degree of innovation involved. Whereas the performance aspects of products with a technical content can often be modelled using

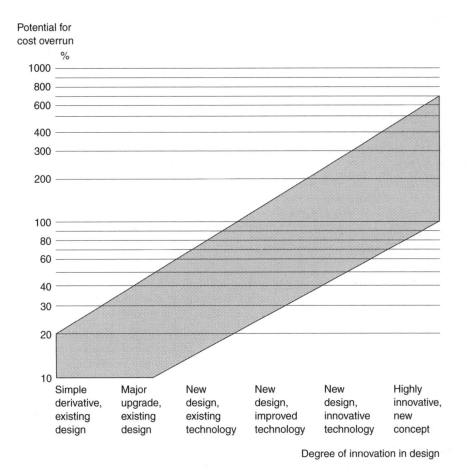

Figure 7.2   Potential for cost overrun versus degree of innovation in product design.

computerized means, what is far less easy to model is the uncertainty that exists between what is modelled and what happens in the real world. This is where the unexpected occurs; because it is unexpected we can have no knowledge of what will occur, when it will happen and what form it might take. A good example is a failure during a test programme; unless something is being tested to destruction or there is very little knowledge of the design, no one expects a test failure although everyone will concede the possibility that a failure can happen. When a failure does occur it often reveals something completely new and unexpected about the design; had the failure been anticipated, it could have been eliminated at the design stage.

The aspect of uncertainty discussed in the paragraph above may have resulted from the initial decisions about the required performance and the choice of technology but it does not directly result from consciously made risk decisions, instead it results from our general lack of knowledge about what will occur. A plan only says what is expected to happen, not what will happen; what actually happens depends on a host of factors, some of which we will not be aware of until reality brings them to our attention. This aspect of project risk I have chosen to call 'conditional risk' as it describes the risks that arise when the conditions on the project differ from those given in the plan and the plan can include performance, cost and schedule aspects.

Uncertainty in the technological aspects of any project can be identified through a number of analytical methods, but predicting how things will turn out is rather more difficult. Furthermore, the extremely wide range of technologies employed on projects of all descriptions means there are no generalized analytical models for predicting the behaviour of the technology in any given project although special techniques have been developed for certain classes of project, for example, software development. The same is not true however for the cost and schedule aspects, these tend to be common to all projects and they are the form in which the plan is generally expressed. From the time when the earliest analytical project management techniques were devised, attempts have been made at establishing the levels of uncertainty in these two aspects.

The critical path method (CPM), when combined with the drawing of network diagrams, led to the first systematic analysis of project plans. The US Navy's PERT system, introduced in 1957, incorporated the idea of variability in project durations and it led to the idea of attaching more information to the activity than just its duration. In particular, resources could be added to the tasks and if cost rates were known for the resources, these could be used to generate a costed plan. The US Department of Defense formally adopted this approach in 1962 under the title 'PERT/Cost' and attempted to force it onto its contractors. It met fierce resistance, in part because suitable software to perform the calculations was not available and, as many firms had made large investments in their accounting processes, they were simply not going to change to a new and untried method. By 1966 PERT/Cost was effectively dead as a working approach but the basic ideas it contained were not wrong.

PERT addressed one fundamental area of uncertainty in project plans: how long will any activity take? Variability between actual duration and planned duration of any project activity is a basic and common form of uncertainty in the project conditions and it introduces uncertainty into three important aspects:

- The start and finish dates of all subsequent activities are now in doubt and thus the end date of the project.
- The critical path to the end of the project may be in doubt and thus the areas where the most effort should be concentrated.
- The costs and resources required to complete the project are in doubt.

Small variations in a few individual activities may have little overall effect but if there is considerable variation over a wide range of activities it could add up to a sizeable problem.

PERT and PERT/Cost attempted to produce a measure of variability and thus confidence in the completion date and the final cost by using a statistical measure – the 'variance'. This measure is calculated as the mean square of the difference between any particular value and the average of all the values of a distributed variable across the complete range of the distribution. It is a single figure measure of the spread of a distribution but it says nothing about the shape of the distribution. Its useful property is that if we wish to combine two sets of probability distributions in the way that the duration of Activity 1 combines with Activity 2 in Figure 7.1 we know that the variance of the duration of the result of Activity 1 followed by Activity 2 is the variance of Activity 1 plus the variance of Activity 2. The square root of the variance is termed the 'standard deviation' and is the commonly quoted measure of the spread or dispersion of a distribution. The standard deviation bears a fixed relationship to the Normal distribution, which is conveniently used to describe the final distribution of the end date of a string of activities. The relationship is: the mean of the distribution covers 50% of all values, the mean plus one standard deviation covers 84.1%, the mean plus two standard deviations covers 97.7%, and the mean plus three standard deviations covers 99.85% of all values. The final value is getting very close to certainty for practical purposes and is often quoted. The standard deviation is generally given the Greek symbol Σ sigma; the formula for near certainty in any distributed value is the mean plus three standard deviations and this is often referred to as the 'three sigma rule'. Sometimes the mean plus or minus three standard deviations is used and this is known as the 'six sigma rule'.

PERT required three estimates to be made of each activity duration – the shortest, the most likely and the longest; from these three values both the mean and variance could be calculated using simple formulae. These values, plus the formulae, could be used by a critical path analysis program to calculate the mean overall project duration, the mean overall project cost and the one, two and three sigma values. From the moment it was launched, PERT was attacked on both theoretical and practical grounds and it soon fell out of favour; however, the principles contained within this approach were important and they have come back in a more modern form.

Simulations

PERT and PERT/Cost contained a method of calculation of the range of possible outcomes for the costs and durations associated with a project plan; however, by using the variance they took a mathematical short-cut to the answer and this was necessary with the relatively low-powered computers of the early 1960s. Today, using modern computers, a different approach can be taken that leads to results with rather more insight.

Figure 7.1 shows how two probability distributions can be combined and it can be extended to cover any number of distributions. Two methods have been devised for calculating the end result:

- direct calculation using the rules of probability – the controlled interval and memory method
- random number simulation.

Direct calculation has already been mentioned in the context of Figure 7.1, but random number simulation uses a completely different approach. Instead of adopting a mathematically analytical method, it works by choosing values at random but whose frequency of occurrence fits the distribution of the given variable. The result, chosen at random, of an activity in a string of activities is combined with the next activity which also has a randomly generated value and this result is combined with the next activity and so on until the end is reached and a single end result is obtained. This process is repeated many hundreds of times, each time with different random values. As each end result is noted, a picture emerges of the spread of possible end results. This method is known as **Monte Carlo simulation** from games using random chance but with fixed probabilities and was first developed in the mid-1940s in the field of physics as a way of combining probability distributions for a group of variables that were not susceptible to straightforward analytical calculation. The method is referred to as 'simulation' as each time it runs it creates a particular set of conditions, thus simulating one possible course for the project, rather than attempting to analytically calculate a general result. Whereas some analytical software has been developed using the controlled interval and memory method, the majority of risk analysis packages available for use in project situations use the Monte Carlo technique.

Monte Carlo methods can be applied to project networks using suitable software. In addition to the basic activity duration, the distribution of the end conditions has to be specified. For practical purposes a number of distribution shapes have been found to be useful; commonly used shapes are shown in Figure 7.3. However, there are many other possible distributions, such as binomial, exponential, Poisson and Weibull, that describe certain phenomena which the more advanced simulation packages can also use.

It will be realized that because of the vast amount of calculation involved, Monte Carlo simulation is only possible as a computerized technique. A refinement of the randomly based method of choosing values for the simulation is to divide each distribution into sections of equal probability and select the values in such a way that an equal number of values is selected from each area. This shortens the simulation process as a smaller number of simulation runs needs to be made to achieve the required accuracy; it is known as the **Latin Hypercube** sampling method.

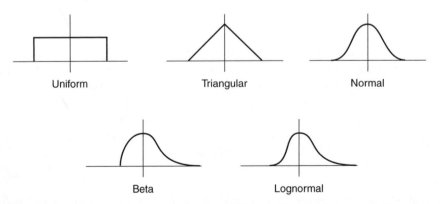

Figure 7.3 Some common patterns of distribution used in project simulation modelling, each pattern has to be specified by its parameters: Uniform by max and min values, Triangular by max, min and most likely values, Normal and Lognormal by mean and standard deviation, Beta by two independent parameters.

Simulation runs on project plans can be done for both durations and costs if data is available and, with some software packages, these two variables may be treated as independent, totally linked, or some degree of linking can be specified on a percentage basis.

Analysing the problem

It was a fundamental feature of the critical path method, and the vast majority of project plans that have been devised since it was created, that when the critical path was calculated it could be considered as a certainty. That is to say there is no doubt about what activities are on the critical path until at least the next update. Once uncertainty has been introduced this is no longer the case, as the project may include a variety of alternative paths, which one will be taken is in the hands of fate and will only be determined as the project unfolds. An example of a project with fundamental issues of uncertainty is given in Example 7.1 below and it will illustrate many of the issues about formulating the plan and interpreting the results.

EXAMPLE 7.1: INHERENT VARIABILITY

A company decides to bid for a contract to design, develop and test a new item of military hardware. The project has a feasibility study phase followed by a full-scale development and pre-production phase. A fixed-price bid is required to cover both phases and the project end-date is also likely to be contractually binding. At the end of the full-scale development phase a production order will be placed but not until a pre-production example has been built and all environmental testing has been completed. The customer also wishes to be in a position to place a production order no later than 45 months from the start of the project. The bidding company notes that an existing item of equipment that it already manufactures can form the basis of the new unit but a significant amount of new design and testing will be needed to meet the customer's requirements. An examination of the programme shows that uncertainties exist in both the areas of pricing and duration but for the purposes of this example only the durations will be considered. The programme can be divided into 6 major activities:

1) feasibility study
2) detail design
3) acquisition of a prototype for testing
4) performance testing
5) environmental testing
6) construction of a pre-production example.

The activities are to be carried out in the order listed, with the exception that sufficient confidence in the design will exist at the end of the performance test for construction of a pre-production prototype to proceed in parallel with the environmental testing. Regarding the activity durations, uncertainties exist over the exact length of time each activity will take and there are further doubts about initial success at the performance testing phase. Beyond the performance test the exact amount of environmental testing is also difficult to establish. It is hoped that some environmental test results from the existing design will be capable of direct translation to the new design and thus shorten the test programme but this cannot be guaranteed. If a performance shortfall reveals itself during performance testing, then it is likely that further alterations to the design will be needed which, in turn, increases the chances of having to perform a full environmental test. Ignoring the cost aspect, the board has decided to quote a duration based on an 80% probability level, but what figure is that and will it be the best option?

This example, loosely based on a real project situation, is typical of many projects where there is general uncertainty not only about the activity durations but what might occur when the activities are complete and the path down which the project might go. If things go well there could be a relatively quick and cheap route to completion, but if failures are encountered and significant changes are introduced then it could result in a much more lengthy and costly project. The difficulty is that at the bidding stage we do not know which it is going to be.

The first step in assessing the future for the project is to express the plan as a logic diagram showing the alternative paths that may be taken. The next step is to estimate the range of alternatives and to assign probabilities to each. Figure 7.4 shows the logic diagram with the assessed durations and probabilities. In this example all durations are given in months and the spread of durations has been kept deliberately small. A simple rule has been used for assessing the probabilities: either they are equal – 50/50, 33.3/33.3/33.3 – or one outcome is more likely than the other – 70/30. In this case it was felt that a satisfactory performance on initial test was more likely than a shortfall; however, if a significant shortfall does occur it is quite likely to delay the end of testing by 6 or 7 months due to redesign, remanufacture and retest. In the event of a satisfactory performance test, a short environmental test is more likely to be needed; however, if significant modifications are introduced following a performance test shortfall then a full environmental test is likely to be required.

The logic diagram has a resemblance to a precedence network but it is different from a conventional network as the same activity can appear twice but in alternative forms. Furthermore, which alternative is taken is governed by a degree of probability. A network of this type contains 'branches' and there are two types. A 'probabilistic branch' exists at the end of Activity A where the following Activity P can either be initially satisfactory, P1, or exhibit a shortfall and be repeated, P2. The respective probabilities are assigned on the nodes and in this case P1 is felt to be more likely than P2. The other type of branch is a 'conditional branch'; this occurs where the branch that is followed is determined by some earlier condition that has arisen. An example of this exists at the node that follows P1 or P2. In this case the condition is not a certain one as there still could be doubt about what will happen so this branch is both conditional and probabilistic. If the route to the branching node is via a satisfactory performance test, P1, then a short environmental test E1 is the more likely; if, however, the route is via P2 then a full environmental test, E2, is more likely. The diagram also shows activities in series, F, D and A where the effect of uncertainty in durations is additive, and activities in parallel, R, E1 and E2 where one activity duration may dominate another. This example shows all the features of the general problem of the durations and routes in a project plan that is subject to uncertainty.

As a common time interval of one month has been used to express all the durations, the controlled interval and memory method of calculation can be used to generate the distributions of times for all the activities. In practice one would be likely to use a

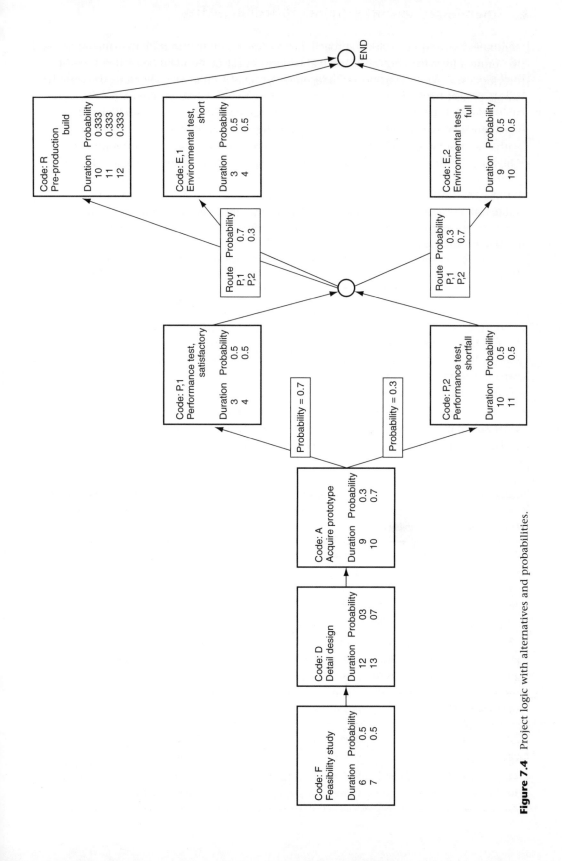

Figure 7.4 Project logic with alternatives and probabilities.

computer-based Monte Carlo approach, but as this does not lend itself to explanation on the printed page the controlled interval method of calculation will be used here. All the distributions have to be treated as independent. Calculation involves working through the whole project from the beginning and generating the distribution of durations at each stage. Here it is felt that the Feasibility study (F) can have durations of 6 or 7 months with equal probability and the next stage, Detail design (D) can take either 12 or 13 months with the latter being more likely. By combining the distributions a new distribution can be obtained for the time to complete the Detail design stage as shown in Table 7.1

Table 7.1 Calculation of durations and probabilities for the completion of detail design (D).

Duration months		Probability p		Combined duration	Combined probability	Cumulative probability
F	D	F	D	FD	p(FD)	Cum. P(FD)
6	12	0.5	0.3	6 + 12 = 18	0.5 × 0.3 = 0.15	0.15
6	13	0.5	0.7	6 + 13 = 19	0.5 × 0.7 = 0.35	
7	12	0.5	0.3	7 + 12 = 19	0.5 × 0.3 = 0.15	0.65
7	13	0.5	0.7	7 + 13 = 20	0.5 × 0.7 = 0.35	1.00

Notice that there are two routes by which the duration 19 months can be derived with probabilities of 0.15 + 0.35 = 0.5 and a cumulative probability of 0.65. By a similar method the position at the end of activity A can be calculated as illustrated in Table 7.2

Table 7.2 Calculation of durations and probabilities for the completion of prototype acquisition (A).

Duration months		Probability P		Combined duration	Combined probability	Cumulative probability
FD	A	FD	A	FDA	p(FDA)	Cum. p(FDA)
18	9	0.15	0.30	18 + 9 = 27	0.15 × 0.3 = 0.045	0.045
18	10	0.15	0.70	18 + 10 = 28	0.15 × 0.7 = 0.105	
19	9	0.50	0.30	19 + 9 = 28	0.5 × 0.3 = 0.150	0.300
19	10	0.50	0.70	19 + 10 = 29	0.5 × 0.7 = 0.350	
20	9	0.15	0.30	20 + 9 = 29	0.35 × 0.3 = 0.105	0.755
20	10	0.15	0.70	20 + 10 = 30	0.35 × 0.7 = 0.245	1.000

Duration, months, FDA	p(FDA)	Cum. p(FDA)
27	0.045	0.045
28	0.255	0.300
29	0.455	0.755
30	0.245	1.000

Using this approach the entire project can be analysed, although the calculation becomes more complex when it comes to a branch as each branch must be calculated separately and the results combined on a probabilistic basis to give an overall result. The numerical analysis will not be taken any further here as few people would attempt to perform such an evaluation by hand calculation, but the final distribution of the project end-date from the controlled interval and memory method is given in Table 7.3.

Table 7.3 Calculation of the end conditions of the preproduction build (R) and thus the end of the project (FDAPER).

Duration FDAPR months	p(FDAPR)	Cum. p(FDAPER)
40	0.005250	0.005250
41	0.040250	0.045500
42	0.123083	0.168538
43	0.199500	0.368083
44	0.193083	0.561168
45	0.110250	0.671416
46	0.028583	0.700000
47	0.002250	0.702250
48	0.017250	0.719500
49	0.052750	0.772250
50	0.085500	0.857588
51	0.082750	0.940500
52	0.047250	0.987750
53	0.012250	1.000000

When the probability of completion is plotted against the overall project duration the result is as shown in Figure 7.5. It will be seen that the distribution has two modes (greatest frequencies) and this project has two distinct futures: an optimistic one with a 70% probability with a duration between 40 and 46 months, centred around 43 months, and a more pessimistic one with a 30% probability with a duration between 47 and 53 months, centred around 50 months. This result springs from the probabilistic branching within the logic and could not have been obtained by analysing a conventional project network. The analysis also shows that when a project hits a problem that results in a major change it tends to shift the entire project, rather than be confined to one area, as changes in one area often lead to changes in another; this is sometimes referred to as the 'knock-on effect' of changes.

The cumulative probabilities of completion for all the activities, F, D, A, P, E and R, are given in Figure 7.6 It will be seen that a marked kink occurs in the cumulative probability line at the $p = 0.7$ point for the completion of the performance test (FDAP) as this is the first major branch. It will also be seen that the probability line for the completion of the environment test (FDAPE) has two kinks indicating that there are three modes in this line. However, the duration of the pre-production build (R) is longer than the environment test and dominates the final result (FDAPER).

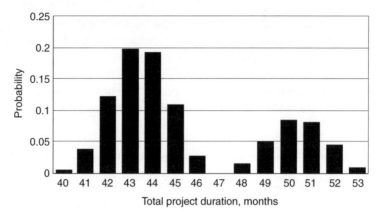

Figure 7.5   Distribution of probabilities against the total project duration.

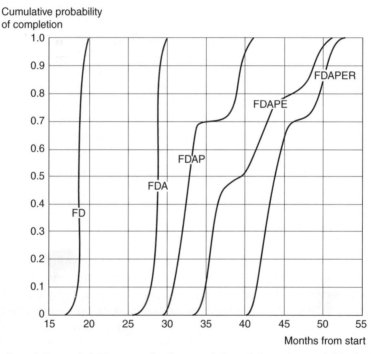

Figure 7.6   Cumulative probability curves for the completion of the various activities in the project.

The result of this analysis raises an interesting question for the Board when it comes to deciding what figures to use in the bid and it also shows how analyses of this type can be used for strategic decision making. If the bid criteria is an 80% probability level then, on the basis of this analysis, the duration to quote is 50 months. As it is known that the customer is looking for a duration of not more than 45 months there is clearly a mismatch. The 45-month duration has only a 67% chance of being achieved, perhaps too low for the confidence the Board is looking for.

However, it should be noted that 45 months' duration is at the 96% chance of the optimistic (70%) future for the project and there is also a production phase to follow after the development work. With new product development projects, all the real profits are actually made on the production phase and this is clearly the main opportunity but it can only be secured if the development contract is won. The Board might therefore decide to bid with a 45-month duration as the prize is still likely to be well worth having, even if there is some schedule overrun and possibly a financial loss on the development phase. The Board might therefore decide that the best strategy is to bid with the 45-month figure but concentrate more effort on the design and feasibility phases with a view to ensuring that the new design passes its performance test the first time around. This might involve more detailed design studies, and additional resources and perhaps a bit more time should be budgeted for this in the final bid. Increasing the chance of a first-time pass from 70% to 85% would dramatically alter the analysis and the confidence in the outcome.

This example illustrates that with any analysis of the future, the result may not be a clear-cut indication of what to do, although there may be pointers. The analysis has indicated the choices open to management but the results have to be seen in the wider context of the overall project and its objectives when it comes to making the final decision.

Chapter 11 shows some examples of alternative software approaches to the problem in this example and it will be seen that the results are identical.

Outputs from Monte Carlo simulations are of two basic forms: frequency distributions of the variable under study, and behaviour indices for each activity. Variability of project attributes such as costs and durations can be shown both as histograms of individual frequencies (Figure 7.5) and as cumulative probability curves (Figure 7.6) as given in Example 7.1 above. The cumulative curve shows the probability that a particular value of cost or duration will be achieved or bettered. Some software can place 'confidence limits' on the probability calculations to show the spread of values associated with a given probability level. It should be noted, however, that the confidence levels are based on an assumption that the input information is perfect, that is, that the plan is adhered to and that no costs or durations go outside the maximum and minimum limits specified. In real projects neither of these assumptions may hold good; the 'confidence limits' may thus give an apparent sense of security that is not really justified.

In addition, some software packages allow the calculation of two index numbers that can help to identify those activities that need special attention: the **criticality index** and the **cruciality index**. These two numbers stem directly from the simulation process, they cannot be easily obtained by direct calculation using the controlled interval method.

The criticality index is a measure of how likely any activity is to become a critical activity in the context of all the variability in the project plan. It is calculated by noting on how many occasions each activity appeared on the critical path during the series of simulation runs. If, for example, an activity appeared on the critical path on 250 occasions in 1000 simulations it would have a criticality index of 0.25 and it would be inferred that it has a 25% chance of becoming critical.

The cruciality index is a measure of the effect the variability of any activity has on the end result of the project. It is calculated by noting on how many occasions did an increase or decrease in the duration of an activity correspond directly with an increase or decrease in the project duration. Thus an activity which always directly affects the project end-result would have a cruciality of 1.0 while an activity of fixed duration would have a cruciality of 0 even though it might appear occasionally on the critical path.

Activities identified as having high criticality represent areas where management effort should be applied to ensuring they are completed on time or their duration shortened. Where activities show high cruciality, management effort should be directed at reducing the variability.

The matter of feedback

Simulation using random numbers is a convenient way of generating probability distributions for later events that derive from the distribution of earlier ones. The principle comes directly from probability theory and, for the theory to work, all activities must be treated as independent. That is to say the result of the first activity in a sequence can have no influence on the distribution of the second and subsequent activities; what result actually arises from the second and subsequent activities is a matter of pure chance. In effect, the principle of independence implies that a project run under such conditions is out of control, for this is exactly what happens if earlier events are not allowed to influence later ones. Some measure of the influence of earlier events on later ones can be introduced by including branches in the plan to show different routes down which the project may go but this does not include an element of influence due to controlling actions. When things begin to go astray and any of the goals are threatened, a project manager would be expected to take some action on future activities to restore the chance of achieving the goal.

This is the fundamental principle of a closed loop control system, however, this is the complete opposite of the open loop contained in the Monte Carlo approach and evidence from actual projects indicates that theoretical simulations may not reflect reality. It has been noticed, with some real projects, that despite large variances between the estimated and actual durations of individual activities, the end result is much closer to the target than theory might have predicted. Obvious examples come from projects in the world of entertainment (the Olympic Games, the Millennium exhibition, etc.) where the event date is fixed well in advance and come-what-may it will be met. In these cases the opening date has 100% certainty at the outset irrespective of the anticipated variability that may be present in many aspects of the plan. The reason is that controlling action is taken throughout the life of the project to compensate for variations when they arise. It is possible to duplicate this effect, to a limited extent without actually achieving a true feedback situation, in systems that can contain conditional logic. However, it results in a significant complication as it involves applying a test to the result of one activity and using that to choose the distribution that will apply to the next. Thus a string of activities whose combined duration is significantly longer than its expected average value may be used to trigger a shorter time with greater intensity of work for the next activity in the sequence. Even so, it may not duplicate the real position as one way that the schedule may be preserved is to sacrifice some aspect of the specification that is not essential but may be contributing to the problem; no simulation can anticipate a situation like this or what decision might be made.

Monte Carlo simulation methods have their place in the armoury of the project manager and valuable insight into the future for the project can be gained from such analyses. They are at their best with situations where the principle of independence largely holds good; with the controlled project situation, the assumptions may not be so valid. From the moment a project simulation is performed the position of the project is altered if only in a small way; the information derived from the simulation affects the view of the project and may immediately set in motion a series of corrective actions which might significantly change things. Feedback is an essential element of project control and the knowledge gained from a simulation is part of the feedback process. The results of a simulation should be seen as a snapshot, at one point in time, of how the project might perform if no further action is taken to preserve the essential objectives – it should never be viewed as a true view of what the future will bring.

Adding contingency

The idea of variability in the outcome brings with it the idea of contingency as a safeguard against uncertainty. The subject of contingency has caused some confusion and discussion about a) the meaning of the word and b) how much to include, if indeed, any should be included at all. Contingency is a reserve for the unknown and unexpected; as all projects involve casting the mind forward into a future that inevitably contains uncertainties and unknowns, no plan for a project can be considered complete without it. To fail to admit contingencies is to assume perfect knowledge of the future and that, for the most part, is something we can never have.

What exactly constitutes a contingency is a matter of debate as there has been a move in some quarters, notably the USA, to define a contingency as something different from a management reserve. This is perhaps a matter of semantics as they are essentially the same thing but it can come down to who holds the contingency. In essence, the management reserve is viewed as that part of the project contingency that is held outside the project by the sponsor. This reserve is extra to any contingency held inside the project. In US government contract practice, under such conditions as earned value management, contingencies are not allowed. That is to say, all work within the project must be priced without any added contingency for overruns; should the project overrun its projected costs, the overruns are covered by the management reserve, if they are accepted. This is a somewhat artificial approach to a particular contracting situation, designed to ensure visibility of contractor performance and tightly defined initial estimates, but many organizations would not make the distinction or fail to admit any contingencies in the project's own budget.

The term 'allowance' has also been used in a similar way to contingency but there has been a move, in some quarters, to distinguish between these two terms to the extent that a contingency covers the unforeseen aspects but an allowance covers the foreseen but undefined aspects. Again, this is a somewhat artificial distinction that some would find hard to make.

The addition of a contingency is the most common way in which a company involved in projects protects itself from the effects of the unknown and unforeseen; it is the most elementary and universal act of risk management. Contingencies can be added to time and cost aspects of a project; it might also be possible to add them to aspects of performance but this is highly dependent on what the output of the project is. With a project output that is essentially a service, for example, a computerized traffic management system, a reserve or back-up can be included to cater for occasional excessive demands, but for something like a one-shot device that must work on demand, for example, an ejection seat, it is not possible.

The amount of contingency that is added can have a significant bearing on the outcome of the project, too much contingency and it might lead to a lax attitude to day-to-day control but too little can lead to a situation where budgets and timescales are exceeded well before completion and this can have ramifications for the overall viability of the project. Projects that include a contingency inevitably demand more funds and a longer duration at the budgeting stage than those that do not. This can raise questions when it comes to competitive tendering and there is often a temptation to leave them out when the competition is fierce. This is not unreasonable as a business decision but it must be realized that contingencies reduce risk and a failure to include them must increase overall risk if the contract is won.

What is covered in the contingency and what is excluded can depend on the contractual arrangement, although this will not be the case for in-house projects such as developing a new product. Contingencies contained within the project contract and its budget typically include sums covering identified risk issues, incomplete scope definition, inaccuracies in estimates, and residual risks. Excluded from the project contingency but possibly covered by the sponsor's or management's reserve are allowances for scope changes, timescale changes and *force majeur*.

Contingencies can be calculated by a variety of methods, some of which are more suitable to particular situations than others. Commonly used methods are:

- **Rules of thumb** – These generally amount to adding a fixed percentage to either the overall project budget or specific parts of the budget if it is known that greater uncertainty exists in some parts of the project than in others. This approach can work well with projects that are well understood at the outset and there is good historical data on which to base the estimate, routine construction work being a good example. As the degree of uncertainty increases, this approach tends to become less applicable, either from the point of view that it might not generate a sufficient amount or the contingency percentage might be forced to grow to the extent that it becomes a major feature in the entire budget.

- **Contingencies based on simulated outcomes** – With this approach all the activities in the project have distributions attached to the end conditions; then, using a process like Monte Carlo simulation, a cumulative probability distribution is derived for the overall project cost and time. This is clearly a more analytical approach than a rule of thumb as it requires greater insight into the likely outcome of all the project activities. However, most projects are one-off affairs, so any distribution attached to any particular activity is unlikely to be made on the basis of objective measurement; for the most part it will be a reasoned guess. The simulation process will produce a probability value associated with any outcome up to the maximum possible – a contingency could be set by adding a sum to the base estimate to give, say, an 85% chance of it not being exceeded; any amount above that is held outside the project. Unless there is very good historical evidence to back up all the individual estimates, it would be wrong to assume this is an 85% confidence level, although this term is sometimes used.

- **Mathematical rules** – Besides the fixed percentage approach it is possible to calculate a contingency value without using a simulation process. If an assessment of the distribution of end conditions for all the activities can be made, then an approach similar to PERT[1] can be used. Both the mean value of the end conditions and the variances have to be calculated; when these are added it will, in the case of the project cost, produce the mean project cost plus the total variance. There is a statistical rule which says that when distributions of any shape are sampled on a random basis the resulting distribution tends to be normal (the Central Limit Theorem[2]). Using this and the calculated overall variance, the probability associated with a particular overall value can be calculated from the normal distribution or the contingency can be set according to one (84.1%), two (97.7%) or three (99.85%) standard deviations (Σ), as shown in Figure 7.7. A variation on this idea is to use the principle of expected values but this must be applied to the outcomes of specific risk issues and could be problematic when it comes to overall uncertainty.

Contingencies are important and they should be given proper consideration; there can however be temptations to reduce or eliminate them particularly where competition is involved. The other fear, often expressed by management, is that contingencies, once they are included in the budget, will be spent whether needed or not. If this is the fear then it is for management, through a businesslike attitude, to ensure that proper controls are in place.

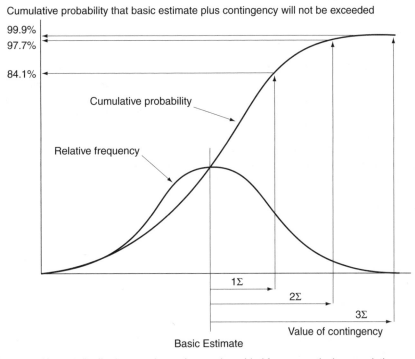

Cumulative probability that basic estimate plus contingency will not be exceeded

99.9%
97.7%

84.1%

Cumulative probability

Relative frequency

1Σ

2Σ

3Σ

Value of contingency

Basic Estimate

Using the Normal distribution, contingencies can be added for any particular cumulative probability; if required, the standard deviation can be used with fixed probabilities.

Figure 7.7 Cumulative probability values, whether derived from a simulation or the PERT formulae, can be used to determine the degree of protection given by the addition of a particular value of contingency to the base estimate.

Notes

1 The PERT formulae for the mean value, the variance and the standard deviation of an activity whose duration is defined by three estimates are:-

Mean duration

$$D = \frac{S + 4M + L}{6}$$

where D = Mean or expected duration
      S = Shortest duration
      M = Most likely duration
      L = Longest duration

This formula has been considered to give a low estimate of the outturn mean value and is sometimes revised to

$$D = \frac{S + 3M + 2L}{6}$$

Variance of duration

$$V_D = \frac{(L - S)^2}{36}$$

where V_D = variance of duration about mean D

Standard deviation of duration

$$\Sigma_D = \sqrt{V_D}$$

where Σ_D = Standard deviation of duration about mean D.

2 The Central Limit Theorem states that the average (mean) of a sample drawn at random from a distributed population will be normally distributed irrespective of the population distribution. This idea has been extended on the basis that any particular outcome of a project with uncertain durations is formed from a random sample from the distributions of all the activities whose total number is fixed. Whereas this may hold good for the cost aspect of a project, the schedule aspect is governed by the critical path which is based on the idea of selecting the longer of two or more durations at any node hence the sample is not truly random. This objection seems to have been overlooked by practitioners; given that many of the distributions used in simulations are only estimates, it may be justifiable. It should also be noted that, like the simulation process, it takes no account of feedback which further undermines the idea of randomness in real projects.

8 *The Risk Management Process*

Considerable efforts have been made by individual workers, the professional associations and the standards bodies to devise a general process for managing risks in projects. Although it is unlikely that any international standard for the process of risk management will be created in the near future, application guides have been produced that are finding increasing acceptance in industry. Notable among them are the British Standard BS-6079-3:2000 'Project Management – Part 3, Guide to the management of business related project risk'[1], the international standard BS IEC 62198:2001 'Project Risk Management – Application guidelines'[2] and the *Project Risk Analysis and Management Guide*, produced by the UK Association for Project Management.[3] The processes advocated are all rather similar and follow the general pattern given in Figure 8.1.

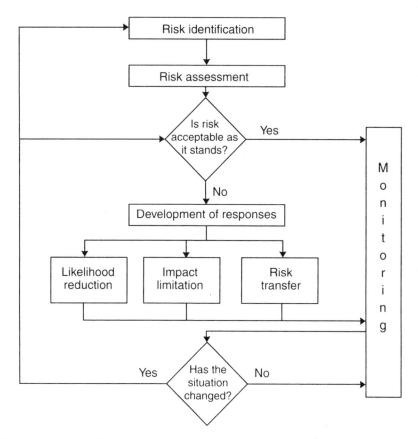

Figure 8.1 The generalized risk management process.

Although the process models may differ in detail and the way they are drawn, they all tend to show a series of discrete activities that together form a feedback loop as shown in Figure 8.1. They tend to agree that the key activities are:

- identification of the risk issues
- analysis and assessment of the risks for their potential impact on the project
- deciding whether anything can or should be done about the identified risks
- developing responses, where required, to the risk issues; some may be proactive while others may be in the form of a contingency
- monitoring the situation
- reassessing the situation in the light of actions taken or risks materializing.

Notice that the process includes risk assessment as a separate activity that feeds into the risk management loop, but the process does not exclude the possibility that risks could materialize even though they have not been assessed or identified in advance. This could occur when the risk-monitoring process detects that the situation has changed but in a way that is unconnected with the assessment process. In practical terms it represents a sudden and unexpected change of project circumstances, for example, a freak environmental disaster such as a flood or earthquake, a catastrophic test failure or a competitor suddenly appearing with a radical new product.

Some aspects of this process have already been introduced, particularly those concerned with analysis and decision making, while others will be new. Risk management is a process that will not necessarily happen on its own although many project control systems that do not include formalized risk management will include elements of this process through regular status and progress reporting, progress measurement and forecasting, project management meetings, project reviews and informal discussions. By these means, problems that are foreseen by the project team are brought to the attention of the project manager and whatever action is required is taken. Formalized risk analysis and management is a relatively recent invention; but risky projects have been successfully completed in the past without a formalized approach, so an effective informal process must have existed. Formalized risk analysis and management simply removes the element of chance associated with an informal arrangement.

Handling risks in an effective way starts with the recognition at senior management level that risk is an inherent feature of projects and to avoid failures and disappointments some measure of active management is necessary. Suitable conditions must be created within both the project organization and the information system for risk issues to identified, monitored and suitable actions taken. Risk management goes well beyond setting up a structure – it is an ongoing process that needs to be carried out throughout the life of the project. Different responses to the risks and opportunities that present themselves will have to be adopted according to the stage of the project and the state of development of the end product. Figure 8.2 shows a schematic process for risk management together with the techniques appropriate to each situation in the risk management process.

Risk identification

At the start it is important to understand the fundamental objectives of the project; these might typically include making a worthwhile return on the venture. However, projects are

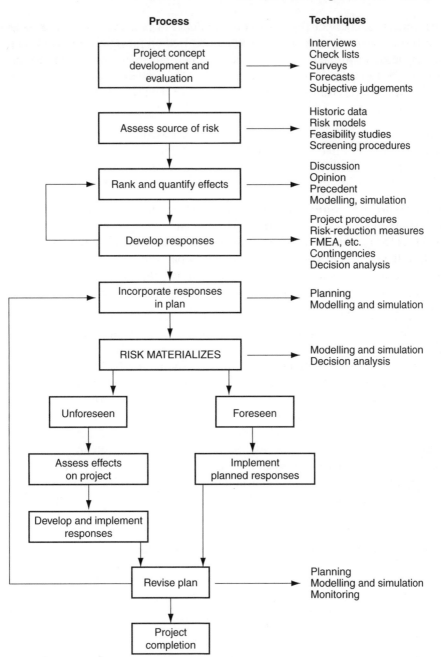

Figure 8.2 The risk management process and associated techniques.

not simply speculative investments in finance, in order to achieve that return some work must be done and it is in that process that most of the risks lie. It is therefore important to identify the sources of risk within the activities of the project; this may be a rather subjective process but a structured and analytical approach, whilst not eliminating the subjective element, can at least ensure completeness. Specific techniques that are generally applicable and simply implemented include:

- The formulation of **checklists** based on experience of earlier projects – Risk issues can be identified through an examination of what occurred on previous projects plus an overall understanding of the issues that are likely to be problematic on future projects. These issues can be formalized into lists and structured in a way that suits the particular type of project. New projects can then be examined against the list and an opinion formed about each point raised.

- **Structured interviews** with responsible or knowledgeable staff, perhaps using the checklist as a basis. Interviews of this type are best done on a one-to-one basis, free of any hint of an inquisition; they can further refine the perception of where difficulties may lie as well as drawing attention to areas that might not be covered in the checklists.

- **Brainstorming sessions** with a group of knowledgeable staff – In an atmosphere of free speculation and without peer criticism, people are invited to produce as many ideas as possible of the risks that might arise. This can lead to a very large number of ideas, some of which will be wild speculation. All risk ideas put forward have to be analysed and categorized into those that are real and need to be either dealt with or monitored, and those that are largely imagined or are extremely unlikely and can be ignored.

- **Assumption analysis** in which all the basic assumptions are listed and challenged – This is often more difficult than it might seem as many assumptions are unspoken and simply never considered; they are things that are so familiar that they are taken for granted, even in new situations. An assumption should not be seen simply as a reversed form of a risk statement, for example, the assumption that there will be adequate staff is the opposite of the risk that adequate staff will not be available. An assumption should be a positive statement that history shows is generally true. The problem can be that there are so many unspoken assumptions: for example, the factory will not be destroyed by an earthquake is something we assume without ever thinking about it; only when an earthquake occurs do we see it as an assumption. Assumptions can be tested against both their importance to the project overall and the likelihood that they might prove false. Any that cannot be unreservedly accepted as being valid are potential sources of risk and can be treated as such.

More complex and specialized methods of risk identification include:

- **Computerized knowledge bases** – These are a new development that combines the checklist of questions with historic knowledge about the relationship of specific risk issues to characteristics of the project. The characteristics are defined to the knowledge base which will then generate a calculated assessment of the levels of risk in key areas.

- **Specialized techniques such as the 'risk diagnosis methodology'**[4] – This approach, developed by the University of Eindhoven, is specifically aimed at product development projects but has the potential for wider application. In essence, it combines several different techniques into a single logical method that aims not only to identify risks but to rank them in order of severity while indicating the types of solution that might be applied. The method starts with detailed interviews with knowledgeable staff who are invited to put forward areas of risk or concern, these are then collated and each risk is turned on its head by stating the 'solution' or risk-free condition. These 'solutions' are circulated to all members who are then asked to make scored judgements about each solution in terms of three criteria: the degree of certainty that the solution can be achieved, the ability to influence the course of events, and its relative importance to overall project success. The scores are then combined to rank the solutions and produce a 'risk topography' for the project. All the staff are then called together for a one-day session at which the topography is presented and the staff then go through each problem and its solution in turn to confirm the overall view or modify it, if needs be. They are then required to propose ways in which perceived difficulties with the proposed solutions might be overcome; this will cause a re-evaluation of some of the risks as the difficulties with some of the proposed solutions may well be resolved. At the end of the session, a new and more detailed ranking of the risk issues will emerge together with ideas of how to overcome the more significant risks.

The external environment is always a source of risk and one over which there may be no direct control; it is important to be able to see this very clearly and such techniques as market surveys, opinion surveys, competitor analysis and technological forecasts may be employed. Maintaining good contacts with interested groups outside the project, including ones that may have the potential to turn hostile, could also be important although this does not apply to direct commercial competitors where secrecy could be very important. Taken together, these actions can serve to direct attention towards changing circumstances or emerging trends which may create uncertainties that could include significant risks but which might also include new opportunities to be exploited.

The output of a risk identification exercise is a reasoned list of risks that can be generally agreed as being more than just figments of the imagination. Whether or not the risks can be ranked and structured can depend on the complexity of the situation; it might not be possible until the next phase has been completed.

Analysis and assessment

Having identified the principal sources of risk, they need to be analysed and assessed for their effect on the project. This is, perhaps, the most difficult task as it involves both analytical thinking and making subjective judgements about the future. A good starting-point is the analysis of historical data, particularly if similar projects have been undertaken in the past. The best guide to a company's future lies in its past; unless some very major organizational change has taken place, things tend to proceed in the way they have done previously. An examination of previous projects including an assessment of similarities, differences, timescales, costs, failures and successes can lead to a more realistic view of each new proposal.

Mathematically based analysis and modelling techniques, as described in Chapter 7, can be used to assess specific types of project risk, particularly those relating to cost and timescale. Ranking according to impact and probability can be done by the approach given in Chapter 10. Analyses can throw light on the range of probable outcomes but they must be treated with some caution as some of the input variables may be both subjective and untested. Analyses can be carried out on both the project itself and on the business as a whole – there could be risks both in going ahead with a project which results in a failure and not going ahead and losing a market to the competition.

Feasibility studies have, as their objective, the testing of specific assumptions. Often they are applied to the technical aspects of a project but they may not go as far as prototype construction and physical tests. Increasingly sophisticated computer-modelling techniques can be used to simulate the function of new products and systems. These models may not be generally applicable and thus may have to be constructed individually to the requirements of each new scheme. Functional and operational characteristics may be tested theoretically and much basic understanding of a new design may be obtained. However, they are abstractions of the real item; they cannot hope to discover all that may be necessary to translate an idea that works on paper or on the computer into a workable product. Besides technical feasibility, cost and timescale may be assessed by direct reference to the product description through the technique of parametric estimating. This approach does not include the probabilistic methods that are contained in the project simulation models but it can still be very useful for assessing costs quickly and rejecting those ideas that have little chance of success for commercial reasons.

The most popular method of recording and ordering risks is through the construction of a 'risk register' specifying all perceived risks with the outcomes, likelihoods and countering strategies. Risks can be ranked in a number of ways, by general category (for example, technical, financial, resources, etc.) and by expected value (impact value x probability), but the approach used by the risk diagnosis methodology seems particularly useful as it requires three aspects to be considered: the probability that the risk can be eliminated or a suitable solution found, the ability to influence the risk situation, and the effect of the risk on the overall success of the project. This three-parameter approach is rather more sophisticated than other methods and simple ranking may not be quite so easy but the additional insight that it gives could be well worth the effort. An example of a risk register is given in Figure 8.3; this is just one of many possible formats.

With any attempt to record risks it is not enough just to identify and categorize them, it is equally important to structure the register in such a way that risks appearing at lower levels are correctly reflected upwards through levels that represent broad groupings of issues and finally determine what, if any, impact they have on the overall goal of the project. Besides the upward direction in which risks may influence higher levels, risks may also exist in a transverse direction where there is an interaction between one group of lower-level risks and another. This can exist where there is an inherent contradiction in some aspect of the project; for example, there may be a desire to increase technical assurance of product performance through extensive product testing while at the same time there is a desire to capture a sizeable market by being first to market through a short overall project development cycle. This kind of situation results in a position where reducing risks of one sort results in increased risks of another. It may well be that risks seen at the lower levels will be deemed manageable within that or the level above and not be reflected upwards. It could also be that a group of risks are developing at the lower level, none of which is individually very significant, but taken as a group they could have a threatening effect on the higher level which could transmit itself to the overall project goal particularly if there is an inherent contradiction. A logical structure will help to identify this problem and ensure that proper consideration is given to the reported situation at each level.

An example of a hierarchical risk structure is given in Figure 8.4, which shows part of a structure for a civil aircraft development project. It will be seen that the highest level is the business case for the project, anything that threatens the overall profitability of the venture would be deemed a serious issue. It will also be seen that there are cross links that relate issues across boundaries at lower levels. Three basic areas have been identified as impinging directly on the business case: the market, the funding and the environment in which the

Project Risk Register						
Project Title: *Engine, Type GO5*		Activity: *Full Dev.*	Cat:	Date: *03/04/2003*		Manager: *P. Turner*
For each Risk Item give Likelihood, Impact and Response						

Risk Item: Specification	Likelihood				Impact	Response
	Nil	Low	Medium	High		
1 Weight too high				✓	Liquidated Damages Liability	Weight Reduction Programme
2 Fuel Consumption too high	✓					
3 Vibration Level too high	✓					
4 Cost too high			✓		Reduced Sales	Value Engineering Programme
5 MTBF too low				✓	Liquidated Damages Liability	Reliability Improvement Programme
6 Etc.						
7 Etc.						

For each Risk in the High category give description and reason:	
Weight Problem	Target is 207kg but initial weight estimate is 219kg. No obvious solution to this at present but suggestion has been made to use light alloy castings in the manifold region, expected saving 6kg.
MTBF Problem	Customer expects minimum of 4,000 hr's MTBF, demonstrated MTBF is currently 3,100 hr's. Extended running will be necessary, known problems are oil seals, new seals test programme may be required.

For each Risk in the Medium category give description and reason.	
Cost Problem	Current cost estimate is £2,345 per unit; this is within 5% of target and should be bettered by current VE programme and selective purchasing, however effects of above high risks may have adverse effect on costs.

Are there any Risks in the Low category that might have hidden effects?	
None at present	
List Related Risk Areas:	Schedule Risk Register, Technical Risk Register.

Prepared by: .....*N. Webb*.....   Approved by: .....*P. Turner*.....

Figure 8.3 Example of a risk register. In this case the register is concerned with road vehicle engine development and risks are categorized initially by risk area: specification, technical, commercial, etc., then by high, medium and low levels.

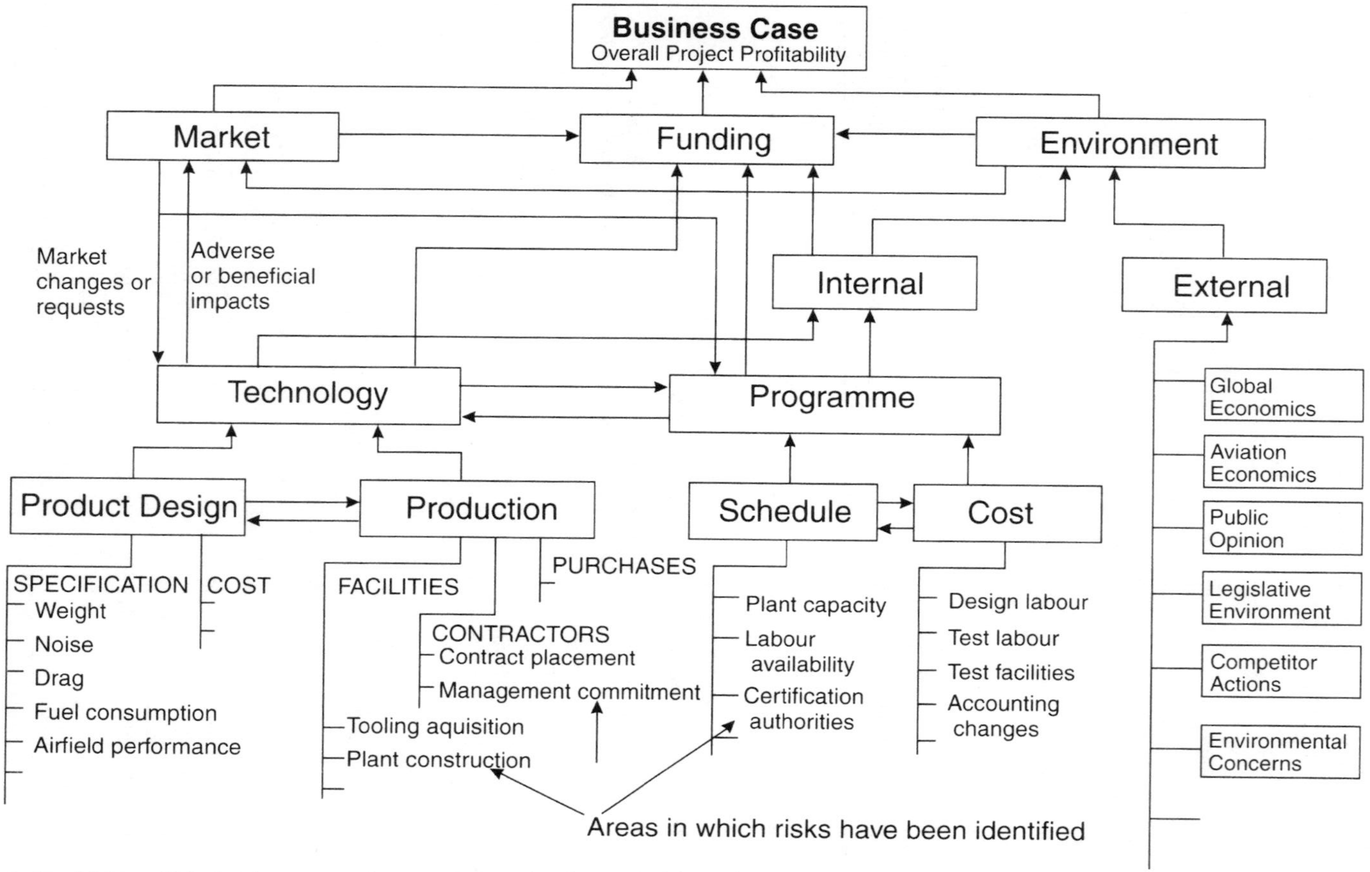

Figure 8.4 Partial hierarchical risk structure for a project to develop a civil aircraft.

project exists. Within the area of funding the principal areas are the technology and the programme, perhaps not surprising as these two factors have the greatest influence on both the demand for funds and its timing. In both areas choices can exist and decisions have to be made, but once they are made the project can become increasingly 'locked in' to a particular way forward. Notice also that issues external to the project figure prominently in this structure as they could have a direct bearing on the outcome but may be out of the hands of the project team.

One of the undoubted weaknesses in the whole process of analysis and assessment is that of subjectivity. What one person may see as a significant risk another may regard very lightly; this is one argument for risk assessments being conducted on a group basis. Using a group gives an opportunity for a range of informed people to make a judgement about any particular issue and hopefully reach a consensus view. That view may, in the end, turn out to be wrong; things that were considered significant risks might be quite simply resolved upon further consideration or more work, while issues that might seem relatively insignificant at the start could grow into thorny problems later on. That does not really matter, providing all concerned agree that the assessment is a realistic, if subjective, view. All assessment of the future is subject to a degree of uncertainty; from the moment a risk assessment is completed, the risk situation is altered as from that time onwards effort will be directed towards resolving the risk issues. A risk assessment should not be seen as a definitive statement about the riskiness of a project but rather as a snapshot of how risks were viewed by a particular group at a particular time – the next time the group meets it could all look different.

Analytical techniques such as those discussed in Chapters 5, 6 and 7 can and should be used where appropriate: simulation modelling can help if a quantitative view is needed about risks associated with costs and schedules, while decision analysis might be useful if choices have to be made regarding alternative approaches to identified risk situations. The output from the risk assessment process should include:

- a detailed description of all identified risks
- a reasoned ranking of all identified risks
- a structure of the risks that shows how they interact and impinge on the project objectives
- an assessment of the likelihood and impact of the identified risks
- some indication of what action each risk might require.

Choosing what to do

Risk management does not end when the assessment is complete, in fact, the hardest part may be deciding what to do about each of the identified risks; some might be deemed acceptable with no further action while others may demand that something is done. The process of decision making in the face of uncertainty is at the heart of risk management and the analytical techniques described in earlier chapters will undoubtedly be useful in certain situations. There might, however, be situations that do not involve simple choices between clearly perceived alternatives as a whole series of interrelated issues might have to be faced and a number of options are open. It is generally accepted that there are 6 courses of action that can be adopted in response to perceived risks although the circumstances of any particular situation may not allow more than one or two to be feasible options:

1) **Risk acceptance** – acknowledging that the risk exists without taking any specific action other than to note it. This course may be taken when i) there is simply no countering strategy available but it does not constitute a reason for stopping the project, or ii) when the risk is considered to be of little significance or its chances of happening are considered remote. Point i) could include the acceptance of a fundamental risk associated with starting the project in the first place; any type of speculative project, such as new product development where the eventual sales cannot be known in advance, contains an element of accepted risk that cannot be eliminated even if things can be done to reduce it.

2) **Risk avoidance** – choosing a course of action in which the risk is not encountered. Obviously this is an attractive option as it eliminates the perceived risk all together and must always be the first solution to be sought. Courses of action could include a direct attack on the risk, (for example, if a particular performance parameter is causing a worry, including a programme of work to ensure that a solution is found), or it could involve avoiding the risk by eliminating its cause (for example, removing a performance parameter that is proving difficult to achieve from the requirements specification). However, taking risks is an intrinsic part of business life and a policy of risk avoidance could, if pursued too rigorously, degrade the project to the point that a new, and possibly unrecognized, set of risks are introduced.

3) **Risk reduction** – taking some action in advance to ensure that either the potential effect of the risk is reduced, its likelihood of occurrence is reduced or both. Reduction strategies take as many forms as there are risk situations. Reduction is not the same as avoidance as it implies that some residual risk will remain after the action has been taken. Much the best approach to risk reduction is to anticipate those risks that are amenable to some form of work that will alter the situation favourably and then include this work in the project plan. Such an approach should lead to a 'robust' plan which is not likely to be blown off-course due to uncertain but foreseeable situations that have not been catered for. Another form of risk reduction could lie in the contractual arrangements that are made between the participants; by choosing the right contract terms and conditions, risks can be reduced for one party although they may increase for another, or they could agree to share risks, perhaps with an equivalent arrangement to sharing any rewards.

    Risk reduction can be applied to any aspect of a project in which the risk cannot be avoided without seriously compromising the whole project, providing risk reducing measures are feasible. In product development projects, for example, one of the most obvious approaches to risk reduction is to include a thorough testing programme that explores all aspects and thus reduces or largely eliminates risks from unsatisfactory products hitting the market. Performing some form of test before any significant decision is made is a generally applicable risk reduction strategy, providing, of course, that a test is possible and time allows it. Risk reduction strategies may come at a price in terms of both cost and time; although they can reduce risks in their intended areas, they have the potential to introduce risks of a different form in other areas.

4) **Risk mitigation** – taking some action after the effect has occurred to lessen its impact. Prevention is better than cure but sometimes the cost of prevention can be excessive in respect of the risk, particularly where the consequences could be serious but the possibility, though real, is seen as rather remote. In effect this is a wait-and-see strategy,

but the difference between this and pure acceptance is that some course of action, even if it is no more than a notional plan, exists that can be pursued to lessen the impact if the risk materializes. One of the most recent examples of a practical risk mitigation strategy is in the preparations governments are making for dealing with the aftermath of a terrorist attack following the events of 11 September 2001. No one can be sure if and when an attack might take place or what form it might take, but emergency plans can be made to deal with casualties and lessen the impact should an attack occur. Mitigation need not be seen as a strategy to be pursued on its own, it can be pursued in parallel with a risk reduction strategy even when applied to the same basic risk; this has been done by governments against terrorist threats through risk-reducing measures such as increased surveillance and improved security.

5) **Risk transference** – placing the risk or its effects with some person or organization better able to deal with it. The reason for doing this may be twofold: i) the organization to which the risk is transferred understands the risk issues rather better and is thus less likely to encounter them (this is particularly so where specialist technology is involved), or ii) the organization is better able to sustain the effects of the risk if it should materialize, possibly because it is more secure financially or can rapidly bring resources to bear on the problem. The most common form of risk transference is taking out insurance as here the financial effects of a risk materializing are transferred to the insurance company in exchange for a fee. Only certain kinds of risk can be covered in that way and the insurance company might demand that risk-reduction measures are implemented before granting cover. For example, for insurance against thefts and break-ins to a construction site, the insurer will demand adequate security measures are in place. Insurance is not the only form of transference as the use of contractual conditions can serve to transfer risks of certain types. The use of fixed-price contracts can transfer risks associated with cost overruns to the supplying contractor and liquidated damages clauses can be used to recover losses associated with late delivery or performance levels below that specified.

6) **Contingency provision** – setting aside or providing some time or resources that can either be called upon in the event of the risk materializing or used to avert a risk materializing. It is, in effect, a reserve against the unknown and uncertain. This subject has already been addressed in Chapter 7 where it states that adding a sum to the project estimate to cover aspects that are not known at the start is the commonest form of risk management. Contingencies are often formalized in the project estimating process, and a structure defining who has control of each level of contingency may be set up. Contingency can be seen as something to facilitate the implementation of Options 3 and 4, although neither option may be defined at the time the contingency is established. It should also be noted that contingency need not be seen as simply a reserve on which to draw when aspects of the project overspend, but also as something to be used to avert a risk situation materializing. In this case the contingency might be spent speculatively but the case for doing so will have to be well founded.

With the exception of risk acceptance and risk avoidance, which are mutually exclusive strategies, the other 4 contain a degree of overlap within their definitions, thus the act of risk transference might also be seen as being a method of risk reduction. Although it is useful to see these strategies from the point of view of understanding the approaches to a risk situation, it might not be wise to try to pigeonhole any practical approach into one or other category in an exclusive way.

Monitoring the situation

Having assessed the perceived risks and decided on how to handle them, it is necessary to continuously monitor all changes in circumstances that could affect the risk either by making it more or less likely to materialize or altering its effect. The popular method of doing this is through:

- the maintenance of a risk register which shows the current status of all recorded risks
- demands for risk reporting from responsible staff
- regular meetings among project participants involved in risk issues at which the status of the risk can be discussed.

Risk registers have already been discussed and can be maintained by a manual process or using contemporary software. Examples of computerized systems are given in Chapter 11.

Reporting on risks is an important aspect and the demands of a formalized process should ensure the position is continuously under review and developing situations do not go unnoticed until it is too late. What reporting demands are made will depend on the organization for risk management, the project complexity, and the general project reporting arrangements. Big and complex projects with a large number of risk issues in a variety of areas may require the identification of specific individuals with responsibility for certain risks and who will be required to report regularly. With small and simple projects, risks can be both monitored and handled through the normal project progress reporting procedure providing it calls for reporting on identified risk issues. Reports will normally demand information against specific risks on such things as:

- actions taken in the reporting period
- changes in risk status (for better or worse)
- actions to be pursued in the next period
- newly perceived risk issues
- overall effects on the programme.

The lattermost point may only be possible to determine through a higher-level analysis based on a collation of lower-level risks. Information from risk status reports can be added to the risk register to give an overall view of the situation at any reporting point.

As has been mentioned earlier, new risk situations can arise at any time in the course of a project; they can result from a sudden and unexpected change in fortunes. These situations lie outside the pre-planned control system but the project reporting system should be sufficiently responsive to bring whatever has occurred to the attention of those in control who need to know. In practice, when serious changes in fortune occur they are usually well perceived and notification quickly finds its way to the top of the management structure. If it does not, there is something wrong with the communication system; this may have its roots in the relationships between individuals, particularly if the project manager or other senior staff are eager to criticize what they perceive as failures in people.

Meetings at which those responsible for handling risk issues can discuss the situation and formulate strategy are a vital feature of active risk management. Meetings may be specially convened for this subject alone or risks may be one item on the agenda at the project manager's regular progress meeting. Where a formalized risk register is being maintained, minutes of any meetings that are held to discuss risk matters should be taken and appended to the relevant issue of the register. Whichever approach is taken, it is important that discussion is free and open and individuals reporting on difficulties are not subject to criticism from peers. Risk, perhaps more than any other aspect in management, has an emotive aspect to it and few can be totally objective about risks where there could be implications for the individual. A rise in the chance of a risk materializing may hold fears for people likely to be responsible for the developing situation; it needs to be recognized that risk is a matter of general concern and team support is likely to be more effective than threats. A climate of blame could lead to a culture that conceals or does not admit to risks existing until it is too late and the effect becomes all too apparent.

Closing the loop

No risk management system will be effective if there is no mechanism for effective decision making when risks arise. An organization structure sets out the chain of command but command will only be effective if proper instructions are given and acted upon. Obvious though this may seem, risks that are clearly seen and could, with the right action, be avoided can turn into reality because the right action was not taken at the appropriate moment. This is a failure of decision making and it can have its roots in:

- **Organizational culture**, one that places a heavy penalty for what are perceived as wrong decisions can result in no decisions at all with the result being a prolonged drift, events left to chance and a defensive attitude founded on excuses.

- **Organizational structure**, one that places responsibility for success without the required authority to act, particularly if significant resources are involved, can result in a laborious decision-making process that might fail to seize chances to avert a risk before it becomes a reality.

- **Paralysis by analysis**: this often results from a general lack of confidence in being able to see the way ahead with any clarity. It can also arise in a complex project situation that has many competing and powerful interests; this is sometimes the case in large-scale public sector projects, some of which have become notorious for delays, overruns and, in some cases, an unsatisfactory product as well.

- **The character and ability of the project manager**: if he or she does not have the intellectual capability to size up situations in a realistic way, take measured judgements on issues of uncertainty and then act with authority, he will simply fail to make the required impact. In difficult circumstances projects need a leader in whom both the staff and the sponsor can have a high degree of trust; it includes being able to handle the difficult decisions that have to be made when really unpleasant risks present themselves. He or she may not be right on every occasion but he does need to be right most of the time.

Once a decision is made about how to handle a risk, action needs to be taken to see that the decision is implemented. In many cases this can be done by incorporating the actions in the project plan and making the appropriate budget provisions. If this is done there should be no excuses for non-compliance. As to what follows: the reporting and monitoring process should show how effective those decisions have been and what, if any, further action might be needed.

Notes

1   BS06079-3:2000 'Project Management – Part 3, Guide to the management of business related project risk'
2   BS IEC 62198:2001 'Project Risk Management – Application guidelines'. Both are available from the British Standards Institution, 389 Chiswick High Road, London W4 4AL <www.bsi-global.com>.
3   UK Association for Project Management (1997) *Project Risk Analysis and Management Guide*, Norwich: APM Group Ltd.
4   Halman, J.I.M. and Keizer, J.A. (1998) 'Risk Management in Product Innovation Projects', *The International Journal of Project and Business Risk Management*, Vol. 2, No. 4, Winter, pp. 333–47, ISSN 1366-2163

9 *Organizational Issues*

The risk management process given in Chapter 8 will not be as effective as it might be if it does not become part of the organization's culture, structure and practices. Each of these can have different effects on the way that risks are both perceived and handled.

Attitudes and culture

Issues of culture may be among the most difficult to deal with as they can go to the very foundation of how the organization sees itself as well as determining the behavioural norms that are expected of individuals. They are often embedded in the overall approach to any situation but there may be different cultures in different parts of the organization as each can be determined by the outlook of a particular profession. Which of these is uppermost may depend on the history of the organization, its function and the character of key individuals; it can show itself in the overall attitude to risk.

RISK-SEEKING ATTITUDES

Risk-seeking attitudes are part of the 'entrepreneurial' or 'enterprise' culture that has characterized many successful individuals and organizations that regularly hit the headlines. What is often less publicized is the number of enterprises that have started and failed. Nevertheless, entrepreneurs are continuously coming forward and major organizations are embarking on enterprises with clearly perceived risks of failure. With individual entrepreneurs it may be a matter of personal choice to start a risky venture, but established organizations may feel they have no choice in a world that is continuously changing – a failure to create innovative products and services or move into new markets will lead to decline and death. Sometimes the choices made might be seriously wrong, even if they are made for the right reasons; for example, Marconi's move out of defence electronics into telecommunications just before the telecommunications bubble burst has led to its virtual collapse. A move into an unfamiliar field of business at a time of unsustainable growth is risk taking of the highest order, although it may not have been seen as such at the time. Given the long-term global trends in telecommunications, Marconi's move might have been seen as essential, although not on such a large scale, but a combination of bad timing and a world-wide reappraisal of the market led to a disastrous outcome.

Entrepreneurial companies tend to focus on the benefits of any project rather than the potential for losses and sometimes it may lead to distorted judgement. When it comes to individuals, it has been noted that people are more prepared to accept risks in areas where they feel they have some special knowledge even if the outcome is very uncertain; for example, people with an interest in football would be more inclined to gamble on the result of a football match than some other sport about which they have less knowledge. The Marconi decision to move out of familiar territory might be seen as the opposite of this and indicate that decisions that we make on behalf of an organization might sometimes be different to those we make for ourselves. Specialists in a particular field might well see risks associated with their activities as being less than those outside might view them; in many cases they may be right, but sometimes close proximity to the subject combined with professional pride might lead to an underestimation of the real risks, particularly if it is coupled with a 'can-do' attitude.

When it comes to individual projects, entrepreneurial organizations may adopt a 'go for broke' approach on the basis that some of the projects will be winners and highly profitable and the losers have to be accepted. This is certainly true of some sectors of the entertainment industry; pop music groups may be formed and marketed in the expectation that enough hit records will be sold to recover the costs. Often sales are insufficient and the costs must be written off, but occasionally groups like the Spice Girls come along and are hugely profitable.

It may not always be possible to foresee which projects will be successful and those which will not, even when the indicators seem to point in a particular direction. Table 9.1 shows how a series of DuPont's product development projects was viewed in 1968 and the position of those projects nearly 30 years later. It can be seen that of the six projects that appeared to be promising a high reward only one was still active. However, of seven projects

Table 9.1   Comparison of how a series of DuPont's new product ventures was viewed in 1968 and the position in 1997.

Project forecast in 1968 and result in 1997

Venture	Commercialization	Forecast first 10yrs earnings	Result in 1997
High reward ventures			
Permasep®	1970	$149m	alive
Polyester microfoams	1973	$286m	sold
UV Imaging	1973	$107m	dead
Office Copier	1971	$150m	dead
Absorbent products	1972	$179m	dead
Qiana®	1969	$217m	dead
Low reward ventures recommended for critical review			
Tyvek®	1967	$12m	winner
Surlyn®	1965	−$1m	winner
Corfam®	1964	−$26m	dead
Nordel®	1964	−$37m	alive
Krytox®	1966	−$1m	alive
Clysar®	1964	−$24m	winner
Symmetrel®	1967	−$4m	dead

Source: E.I. du Pont de Nemours and Co.

that were looking very doubtful and under threat of cancellation, three turned out to be highly profitable and two more were still active. In at least one case (the packaging and coating material Surlyn®) a marketing breakthrough was needed to turn a troubled project into a winner.

MEASURED RISK ATTITUDES

A more usual approach within well-established organizations is to take a measured view of risks in which they can be seen in relative terms for their potential effects on the project's objectives. Evidence of taking such a view can be seen in the assessments made of the potential worth of project ventures by a mature organization like DuPont. However, Table 9.1 also shows that sometimes maturity and measurement are not enough; it also requires a degree of commitment, sometimes against the odds, to turn a good idea into a winning product. Measuring the risks and taking reasoned decisions is the subject of this entire book and firms that take up some of the principles it sets out will have matured enough in their attitude to realize that risk is an inherent feature of business. It is not to be feared or avoided, but respected and handled with the care it deserves. Mature organizations will have the processes in place to deal with it.

Measuring risks implies a significant base of knowledge: if things cannot be measured then knowledge is likely to be scanty and decisions are likely to be made on the basis of guesswork or assumption. All the analytical techniques given in this book can be used where appropriate to measure risks and take reasoned decisions. Organizations that take a measured approach are those that are prepared to invest in knowledge; they will expect studies to be undertaken regarding risks that are identified and thorough evaluations of alternatives may be required. General agreement through some committee-based process may be required before the important decisions are made. They may have very good reasons for adopting that approach as the projects may be large with a high profile, demanding a big investment in resources, and they could be very costly if things go wrong. Organizations that work in that way will be less able to deal with rapidly changing situations as their approach requires both time and effort. In this respect they may be at a disadvantage in a changing world compared to entrepreneurial companies that may adopt a more intuitive approach to risk decision making.

RISK-AVERSE ATTITUDES

At the most extreme, a totally risk averse culture may exist. This can occur in highly institutionalized organizations that have pursued a single approach for a very long time or see themselves in a position where mistakes cannot be tolerated, possibly because they are subject to public scrutiny or a loss of public confidence may be involved. When risk situations do arise, a risk-averse attitude can lead to either a rejection of a perfectly reasonable business case or management inaction. When important decisions must be taken, 'paralysis by analysis' sets in or a 'wait and see' approach may be adopted allowing events to proceed in their way until only one course of action is left open – management then 'decides' to go down that route. Behaviour of this sort stems from the desire not to be seen to make a wrong decision and it can result in the kind of action that was taken by the programme manager in the stabilizer fin Case example 6.3: to have made a wrong decision involving large sums of money might have called into question his competence as a manager. The risk-averse culture of the organization can find expression in high risks for the individual; it may also lead to high risks for the organization although these may not be recognized at the time.

The general culture of an organization can lead to the three attitudes to risks given above but risks can exist for any project if the various cultures within the organization are not aligned with what is needed to complete the project successfully.

CULTURAL DIFFERENCES

Although organizations can have some overriding cultural approaches to certain aspects of their business, there can be lower-level cultural differences between parts of the organization that can represent real risks to any project if they are not recognized and dealt with. A study in 1986 by McDonough and Leifer[1] on the success of new product development projects has highlighted how the success of the project as a whole can be influenced by a situation where the culture within the design department is at odds with the business objectives.

The different cultures that can exist within an organization derive, in part, from the professional training that individuals received in their early years and the role they take on in their current positions. Board members should have a 'business culture' that sees the world in terms of the opportunities that exist, the gains that are to be made and the risks involved. Accountants may have a less visionary culture, that stresses accuracy, monetary quantification of management issues and avoidance of risk. Designers and technicians are different again, their culture stresses innovation, creativity, problem-solving ability and attention to detail; it could be termed an 'R & D culture'. All of these cultures coexist within any organization and it is the mix and tension between them that provides both the creative drive and the hard-headedness that are necessary for a company to survive. An organization may set out written procedures that define its way of working but culture dictates the way things are actually done. Culture defines the unwritten rules of behaviour by which employees recognize what is appropriate or acceptable within their group and what is not. The problem comes when the culture of individual departments is not aligned with the objectives of the project as a whole. Whereas an R & D culture that values inventiveness and problem solving is an essential asset to any commercial organization, its effectiveness may be reduced if it does not align itself with other, equally important values.

Professionals in one discipline may see their own goals as being those of the profession as a whole; this may lead individuals to pursue activities that they see as increasing their professional standing, perhaps by performing activities that may lead to published papers, but which have only a marginal bearing on the project's goals. McDonough and Leifer found that projects that involved developing novel products tended to be more successful in organizations where the 'business culture' was dominant over the 'R & D' culture in the design department. The business culture stressed the commercial viability of the product at every stage and when a technical decision was necessary, commercial necessity took precedence over technical sophistication. Where projects to develop new products were less successful, the R & D culture prevailed; inventiveness was pursued at the expense of the original specification with the result that the product no longer met the business requirements that were the reason for starting the project in the first place. The quotations below illustrate the point:

'The program grew. [We were] forever changing the moulds ... There were lots of design changes, when we finally got it, the costs were out of line.'

'This project was not very successful. It was too sophisticated. We needed to develop a less costly, less sophisticated product ... The project went on and on.'

'Our current product is the best in the world. Unfortunately this is not what we wanted. We have the Cadillac; but we wanted the everyday market.'

Such comments demonstrate that in these projects the design engineers were more interested in advancing the state of the art than they were in producing a commercially viable product. Advancements in technology may be vital to the survival of the company but in these cases the R & D culture of technology for its own sake had taken over to the detriment of the project as a whole. Cultural attitudes stem from early industrial training, they tend to be reinforced and ingrained through membership of a group of like-minded individuals. To attempt a cultural change may not be a very rewarding experience; it might have the effect of causing valued individuals to leave. Instead the R & D culture needs to be kept in check through close control. If the business culture is not reinforced by the appropriate leadership style, the R & D culture tends to prevail and in consequence the project suffers.

These issues raise the question of the project manager, whose first objective must always be the overall success of the venture. For this, a business attitude is essential yet some companies insist on drawing their project managers from the Technical or Engineering division. They reason that as developing products and systems is a technical job, a technician is the best person to lead the project; in effect, they are saying that the first priority in a project is a technical success. In fact, the first priority should always be to meet the project's objectives, often this requires it to be a business success but a technical specialist, however competent in his field, may not be the best choice to ensure that. Project leaders that are primarily concerned with the technology may become fascinated by its possibilities or engrossed with the detail. Either way, they can fail to see the broader picture and may not take time to establish proper control procedures or set up lines of communication to other departments whose input is necessary as the following quotations illustrate:

'[The project] broke some technical boundaries but these were not of great benefit to the end user. The leader needs to have a broad scope and this leader didn't have it. He wasn't concerned so much with sales.'

'He will not get a direction from Marketing, he will set one as project leader. [The project leader] said "Here's what I'm going to do, take it or leave it".'

'[The project leader] was not flexible; it had to be done his way. [The design] was done only 1–2 months late but it took 6–9 months to get it through manufacturing.'

In each case, the statement clearly reflects the narrow, parochial attitude adopted by the project manager. With more successful projects, a broader and more businesslike approach was taken by the manager who ensured that design specifications were set out at an early stage with the full involvement of both Marketing and Manufacturing. Boundaries were drawn around packages of work and the designers were expected to conform to them;

deviations from specification were only allowed with the agreement of the whole team. In short, a business culture that stressed commercial value above novelty, and practicality above inventiveness was imposed upon the designers. It did not replace the design culture or make them designers in any lesser sense but it focused their efforts on achievability and directed them towards a more profitable goal.

OVERALL

Cultural issues represent a major area of uncertainty in any project, attitudes on the part of both the organization as a whole and the individuals can shape the course of events and the decisions that are made when risks or uncertainties present themselves. However, this is rarely a risk that is noted on the risk register; for the most part, culture is a quality that is simply assumed and rarely challenged. Culture embodies the attitudes, values and practices of the organization and can be very deep-rooted. It has been noted that in companies that were originally family businesses, the family culture can persist for a generation or more after the original owners have sold out and the firm has become a large public company unconnected to the founders. The project manager's first task is to recognize the culture for what it is; it may be beneficial if the accent is on adaptability, responsiveness and a focus on project goals but less than helpful if it lays a strong emphasis on risk aversion, departmental loyalty and strict adherence to procedure. Brave project managers may try to bring about a cultural change on their project but without backing from the most senior level they are unlikely to succeed. To try to change the culture and fail to do so may do more harm than good and the person that suffers most could be the project manager who may be perceived as 'not fitting-in'.

Project contract structure

How the project is organized among the participants can have a major impact on its performance. This has been recognized to a greater extent in the last ten years than at any time in the past. It has led to new forms of organization that specifically address aspects of project risk. The way that projects have been organized and executed has undergone a revolution in the last fifty years and never more so than in the area of very large, multidisciplinary projects. Often these projects involved large expenditures and advanced technology and sometimes had outcomes that were decidedly less than satisfactory. The organizational structure and the contractual arrangements have been identified as two of the root causes of some of the failures and this has stemmed, in part, from the attitudes to managerial control and to apportioned risk embodied in the organizations that were created.

FORMS OF CONTRACT

The type of contract used when sponsors engage contractors to carry out their projects will reflect both the nature of the project and their attitude to risk in financial terms. Contracts for projects fall into two basic categories:

- those in which the greater risk, in cost terms, lies with the sponsor
- those in which the greater risk lies with the contractor.

COST-REIMBURSIBLE CONTRACTS

Contracts in which the principal risk lies with the sponsor are of the 'cost-reimbursible' type; here the contractor can spend time, money and effort at the direction of the customer and whatever costs are incurred are repaid to the contractor with an additional fee. They are referred to as 'cost plus fee', 'cost-plus' or sometimes as 'limit-of-liability' contracts as it is usual for the sponsor to control spending on the part of the contractor by setting limits to the amount that the sponsor is currently willing to pay. When the limit of liability is reached, the sponsor can either increase it, in which case work can proceed, or decide against doing so, giving the contractor the right to stop work.

Contracts of this type were common in the public sector for development work until the early 1980s since when there has been a move away from using them. The chief criticism has been that they contain little incentive for the contractor to complete the work as cheaply and quickly as possible; in fact, the very reverse may prove to be the case as the more that is spent, the greater the profit, in real if not in percentage terms. Cost-plus contracts are still let for projects where the outcome is so uncertain or the chance of failure is so great that contractors are unwilling to undertake the work on any other basis. This can occur with feasibility studies, research projects or projects for the development or exploitation of new and untried technologies where the innovative nature of the work may mean that success is not guaranteed or excessive effort may be needed to generate a worthwhile result.

Several types of cost reimbursable contracts have been devised, some with the specific intention of introducing a measure of incentive.

Cost-plus fixed fee

This is the simplest form of cost-plus contract and is used where it has been shown that making an accurate estimate of the work content is impossible, usually because of the exploratory nature of the project. Here a fixed, agreed fee is paid to the contractor on the basis of the costs incurred. The fee is often expressed as a fixed percentage of the costs submitted. From the point of view of the customer, this form of contract is the least preferable as the customer must bear all the cost risk and there is no incentive for the contractor to hold down costs or maintain the schedule; it requires the greatest degree of managerial control.

Cost-plus award fee

With this arrangement, the customer reimburses the contractor for all costs incurred but the fee is awarded on the basis of some agreed measure of project performance. To protect the contractor, a base fee is established and an overall maximum fee is also set. Between these limits an award can be made by the customer according to agreed criteria. However, some criteria may be subjective and this can lead to disputes over the size of the award. Some customers may insist on a clause that states that his decision on an award is final and not subject to a disputes procedure.

Cost-plus incentive fee

Where the project goals, in terms of cost, schedule and performance, can be specified with reasonable certainty, it may be possible to introduce an incentive based on achieving these parameters. For this to work, a target cost is agreed between the contractor and customer together with a target fee that should be obtainable if the target performance is met. On either side of that figure, both a maximum and a minimum fee are set and are payable depending on the project outcome. Adjustment formulae must be agreed and they should include reference to project milestones as well as demonstration of performance attainment. Considerable care must be taken in devising formulae, particularly where three parameters: cost, schedule and performance all combine. For example, a customer might not find it acceptable if it was found that the formula awarded a high fee to a contractor that was running ahead of schedule and generating good product performance but at excessive cost. It is essential that whatever formula is chosen, it should be simple and straightforward. Complex formulae run the risk of being difficult to interpret and administer: they are also less predictable in their effects when a large number of variables is included.

FIXED-PRICE CONTRACTS

In recent years there has been a move away from cost-reimbursible contracts and sponsoring organizations are attempting to procure project work for fixed prices. This is a response on their part to the growing financial risks associated with projects and an attempt to place more of the risk with the supplying contractor. There are, however, a number of preconditions for this type of contract to be applicable:

1) The basic feasibility of the project must have been established and be agreed by both parties.
2) The end-product or system must be capable of being defined in sufficient detail that no doubt exists with either party as to what is expected.
3) The work content can be clearly identified and costs can be estimated with reasonable accuracy.
4) Competition exists among potential contractors (this is not an absolute requirement but it helps).

In recognition of Point 1), with larger and more complex projects it is common to let feasibility study contracts before a full development or implementation contract. Both parties have the opportunity to assess the results before proceeding to the next stage; it is beneficial to both and should reduce the risks as greater realism should be contained within the specification and the plan. Feasibility studies typically include an analysis and, sometimes, a practical demonstration of the key technologies; this is fundamental to establishing the areas of potential risk. Promising feasibility studies usually conclude with an outline development plan including provisional costs together with a product specification. Analysis of the feasibility study reports and proposals by the customer often results in a rethink and refinement of the project goals. Before a full implementation programme is agreed there is usually a period of negotiation between the customer and the potential contractor over both the plan and the product. To obtain a range of possible solutions, customers sometimes let several feasibility study contracts with alternative suppliers but the product specification is likely to be based on the most favoured concept to emerge although that could be an amalgamation of ideas from different contractors. It is important that all parties should feel the final specification is complete, unambiguous and clear as to what is required. It then becomes a matter of judgement as to what contingencies should be allowed to cover the remaining risks.

Some contractors have taken the view that the lowest possible quotation should always be submitted in a fixed-price tendering situation as this is most likely to secure an order. Once the project has begun, the expectation is that the customer will begin to ask for changes to the programme or specification and these will provide opportunities to negotiate price increases which, if skilfully handled, can camouflage cost increases that may have arisen in the basic programme. Whatever one may think of this practice it can be viewed as response by the contractor to an attempt by the customer to offload both the technical and cost risks and still obtain a low overall cost. If serious difficulties do arise it is for the sponsor to consider his best interests; it may be far better to negotiate a new price than to see a supplier ruined, as that could lead to far greater expense.

As with cost-reimbursable contracts, alternative forms of the fixed-price contract have been devised for use in different circumstances:

FIXED PRICE, ALSO CALLED 'FIRM, FIXED PRICE' OR 'LUMP-SUM'

This is the simplest form of contract. For the contract as a whole or for each identified and separately priced element, a single figure price is agreed and unless there are specifically agreed changes to the programme or specification, no variations in the price are allowed. From the sponsor's point of view this is the ideal form, as the entire cost risk is borne by the contractor; it is also the simplest to administer. It does, however, place a burden on the customer to be very accurate in terms of design and performance specifications as well as assuring himself that estimates submitted by the contractor are realistic and achievable. It is thus worthwhile assessing the technical and financial strength of a potential supplier when selection is based on the lowest price. The sponsor should satisfy himself that the true nature of the project, its technical and programme implications, the scale of the work and the potential risks, are fully understood by the contractor.

The fixed-price contract is a two-edged sword, useful in situations such as repetitive production programmes or projects with low levels of technology but increasingly less applicable as the degree of innovation or uncertainty increases.

FIXED PRICE WITH ESCALATION FOR INFLATION

The effect of inflation on programme cost appears in two ways: i) inflation above that allowed for in the estimate generates additional cost over which the contractor has no control, and ii) if the project is subject to slippage, not only is there more work than expected but also more is being done at a date later than planned and thus at a higher than expected cost. To remove this risk it became common practice, particularly during the 1970s and 1980s when inflation rates were relatively high, to include a clause in the contract that allows the sum of money paid at any point in the project to be varied according to the prevailing rate of inflation. Contracts of this type have much to recommend them; they remove a contentious element of risk by being seen to be fair to both parties. The relative value of the contract in terms of purchasing power remains fixed, neither party being expected to shoulder the total burden of cost increases if inflation turns out to be higher than expected or make an excess profit if it is lower. Price adjustments are made by the application of formulae which use published index number series as the impartial measure of price movements.

The formulae are of the general form:

$$P_1 = \left\{ a \times L_0 + \left(\left(\frac{I_{lc}}{I_{lo}} \right) \times (1-a) \times L_0 \right) \right\} + \left\{ b \times M_0 + \left(\left(\frac{I_{mc}}{I_{mo}} \right) \times (1-b) \times M_0 \right) \right\}$$

$$L_0 + M_0 = P_0$$

where:

P_0 = The original contract price for the work under consideration at the economic date point (time zero).

P_1 = The price for the work under consideration at the date of raising the claim.

L_0 = The labour cost portion for the work at time zero

M_0 = The material cost portion for the work at time zero

I_{l0} = The labour cost index at time zero

I_{lc} = The labour cost index at the current time

I_{m0} = The material cost index at time zero

I_{mc} = The material cost index at the current time

a and b = Factors of value less than one.

The formula is self-explanatory but the factors a and b which retain a portion of the contract price at the original level serve to reduce the calculated price slightly. This offsets a tendency for the formula to generate a figure higher than the actual costs to the contractor, as it often happens that he can benefit from materials being paid for at a price agreed at the time of order placement which may have been some months earlier. Typically a and b are set to 0.1, in which case the formula simplifies to:

$$P_1 = 0.1P_0 + 0.9L_0 \left(\frac{I_{lc}}{I_{lo}} \right) + 0.9M_0 \left(\frac{I_{mc}}{I_{mo}} \right)$$

The constants a and b can be varied to reflect circumstances but this must be agreed before the start of the contract.

FIXED PRICE, INCENTIVE

Occasionally situations arise where there is a possibility that cost savings can be made during the course of the project. This can happen where such uncertainties exist that it is impossible to agree a fixed price without including excessive contingencies. Sponsors will naturally want to avoid this and may therefore propose a contract that includes an inducement for the contractor to finish the project at a price lower than the fixed, maximum amount. The inducement is in the form of increased profit even though the total contract value may be less. It means that the customer is sharing a proportion of the cost saving with the contractor. Inducements can be in the form of a price adjustment formula that relates to the final profit or a bonus payable if agreed cost thresholds are met.

It is normal to fix at the start both the maximum price (the 'ceiling price') and the assumed minimum level of profit. Below the ceiling price, a lower figure is agreed as the 'target price' which contains a higher level of profit and which the contractor feels he should be able to achieve. As the contract proceeds, claims are made in stages according to a payment plan and the observed progress. Profit at the low level can be included in the claims. At the end of the contract, a formula is applied to the value of the claims and if the total value is below the ceiling price an additional payment is made. Profits under the formula can exceed the target figure but it is usual to limit this by fixing the maximum profit whatever the final cost.

In the right circumstances the fixed-price contract can be beneficial to both sides. However, using it in conditions where there are too many unknowns can lead to a breakdown between the sponsor and the contractor, particularly if issues come to light during the project that were not recognized at the start. Occasionally these can be very serious for one party or the other and disputes can arise over who is responsible and who bears the cost overruns; no project benefits from this. Well-publicized examples of this occurred with the disputes between Eurotunnel, the sponsor, and TransManche Link, the contractor, over payments on aspects of the Channel Tunnel construction costs; the contractor claimed the sponsor had revised the scope based on new and hitherto undefined design criteria, while the sponsor claimed this was a risk the contractor should have considered. This hard stance was undoubtedly inspired by the serious financial position into which Eurotunnel was sliding, a position that stemmed from Eurotunnel initially understating the costs of the tunnel in order to attract funding.

Contractual organizations

Straightforward contracting principles, as outlined above, can be used on relatively simple (though not necessarily low-cost) projects, but complex projects involving a variety of technologies and significant risks have demanded a special organization that is usually specified by the contractual arrangements. The organizations that have been created reflect both the complexity of modern projects and a changing attitude to risks that has come about in the last forty years. Experience with these different organizational forms has shown that while they may reduce risks of one sort there can be drawbacks that result in new and different risks.

RISK OWNERSHIP WITH DELEGATED AUTHORITY – PRIME CONTRACTORSHIPS

In the period up to the end of the 1950s, project sponsors generally organized their projects by letting contracts on those suppliers deemed able to do the work; they managed the contracts and integrated the suppliers to get the products and systems they wanted. By the 1960s, in some sectors, product complexity had grown to the point where the sponsor could no longer perform all the technical tasks involved in managing the design, manufacture and integration. The solution lay in the appointment of a **prime contractor**, that is, one organization, with the required technical and managerial competence, charged with overall responsibility for delivering the project. The prime contractor had delegated authority over technical and managerial matters connected with the running of the project, although he may not have had control over the selection of the subcontractors who may well have made their bids directly to the sponsor and who would be selected on the basis of merits that the sponsor perceived.

With this arrangement, control was exercised by the prime contractor through the plans and instructions that he issued and the contracts that were in place with the subcontractors; although the contracts may have been written by the prime contractor, the basic terms would have to be in compliance with the sponsor's requirements. Although this was quite an effective way of managing large and technically complex projects, its weakness lay in the fact that there was no effective team commitment. With the exception of the prime contractor, the various parties were only bound together by their contracts and their own expectations from the project – they had no real stake in the overall outcome other than they would all lose if the project was cancelled. The directors of the prime contractor and the subcontractors did not meet to form a steering group to take a combined responsibility for progress and results; all the steering was done by the sponsor. Inevitably, tensions arose between the prime contractor and the subcontractors whenever one subcontractor observed that another was not making the required progress. As each subcontractor was in the project for his own benefit there was a clear temptation to conserve resources and slow down to the pace of the slowest contractor; this could actually be financially beneficial as often the contracts were let on a cost-plus-fee basis. Some attempts were made to generate an incentive through the use of fixed-price contracts and liquidated-damages clauses but inevitably these led to tensions. It is thus not surprising that this form of project organization, whilst often delivering on the technical aspects had the potential for making slow progress and generating cost overruns; for the most part it was the sponsor that bore all the risks of cost overruns and delayed deliveries.

RISK TRANSFERENCE – TOTAL PACKAGE PROCUREMENT

In the late 1960s an attempt was made in the USA to rectify this situation by passing as many of the risks as possible to the prime contractor and his subcontractors through a process instituted by the Department of Defense and called 'total package procurement'. Prior to this time, contracts for development were priced separately from those for production and agreement over pricing each phase was made as more knowledge became available. Although this is a sensible way of working and generally reduces risks for the contractor, it was seen as leading to unacceptable growth in overall project cost. Total package procurement did away with the staged approach and bundled all the phases into one contract with tightly defined performance guarantees at the start. The risks of failure were placed firmly with the contractors, or so the DoD thought. The first contract to be let under total package procurement was for the Lockheed C-5A *Galaxy* freighter for the US Air Force. Under this regime a number of significant items that would normally have remained estimates until well into the project became contractual guarantees at the start, thereby sowing the seeds from which thorny problems would later grow. As it became clear that guarantees regarding aircraft weight could not be met, poorly thought-out design compromises were made in an attempt to rectify this situation, but this led to a seriously weak wing. By the time the problem was realized more than half the production had been completed; worse was to come as a later study revealed that the wing would only have a quarter of its target design life and the Air Force had a real problem as some service aircraft were already approaching that figure.

Total package procurement was a contractual approach to reducing sponsor risk but it backfired: it attempted to tie down too many features at too early a stage in the design cycle and across too great a period over which the whole project would run. Its most serious flaw was that the guarantees that were set in the original specification robbed both parties of flexibility at times when difficult technical and commercial decisions had to be made. It was later realized that flexibility, based on a proper appreciation of the true costs of development, the associated risks and the value to the sponsor of particular features, is exactly what development projects need if they are to result in the product the customer really wants. The fixed-price arrangement that was originally part of the contract had to be changed to cost reimbursement, but even so contractors like Lockheed suffered substantial losses. The Air Force later instituted a programme to fit new and much heavier wings to its *Galaxys* and, with the modification of all existing aircraft, the US Air Force finally got the plane it needed, though ten years later than planned and at excessive cost. Total package procurement's deficiencies as a procurement process were clearly recognized and in 1972 it was formally abandoned. As an attempt to reduce performance and programme risk through a purely contractual approach, it failed completely in its objective. By failing to acknowledge that the inherent risks in technological projects have to be shared equitably between the sponsor and the contractors, it resulted in a much more risky situation than the sponsor ever envisaged.

The failure of total package procurement ought to have consigned it to the dustbin of history but there is evidence this type of contract is beginning to make a reappearance as customer organizations with tight financial constraints, and possibly competitive pressures, try to further reduce their risk exposure where complex technology projects are involved. It would seem that its dangers have been forgotten.

RISK SHARING – PARTNERSHIPS AND ALLIANCES

The prime contractor approach was one that was aimed directly at clearly seen risks for sponsors who were increasingly less able to deal with the growing complexity of technological systems, while total package procurement was an attempt to use contractual terms to pass significant risks on to the suppliers. Both these methods contained something of an adversarial approach, based on tightly defined contractual arrangements, between the sponsor and suppliers and neither delivered what was hoped of them. In the case of total package procurement, the risks for the sponsor turned out to be far greater than anything that could have been imagined which resulted from both an unequal division of risk and a failure to recognize that risks apply to both parties and have to be faced and dealt with properly – they cannot simply be contracted away. The sheer complexity of some multi-national projects and the desire at a national political level for a stake in the project that was more than simply a contractor, led, in the 1960s, to the formation of joint venture companies that acted as the prime contractors and whose shareholders were the main participating contractors. The principal contractors in this new company were now bound together in a way that the older prime contractorships did not allow. A good example of this is PANAVIA GmbH, a company registered in Germany formed from BAC, MBB and Fiat, that was created to design and produce the *Tornado* aircraft to the requirements of the UK, Germany and Italy. With this project the sponsoring governments also formed two joint organizations: a top level organisation, NAMMO, and day to day management agency, NAMMA, to collectively handle the project from the defence ministries' side.

The 1980s saw a move towards a more inclusive approach in which the sponsor and the contractors work in a mutually beneficial 'partnership'. Unlike the government-inspired initiatives that created prime contractorships and total package contracts, project partnerships, or 'alliances', started in the private sector. These were formed among companies that were collaborating on projects that resulted in a capital asset that could be exploited for profit. When the project was finished there could be a reward to be shared among the participants if the project was completed within its time and budget and there was the potential for a further reward if the asset could be operated profitably. The idea was taken up by the oil and gas industry who applied it very successfully to projects to build oil rigs and exploit the reserves. It led directly to the concept of the 'risk/reward' or 'gainshare/painshare' contract and the alliance approach to project organization and management. An alliance is a particular form of contractual joint venture, but it is not the same as a joint venture company as no separate legal entity is formed. Members of the alliance, both the sponsor and the contractors, are part of a team bound together by a contract that agrees to share the costs and the rewards and each has a member on a project steering committee. This approach overcomes the principal weakness of the prime contractor arrangement and also gets away from the old idea that the only effective way to encourage the contractors to perform is to apply penalties. Providing trust can be maintained, alliances have delivered some spectacular successes; in particular, because they have allowed contractors to 'think outside the frame' and propose novel solutions that would never have come forward under the older and more formal arrangements. Because of the risk/reward framework, every member of the alliance stands to gain or lose depending on the outcome of the project. It means that risks are no longer seen in isolation, as a problem for one contractor, but as issues that concern the whole team.

REMOVING THE BARRIERS

The principle of sharing the rewards amongst all the members is aimed directly at breaking down traditional barriers to cooperation that have been built up over years and set in the concrete of conventional wisdom. But deeply-rooted traditions die hard in industries where commercial confidentiality, competitive tendering and liquidated damages have set the tenor of current practice. The old arrangement was based on a desire for control from the centre and a belief that those with whom one does business cannot be trusted or be relied upon to do what they promised; it was only through the application of exacting contractual terms that any confidence in the outcome of a business deal could be guaranteed. There can be little doubt that, when difficulties arose on projects, thinking of that type often made matters worse for it promoted a recourse to legalities and a defensive position rather than a willingness to face up to difficulties and propose solutions. Although the adversarial quality that underlies much current contracting practice may have sharpened contractors' focus on the expected results, it has weakened the whole project organization in terms of its ability to function as a committed team.

Becoming a member of a partnership or alliance requires a cultural change, from a defensive stance based on self-interest to one of openness and cooperation; some firms will find that relatively easy while others with a more conservative outlook may find it more difficult. However, it is not just a matter of cultural adjustment for the contractors that do join, as success relies equally upon the actions of the sponsor. Being part of a risk-sharing arrangement means that the sponsor must divulge to the members far more information about the prospects and progress of the project than would have been deemed prudent before. A trusting attitude is the basis from which cooperation springs and the sponsor, more than any other member, must take the lead and be seen to act in the spirit of the alliance.

The amount of exposure that can be borne by the contractors in the partnership will be determined by their willingness to accept losses or reductions in profit up to some maximum figure they must decide individually. Losses over and above that maximum are borne by the sponsor and any partners that are also funding the project. It might be expected that the contractors will take 50% of the risk exposure while the sponsor shoulders the other 50%. This split may or may not be achievable depending on the view of the risk each contractor takes. If the project is completed for less than its budget or it makes an operating profit, the rewards are shared between the sponsor and the partners in the alliance in the same proportions as that for the risk exposure. Even though there is a maximum risk exposure limit for each contractor, there is no maximum for the reward that each contractor can receive; whatever savings or profits are achieved, they are shared in the same proportions.

METHOD OF CALCULATION

To see how the gainshare/painshare arrangement works, suppose the members of an alliance have agreed that a project has a target cost for completion, up to the point that exploitation of the asset can start, of £400m. This is the sum that the alliance as a whole should aim to complete the project for; it is often referred to as the 'Overall Target at Sanction' and it will be used to calculate the gainshare loss or reward. Now assume that, after a thorough risk assessment of the whole project, but excluding the exploitation phase, an additional risk budget of £50m is agreed among the alliance members. This budget can be assumed to represent a sum that will take the project from the sanctioned level of expectation (for example, 60–70%) to something greater than, say, 95%. The contractors must decide how much risk money each is willing to contribute to the £50m; the value of each contribution determines the contractor's percentage share. The percentage risk contributions need not be in the same proportions as the contractor's individual shares of the project budget.

The reward or loss can only be calculated at the point where it is agreed by all the alliance members that the development or construction phase of the project is complete. Figure 9.1 shows how the calculation is done; it will be seen that there is a simple relationship between the final out-turn cost for the project, the original target cost and the division of rewards or losses. If, for example, the project is completed for £370m there is a £30m saving on the total target cost and this is shared among the members in direct proportion to their contribution to the risk budget. Contractor A, who put up 12% of the £50m risk budget (£6m), could expect to receive a reward payment of £3.6m. Conversely if the project had overspent by £30m, Contractor A would be expected to contribute £3.6m from his risk provision. As each contractor is only willing to contribute a limited amount to the risk budget, once that budget is exceeded all further losses are carried by the sponsor.

Despite the apparent simplicity of the mathematics and the attractions of an increased reward for good work, there are obvious problems with this arrangement and some potential contractors would clearly be wary of it. In particular, if a given contractor does well on his part of the project but the rest of the team perform poorly he could end up paying an additional sum, thereby losing most or all of his profit, even though he has done nothing to deserve it. From the sponsor's point of view he should be cautious about the prices tendered by the contractors for if they are too easily beaten he could find himself paying out far more than was necessary.

The counter to the first of these objections lies in the second phase of the gainshare contract. If the newly created asset or product is profitably exploited in the market, each of the alliance members stands to receive a share of the profits and thus offset any losses made in the construction phase. The profit shares will again be calculated from the percentage risk contribution and payment will continue over a period that is agreed with the sponsor at the

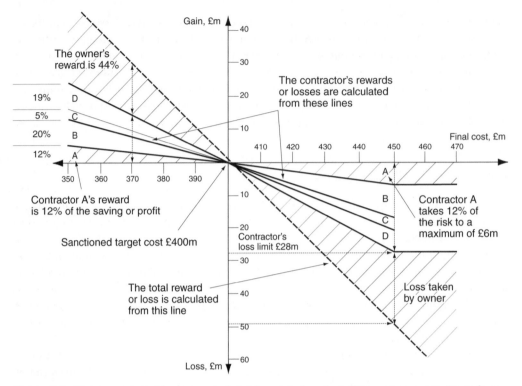

Figure 9.1   How rewards or losses are calculated in a gainshare/painshare arrangement. Rewards or losses to contractors are proportional to their risk contribution and the overall project outcome.

outset although it is not likely to cover the complete production life of the asset. Without this additional opportunity for profits many companies may feel that gainshare/painshare in the construction or development phase alone offers little benefit over a simple fixed-price contract except that it has the added risk that their fortunes are now tied into a group of companies over whom they have very little control and who may perform poorly. Furthermore, the actions of the sponsor to secure his position might, if not handled properly, serve only to heighten these fears.

PROJECT APPLICABILITY

Alliances may not be so suitable for owners or sponsors who have a preference for fixed-price contracting as a way of reducing financial risk and may be even less applicable in situations where there is no profit from the operation phase to be shared with the members. One of the attractions of gainshare/painshare in a capital project is that even if costs exceed target in the development or construction phase, there are still rewards to be had from the profits from successful commercial exploitation. Thus there is always an incentive to perform well and propose ideas that will increase overall profitability, even if it means some increase in the construction and development cost. Examples of this have been observed in successful alliances. However, these profits are not present if the sponsor is a non-commercial organization. This can arise with sponsoring organizations such as a government department; for example, a defence ministry will not seek to make any profit by selling the weapons and systems it commissions in the production phase as it requires them for its own use, although it may assist in sales to foreign defence organizations. As an incentive to better performance, cost saving is not an effective substitute for increased profit; in a gainshare agreement an operating profit in the exploitation phase represents something of value coming into the project from outside, thus contributing to the overall worth of the venture and the sum of money to be shared. On the other hand, cost saving may not reduce the overall worth of the venture, if all the savings are shared out, but the value to the contractor decreases as costs go down even if profits rise in percentage terms. The only member that really benefits in this situation is the sponsor because his function is that of a purchaser rather than a vendor.

It must be said that not all partnerships and alliances have been successful. Some public sector alliances for construction projects have failed because the ingrained culture within organizations that are subject to public scrutiny simply does not allow the degree of trust and cooperation to develop. This has often been made worse by selecting partners on the basis of lowest tendered price rather than reputation and quality. The problems seems to arise if it starts to be recognized among the partners that there will be no reward, which can stem from the fact that there is no capital asset at the end to generate a profit to be shared by all. At that point trust can break down, profit protection becomes the overriding goal and contractors may shift their effort into other activities they see as more profitable, leaving the alliance to go its own way.

Despite the problems, some of the principles contained in the idea of partnerships and alliances are being adopted by government departments. In 1996 the US Department of Defense formally abandoned its adversarial way of contracting for major weapons procurement with a new initiative aimed at the formation of 'integrated product teams'. It completely changed its emphasis from one of detailed control at every level to a total system acquisition process that made compliance with user needs, effective integration of complex systems and best-value products the principal programme drivers. This represented a significant shift and a recognition of the nature of contemporary advanced technology products. In particular, the growing cost of ever more sophisticated products is becoming unsustainable and integration of complex systems, so that they can work together satisfactorily, is becoming one of the greatest technological challenges and thus one of the most significant sources of project risk. At a lecture to the Institution of Electrical Engineers in November 2002 the UK's Future Joint Combat Aircraft Team Leader stated, 'Fourteen of our top twenty risks are associated with systems integration.'

History has shown that technologically based projects exhibit significant risks; history also shows that the type of contractual arrangement that is created to govern the project can have a major impact on its performance. Where it is recognized and accepted by both sides of the project organization that major risks are involved, success is more likely to come through an open and mutually supportive contractual arrangement than through an adversarial one, particularly if the division of risk is unequal.

Managerial organization

A number of different organizational approaches have been developed for handling risks in projects; in general, they reflect both the degree of risk to which the project is exposed, the scale of the project and the sophistication with which risks are handled. Small and simple projects may require no more than a notional assessment of risks; most will, by the nature of the project, be relatively insignificant and easily dealt with if one should arise. There may, however, be one or two issues that represent significant risks. Generally, these will be well perceived and, through discussion, observation and regular progress reports, they can be kept under review by the project manager; such actions would be seen as a normal part of the project manager's job.

As projects grow in size and sophistication, more risk issues may arise and their interrelationship may become complex. In this situation, risks may have to be treated in a more formal way that ensures they are identified, monitored and acted upon. This is normally done through two activities: the generation of a risk management plan, and the creation of a formalized risk-handling structure.

THE RISK MANAGEMENT PLAN

The scope and scale of the risk management plan will vary according to the size and complexity of the project and the perceived level of risk. It will set out the approach and procedure for identifying, assessing and dealing with risk issues although it will not normally contain any discussion of the risks themselves or what might be done about them. As a general guide a risk management plan could contain:

- **General project organization**
  - an outline description of the project
  - a statement of the project's primary and secondary objectives
  - the project's basic organization structure, including the reporting and command structure
  - the division of responsibility among the project participants
  - the details of the principal participants

- **A statement of the purpose and scope of the risk management function**
  - what is expected of the risk management process, where and how it fits into the project management organization

- **The organization of the risk management function**
  - roles and responsibilities
  - reporting structure

- **The risk management process**
  - risk identification procedure
  - maintenance of risk status information
  - risk reporting procedure
  - risk status review
  - risk decision-making procedure
  - application to the contingency fund procedure (if applicable)

- **Financial and contractual issues**
  - basis of risk apportionment contained within the contract structure
  - allocation of contingencies (if applicable)
  - risk/reward-sharing procedure (if applicable)

- **Additional information**
  - job titles of persons responsible for specific risk issues
  - risk status report formats (inputs and outputs)
  - reporting calendar
  - review procedure
  - contract terms applicable to risk matters (if applicable).

A list of topics such as that given above is very general and would need to be tailored to the requirements of any particular project situation.

Management structure for risk handling

Both the scale of the project and the associated risks will have a bearing on how risks are dealt with. With relatively simple projects, the project manager may handle risks as part of the everyday work but with complex projects, a more structured arrangement may be put in place. The structure will reflect both the nature of the work being done and the overall organization of the project; there is thus considerable scope for alternative approaches to this issue.

Whatever structure is put in place it should embrace certain key managerial principles:

- The risk responsibility and decision-making structure should reflect the overall project organization structure.
- Responsibility for handling risks should be placed with those who have the greatest ability to deal with the issues that gave rise to those risks.
- Responsibility for risk handling should be associated with the required authority to act.
- Risks should not be unfairly apportioned within the organization.

It was said in Chapter 8 that a risk breakdown structure should be devised that shows how lower-level risks relate to one another and combine to influence the entire project's objectives. This structure needs to be mapped onto the organization of the project participants and their contractual relationships. This should produce a rational division of risks among the participants together with their organizational arrangement. When risks arise, it should be possible to associate them with both the source of the risk and the organization structure. In general, the organization structure reflects both the technical competence and the authority levels within the project and thus the ability to act.

RISK OWNERS

Responsibility and authority must be made equal; if they are not, tensions will inevitably arise and decision making may become irrational. The result is both managerially inefficient and possibly a new source of risk in itself. The most basic principle is to place responsibility for handling risks with the people most closely associated with the risk area and give them the authority to act when appropriate. This principle has led to the creation of the 'risk owner', that is, a person deemed responsible for monitoring and dealing with an identified risk. The risk owner normally resides in the functional area where the risk issues arise and is required to report on risk matters to the project manager. Ownership in this context is not the same as the legal concept of ownership, as one feature of legal ownership is the right to dispose of something you own. Clearly a risk owner in a project management sense cannot do this neither can he take advantage of another feature of ownership: the right to use what is owned for one's own ends. Thus ownership of a risk implies something rather different from the conventional view in that it carries with it the idea that the owner has some special knowledge of the risk or the situation that brought it about and is in a position to influence the outcome. The idea of a single person with responsibility for handling specific risk issues is a useful one; it allows authority to be concentrated in people who can have the greatest impact and it ensures that all risks are covered by individuals with accountability for what occurs. How much influence any risk owner has will depend on his or her status in the organization and the magnitude of the risks involved. Risk owners should be appointed by the project manager, they can be individuals or organizations depending on the project structure; ideally it should be individuals (or job titles) and they should be named, as they will be the first point of contact regarding any issue associated with their risks. Risk owners are required to monitor the status of their risks, report on changes in status and initiate risk-countering strategies. Where risks can be contained within one area, spending limits or an overall risk budget may be set and risk owners allowed to spend freely within them on reported risk issues without recourse to higher levels in the project structure.

Handling risks could involve spending time and resources on speculative work to avert a potential problem or it could involve extraordinary and unplanned mitigation actions if risks materialize. People with the delegated responsibility need to be given the power to act but some organizations have failed in this respect, with the result that risk issues have not been dealt with efficiently due to lengthy decision-making processes. However, authority must be tempered with realism; risk owners are responsible for continuously monitoring and reporting on their issues, including what actions are being taken and what impacts they are having. They are ultimately responsible to the project manager and must ensure, through formal or informal routes, that the manager fully appreciates the developing situation. If risks are becoming apparent and require action or expenditure that is outside of their authority, risk owners must reflect this upwards through the reporting chain and ensure, to the best of their ability, that appropriate actions are taken.

RISK MANAGERS

In addition to risk owners, some large projects have included the appointment of a 'risk manager' specifically to control the risk issues that are identified but the question remains about the process of management itself. It could be argued that the only sectors that can truly manage risks are financial speculators and the insurance industry, as insurers are in a position to take or refuse risks and set the fee. Insurers can see the extent of their risk exposure, the likelihood of making payments and the level of fee income; every new risk can thus be judged against this background and either accepted or rejected. This is a quite different situation to that in a company undertaking projects as often it faces risks that it would not willingly have taken on. These risks may arise at any time on a project and need not have been envisaged at the start. Thus risk management on projects is not a precise act of management in which the losses and gains can be balanced and the degree of exposure controlled. Risks that are very unwelcome can arise at any time and the degree to which they can be controlled can be very limited.

The appointment of a risk manager indicates that risk is both a significant issue and one that requires more specialist effort than the project manager can spend on it. Risk managers have overall responsibility for:

- developing and maintaining the risk management process
- monitoring the risk situation
- collating all risk information to develop an overall view
- providing risk analyses when requested
- organizing risk reviews
- appraising the project manager of important risk issues that require action
- providing advice and assistance where required.

Notice that this description of the risk manager's role does not include having to make risk decisions. Low-level risk decisions that are within the authority of the risk owners can be taken at that level while high-level decisions that have implications across the whole project remain the responsibility of the project manager and possibly the project sponsor. Anyone in the position of risk manager may find their real ability to manage the situation restricted both by the nature of the risks that arise and the decision-making structure on the project; the position of risk manager might be better described as 'risk information and process manager'. However, a risk manager should not be seen as having a purely passive role of collecting and disseminating risk information for others to act upon, but as having a policy-making role that encompasses defining the entire process by which risk information is obtained and evaluated, defining responsibilities for handling risk issues and ensuring that decisions are made at the appropriate level in a timely fashion. In a complex project, the role of the risk manager can be an important one; without such a person the only individual with an overall view of the risk situation might be the project manager and there is always the danger with a large project that he or she might not have the time to devote to it and developing situations might be overlooked until it is too late.

Whatever contractual arrangements or organization structure is created, one must always remember that no risk management process will be effective if risks are not viewed as reasonable by those called upon to bear the consequences if the risk materializes. Attempts have been made to offload risks in an unreasonable way and these have led to disputes, lack of cooperation or bad decisions which in the end have seriously damaged the project – the very opposite of what was intended.

Note

1 E.F. McDonough and R.P. Leifer, (1986), Effective Control of New Product Projects: The Interaction of Organisation Culture and Project Leadership, *The Journal of Product Innovation Management*, Vol 3, pp 149–157.

10 *Managing with Risk Analysis Methods*

Analysis of risk starts by identifying risks and classifying them. Identification methods have been outlined in Chapter 8 and, having identified the risk, they can be recorded in a register.

Classification of risks can be done in a number of ways depending on the view of the situation that is required; with a complex project a hierarchical structure such as that shown in Figure 8.4 could be appropriate. Simpler representations might however be just as useful when it comes to individual risks that can be treated as issues in their own right.

Impact and probability

One method of establishing the picture with regard to individual risks and their place in the overall project framework is to rate risks according to a probability-impact scoring grid, an example is shown in Table 10.1.

Table 10.1 Example of a probability-impact rating grid. Each identified risk condition is rated with an impact value V.Hi., Hi., Med., Lo. or V.Lo. according to how it is viewed with respect to its impact on overall project cost, overall timescale or the general effect on performance. Whichever of these is deemed to have the greatest effect determines which impact rating is adopted. The probability rating is derived from the likelihood of occurrence. If a risk condition was viewed as being likely to result in an 8% increase in project timescale, while having less impact on cost and performance, but have only a 1% chance of occurrence it would be rated as Med. impact, Lo. probability.

Rating	Probability	Impact on the project		
		Cost %	Time %	Performance
V.Hi.	> 0.71	30+	30+	Significant failure involving major rework or major setback that directly affects the project's objectives.
Hi.	0.7–0.41	10–29	10–29	Failure that involves significant rework, modification or reassessment.
Med.	0.4–0.11	2–9	2–9	Failure or setback that causes additional work and reassessment but containable.
Lo.	0.1–0.01	0.1–1.9	0.1–1.9	Impact has some effect causing rework or reassessment but easily handled.
V.Lo.	< 0.01	< 0.1	< 0.1	Little impact, minor inconvenience, effects easily remedied.

Numerical values can be attached to the conditions V.Hi., Hi., Med., Lo. and V.Lo. in an attempt to further refine the scoring to produce a reasoned overall ranking when a series of risk conditions are evaluated. An example is given in Table 10.2

The probability and impact scoring system should allow the rational ranking of risks but there is a complication. It might, at first glance, seem that the obvious way to put the risks in the order of the most serious to the least would be to multiply the probability and impact scores together to produce a type of expected value. This can, however, produce a misleading result as anything with a low or very low probability will tend to have an overall low score and thus appear well down the list even though it may represent a very serious condition. Another problem with the expected value approach is that it can produce a large number of similar scores in the middle region and thus obscure the distinctions between the various risk issues. An alternative method of ranking is to take the overall rating for any issue as being the larger of the two scores, this approach emphasizes those issues that are either very serious, very likely or both. A third method of scoring is to add the two scores and this approach falls somewhere between the two previous methods. A comparison of these methods is given in Table 10.3 for a set of risk conditions. It will be seen that quite different rankings are attached to each risk condition according to which rule is used.

Table 10.3 indicates the general problem associated with trying to produce a true and unambiguous ranking of risk issues according to their importance; it can all depend on the rule that is adopted and no rule is guaranteed to provide a true view. This might not matter much if there is a small number of easily identified risks but it can be more of a problem if there are a large number of perceived risks, each with relatively small probabilities. An alternative way of looking at risk conditions is not to try to rank them in any particular order but classify them according to how the condition might be dealt with. Using the V.Hi., Hi., Med., Lo. and V.Lo. ratings would produce 25 combinations of impact and probability but this can be simplified for practical purposes. Table 10.4 gives a set of rating combinations with the optimum course of action with respect to each condition.

In terms of impact and probability, four highly significant risk situations are possible and there are less extreme possibilities in the middle region, the four extremes are:

Table 10.2 Scoring system for probability and impact ratings. The scores can be made equal for convenience or, if required, they can be made different as is shown in the table which attaches slightly more importance to probabilities at the lower end.

Rating	Scores	
	Impact	*Probability*
V.Hi.	1.0	1.0
Hi.	0.8	0.8
Med.	0.5	0.5
Lo.	0.1	0.2
V.Lo	0.01	0.1

Table 10.3 Ranking the risk conditions according to three rules: a) probability x impact, b) greater of probability and impact, and c) probability plus impact, using the scoring of Table 10.2. There are considerable differences between the overall rankings of the risks according to which rule is used, note the differences associated with Condition 4.

No	Risk condition	Impact	Prob.	P x I		Max P,I		P + I	
				Score	Rank	Score	Rank	Score	Rank
1	Commissioning failure	Hi.	Lo.	0.16	**5**	0.8	**3=**	1.0	**5=**
2	Delays in drawing office	Med.	Med.	0.25	**3**	0.5	**7=**	1.0	**5=**
3	Material supply hold-up	V.Hi	Lo.	0.2	**4**	1.0	**1=**	1.2	**3**
4	Adverse weather	V.hi	V.Lo.	0.01	**8**	1.0	**1=**	1.1	**4**
5	Planning delays	Lo.	Hi.	0.08	**7**	0.8	**3=**	0.9	**7**
6	Tooling problems	Med.	Lo.	0.1	**6**	0.5	**7=**	0.7	**8**
7	Funding difficulties	Hi.	Med.	0.4	**1=**	0.8	**3=**	1.3	**1=**
8	Single test failure	Med.	Hi.	0.4	**1=**	0.8	**3=**	1.3	**1=**

Table 10.4 Rating combinations with the optimal courses of action. Using this as a guide, ways of handling each perceived risk can be devised. If a very serious risk situation is identified with a significant probability and there is no obvious preventative course of action, it might require reassessing the whole project or viewing it in a different light.

Rating combination

Impact	Probability	Optimum course of action
Hi. V.Hi	Hi. V.Hi	Assume risk condition will arise, assess overall impact on project and its objectives. Make provision in project plan and budget for preventive and mitigating actions, implement preventive measures where possible otherwise put mitigating actions into effect upon condition arising.
Hi. V.Hi.	Lo. V.Lo.	Most difficult of all conditions. Make provision outside normal project plan and budget for mitigating expenditure should condition arise. Attempt to reduce probability to zero if possible. Keep condition under review, be prepared to reassess overall objectives if probabilities begin to rise.
Lo. V.Lo.	Hi. V.Hi.	Provide a contingency within the plan to cover these conditions, with V.Hi. probabilities include events in plan, this removes uncertainty for minimum impact and allows management attention to be focused on more pressing issues.
Lo. V.Lo.	Lo. V.Lo.	Note condition but take no action other than to keep under review. In the unlikely event that the condition does arise it should be possible to deal with it simply and with minimal impact at the time.
Med.	Med.	No particular course of action indicated, treat each risk on its merits, identify opportunities that exist to reduce its impact or probability so that it can be dealt with as indicated above. Ensure there is adequate overall contingency in the plan and budget and expect to draw on some or all of it during the course of the project.

- high or very high impact and high probability
- high or very high impact and low probability
- low or very low impact and high probability
- low or very low impact and low probability.

Of the four, high impact/high probability and low impact/low probability are the easiest to deal with. With high-impact/high-probability risks, it should be assumed that they will materialize and that occurrence should be included in the project plan with whatever actions are necessary. Low-impact/low-probability risks can be noted but beyond that they can be largely ignored on the basis that they are unlikely to materialize and if they do their impact can be simply dealt with at the time. Low-impact risks with a high probability can be seen as an irritation. If there are a lot of them, collectively they can add up to a high impact so they cannot be ignored; action should be directed at reducing the uncertainty rather than mitigating an already low impact. High-impact/low-probability risks are the hardest to deal with unless it can be shown that the probability is in the infinitesimal category. Risks of this type are seen with such things as bad weather seriously affecting operations where there is a low but well-established frequency of freak weather occurrences, or the loss of a satellite due to the rare but not unknown explosion of the rocket launcher. Here the principle of expected values will not work as the expected value that results will be much too low to provide an adequate contingency unless there is a large number of risks of this type; if that is the case the whole basis of the project is questionable. Very high risks, where the probability, although low, is clearly seen as a real one, are best dealt with outside the formal project arrangement. They should be transferred to some higher authority, possibly at board level, where adequate funds may be available or insurance can be provided, or they could be transferred to the sponsor if he is outside the project organization and can be made to agree that special circumstances apply. In the middle are the combinations of medium risks; although none may be individually very significant, collectively they can add up to a big overall risk. They do, however, need to be considered individually as each risk may offer different opportunities for countering actions. If there is a large number of small to medium risks, the principal of expected values can be assumed to operate as some will materialize but perhaps the greater number will not. A contingency needs to be included in the plan and the budget to cover these risks and it can be expected that the contingency will be drawn upon as the project proceeds and some risks become reality.

Robust projects

Once the broad spectrum of risks has been identified, a programme can be constructed that addresses many of them and hopefully their effects can be eliminated. Such a plan is said to be 'robust' as it contains measures designed to eliminate or reduce risks and, if some should materialize, it is not likely to be blown seriously off course.

Robustness can be introduced into projects by:

- Satisfying all parties to the project that the overall objectives of the project are realistic and achievable within the perceived constraints.
- Identifying and addressing significant risk issues early in the development of the project plan and including activities that specifically deal with them, if possible.

- Constructing a plan that allows the acquisition of knowledge to advance in a rational way so that decisions can be based on acquired knowledge rather than assumption or guesswork.
- Building in decision points in advance so that, when significant steps forward must be taken, possibly involving major commitments, decisions are taken with proper regard to what has been achieved so far and a realistic view of what the future might hold.
- Choosing 'best practice' as the decision criteria for any issue (technical, managerial, organizational, choice of contractors, etc.) rather than cheapness or expedience.
- Using the best people and ensuring they are properly trained for the job
- Adopting a contracting arrangement that is suitable to the work in hand and the degree of risk or uncertainty involved. The apportionment of risk should be seen to be fair to all parties.
- Monitoring the risk situation so that risk issues do not arise without being perceived until it is too late to do anything about them.
- Facing up to significant risks when they are identified, however difficult it might seem.
- Placing responsibility for dealing with risks with those who have most knowledge and giving the appropriate authority to act.
- Ensuring that decisions are taken in a rational way, given that significant uncertainties may be involved, that always seeks to preserve the overall objectives.
- Ensuring that actions, when they are taken, are done in a considered way that ensures no conflicts arise with other aspects of the project that may affect the overall objectives.
- Including a contingency against the unknown that will inevitably occur.

The above list of conditions is applicable to projects of any kind although how significant any particular one is will be dependent upon just what the project is. With routine projects that are largely repeats of well-understood tasks, such as building a housing estate, some of these conditions would seem rather less relevant than others. However, with complex technological projects that involve a significant contractor organization and a research and development element, all the issues could be highly relevant as such projects have significant uncertainties; experience indicates that many run into significant difficulties at some point in their life-cycle, some of which might threaten the very existence of the project.

Some of the points given in the list above relate directly to the conduct of the project and the relationship between the parties but others relate to the technical aspects and the plan of activities. Where risks associated with the technical aspects can be identified, countering strategies can be incorporated into the plan. An example of such a plan is given in Figure 10.1 which shows a schematic programme for developing an electro-mechanical type of product; it is divided into three major phases. This is a common arrangement that starts with a prototype phase aimed at testing the basic functions of the product although without much engineering refinement. This is followed by a full development phase in which items that are much more refined and representative of the production unit are built and tested. Breaking the project into discrete phases allows decisions to be made at significant points where sufficient information is available to make an informed judgement before proceeding to the next phase.

Although some of the risks of technical failure are reduced and even eliminated by the two-stage approach to development and testing, the project programme can be made more robust by a recognition of specific technical risks and inserting into the plan responses to

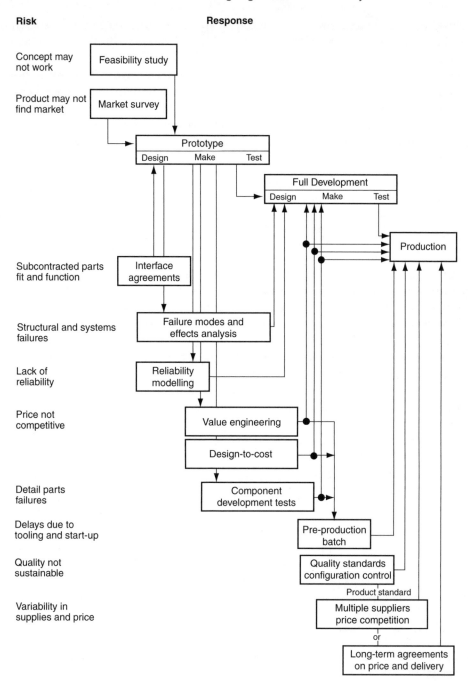

Figure 10.1 Technical risks and appropriate responses.

each risk at the appropriate point. Figure 10.1 shows some of the principal areas of technical risk along with methods that can help in overcoming them. This is only one type of project, others will exhibit different characteristics and thus require different strategies. Given below are brief explanations of the countering strategies indicated in Figure 10.1 to demonstrate how they collectively result in a robust project plan for a project to develop a new product aimed at volume production.

- Structural and systems failures can have some of the most damaging effects on the project. Sometimes major redesigns are necessary as well as repeat testing; it can lead to both cost and time overruns and, possibly, liquidated damages payments. Finite element analysis can predict the behaviour of structures while the technique of Failure Modes and Effects Analysis has been devised to investigate the effects that failures in one area have on the design as a whole.

- Many modern control systems feature computers – such systems can be doubly vulnerable as they can exhibit failures in both the hardware and software. In some industries, good design practice has insisted that critical systems are made in triplicate or quadruplicate and are capable of functioning normally with one system either out of action or behaving abnormally.

- Besides significant structural or systems failures, general reliability may be an area of risk. Reliability modelling techniques that make use of statistical methods have been devised; they are particularly useful in the design of electronic circuits where the life characteristics of standard components are well known. Reliability can be kept to high levels by good design practice such as:
  - Choosing high-quality materials and high-reliability components
  - Designing fail-safe systems and structures
  - Incorporating redundancy and robustness in critical features
  - De-rating electrical components according to the stress and environment they experience
  - Providing environmental protection for critical items through seals, covers, filters, finishes, etc
  - Selecting compatible materials
  - Avoiding dust and water traps.

- Some of the features listed above will have cost implications for the end-product whilst others can be obtained through careful design at no extra cost. Obviously, cost is a major factor in the commercial attractiveness, particularly at the initial purchase stage but poor reliability can lead to excessive warranty claims and, if it becomes generally recognized, loss of market share or a premature end to the product's sales life. Clearly, there are risks in whatever design approach is taken and reliability is one area where the technical response to the risks associated with low reliability can, if not handled properly, lead to a commercial risk in terms of product acceptability.

- Basic product cost must represent one of the largest factors that determines the overall profitability and success of any project that aims to generate goods for sale on the open market. A substantial risk may exist that the product, when it emerges, will be too expensive to compete effectively. The greatest savings in product cost are made at the design stage, not at the tooling-up or purchasing stage and complex designs will always remain more expensive to produce than simple ones. The techniques of Design-to-Cost and Value Engineering have been developed as an effective way of forcing design activities along a route that ensures that, in formulating the product, cost is considered alongside all other parameters.

- It is a simple fact that in most products it is the detail of the design that determines whether or not it will work satisfactorily under all circumstances and if failures do occur what form they will take. Significant risk can be taken out of the design process by a properly constructed programme of tests on detail parts. This can be particularly useful where parts are subject to high stresses or harsh environments. With automated systems involving complex interfaces, a thorough programme of integration testing should be included in the plan.

- Production start-up problems are traditionally dealt with by making a preproduction batch. This can be useful for proving tooling, checking assembly methods and assessing supplier's quality; it can also provide items for additional testing to ensure that any changes that have been made between the full development item and the production item are not detrimental to performance.

- Beyond the development stage, the technical risks in the production programme tend to lie more in the areas of quality control and supplier performance. As such, they tend to cross the boundary between the technical aspects and the purely commercial. Setting quality standards for suppliers to observe is one obvious safeguard against poorly made goods.

- Changes of one sort or another are to be expected in the first few months of production as new problems, often associated with the production methods, come to light. Sometimes, however, correction of the problem can only be overcome by a design change. When this occurs, changes must be controlled rigidly; changes that are incorporated in an uncontrolled fashion can lead to the wrong standard of parts being ordered with all the consequent disruption and costs that ensue. Configuration control procedures can be employed to combat this.

- Once standards have been set for both design and quality requirements, competitive quoting and the use of several suppliers can serve both to ensure continuity of supply and favourable pricing. However, heavy investment in special tooling or the use of proprietary techniques may make using alternative suppliers difficult; in these circumstances protection may be obtained through long-term agreements that cover price and delivery.

Exposure to technical risk in product development projects can be limited by creating a plan which addresses the risks and includes measures to reduce them as shown by the points above. The actual decision to incorporate any or all of the techniques mentioned will depend on the perception of the likelihood of the risk materializing. There is, however, a price to be paid; plans that include risk-reducing measures are more expensive as they contain additional work and they may also increase the project timescale. They tend to involve spending money early on investigative work and if the project is subsequently cancelled this money is lost. It is this cost and time penalty that must be judged against the possibility of a technical failure at the end of development or unsatisfactory products being released onto the market. These may not be the only considerations as timing of market entry might also be a factor, particularly if it is known that competitors are active. A robust plan that addresses all the risk issues might well result in a lengthy project but the market could be lost to a competitor that takes a more entrepreneurial view. This fact tends to emphasize the point that reducing risks of one sort can sometimes result in increased risks of another. It is thus very important to see the whole spectrum of risk issues and ensure that a desire to reduce risks in one area does not seriously compromise an important objective.

Business risk

Robust plans can certainly aid project stability and increase its chances of success but they will not help if the project is founded upon a bad business deal. Although many of the project objectives can be stated in technical, cost and delivery terms, this may not be the primary objective for some of the participants. Whereas the sponsor might well see all the technical, cost and delivery issues as paramount, the contractors will have as their primary objective a profitable return on their work. Projects have gone seriously wrong when contracting arrangements between sponsors and contractors are not attuned to the risks and uncertainties that are inherent in the project and one party is expected to shoulder an unequal portion of the risk. This can certainly happen when work involving a significant degree of innovation is undertaken on a fixed-price basis. There are many occasions where fixed-price contracting for project work is a good approach and potentially advantageous to both parties, particularly where repetitive production or routine construction is involved. For the sponsor, cost uncertainties can be greatly reduced while the contractor has the opportunity to increase his profits by improving overall working efficiency if he is able to. With projects with high inherent uncertainty, this may not be the case, particularly if the contract is let following a competitive tendering process.

As has been shown, project plans that are robust address all the identified risk issues and incorporate countering measures; they could also include significant contingencies against the unknown. Inevitably such plans tend to be expensive and bidding contractors might feel they would have little chance of winning with this approach in a competitive situation. The temptation is therefore to revise the risk assumptions to arrive at a plan that can be costed to produce an attractive price. Sponsoring organizations may be only too pleased to believe the quoted prices as they will certainly not have bottomless pockets. They may also feel that the legal obligations embodied in a fixed-price contract isolates them from the risks associated with a significant cost overrun. In one sense this may be true, but if it starts to become obvious that the contractor is going to lose a significant sum on the contract it can all go wrong. Disputes will break out, corners will be cut, claims will be made, the legal department will get involved. Management attention will be increasingly diverted from managing the progress of the project to arguing with the sponsor over any issue that can be deemed even the smallest deviation from the original requirement, and morale will drop as staff become uncertain about what the future of the project is. Whatever trust existed between the sponsor and the contractor will be lost; from that point on, the overall position of the project will deteriorate unless something can be done to resolve the situation. Ultimately it will be for the sponsor to consider what is in his best interests; in some cases it might only be resolved by changing the contract conditions to reflect a more equitable distribution of risk.

Situations such as that described can arise from a number of causes and the attitudes to risk adopted by the contracting parties is one of them. The desire to reduce risk as far as possible can lead to distorted judgement as can the desire to win in a competitive situation. It can result in a project that starts from a bad business deal and neither side tends to come out well from that. The alliance or partnership arrangement was founded on the idea of sharing risks and rewards and is one way in which poor business deals can be avoided; however, these work best in situations where the risks are not too great and there is an adequate contingency or where there is an additional reward to be shared because the project generates some overall value from outside. For an alliance to work well requires a thorough risk analysis at the start and one in which both the sponsor and the contractors have been fully involved. This principle tends to cut right across the concepts contained in competitive tendering and sealed bids, a process in which much of industry and government continues to place a good deal of faith.

Robustness in projects can be achieved through a thorough assessment of the risks the project is likely to face and the inclusion of countering measures in the plan. However, the organization of the project represents a risk in itself if it is not properly attuned to the conditions that pertain. Using contractual arrangements that are suitable to the work being undertaken is a vital element and it can only be accomplished if all parties recognize the risks involved and come to an agreement in which they are fairly distributed.

Risk analysis and management within the organization

The process of formal risk analysis and management within projects is a relatively recent invention. Prior to the early 1980s it was hardly mentioned within project management circles and no clearly recognizable processes were apparent. There is no doubt that some of the old optimism that was associated with 'project management' in the 1960s disappeared in the 1970s as the world went through a difficult period and a change came about in attitudes on the part of the general public. Major projects ceased to have the appeal that they once had and issues of conservation and the environment came to prominence. Even prestigious projects such as *Concorde* came to be regarded as failures although they were considerable technical successes. In this climate projects began to be viewed not as opportunities but as risks. Risks seemed to exist at every level from government, through to industry and right down to the individual: if it all went wrong he or she could be out of a job. And go wrong it did with such examples as the massive cost overruns on the Thames Barrier and the cancellation of the *Nimrod* AEW.3 with £900m spent. The time was thus right for a reassessment of project management processes and by the late 1980s risk analysis and management was being touted as the new panacea for project ills. Just as critical path analysis emerged as a process that would give project management its unique identity, the advent of Monte Carlo simulation brought respectability to risk analysis. Software developers created packages that would interface with project planning systems and risk analysis based on a reasoned assessment of variability in costs and durations got started. For many project managers in the mid-1990s, Monte Carlo simulation became synonymous with risk analysis and that was where the process began and ended. In fact, risk analysis and management is a much more comprehensive process, and workers in the field began to give the approach a proper methodology which was supported by a range of software tools that emerged in the mid-1990s covering risk registers, identification techniques and decision making. By the late '90s the process had been sufficiently established and used by a variety of organizations for the concept of 'risk maturity' to emerge. This was an attempt to define how far an organization's risk management processes had developed. The work was done in the UK and an example of a risk maturity model is given in Figure 10.2.

The risk maturity model allows any organization to assess its own processes for risk analysis and management and decide how close to a fully mature operation it is or needs to be. The latter point is important as the degree of risk involved in a project can vary enormously as can the degree to which any organization is willing to become involved in risky projects. Those organizations that engage in complex projects and innovative technologies will be exposed to

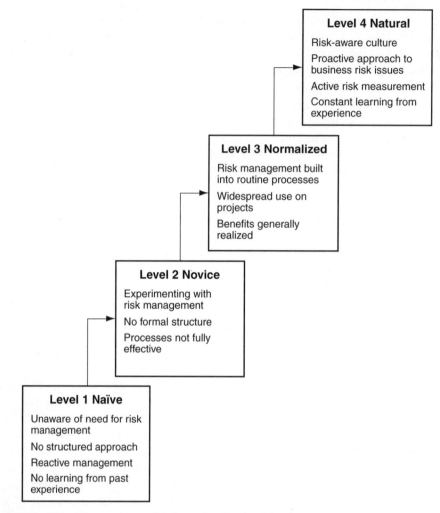

Figure 10.2 This risk maturity model shows four levels of development in terms of the application of risk analysis and management techniques to project work. Organizations can compare their level of development against this structure. Many would be content to remain at Level 3, the heavy emphasis on managing through a 'risk-aware culture' as shown at Level 4 might be seen as counterproductive in some situations. (Source, Dr D. Hillson (1997) 'Towards a risk maturity model', *the International Journal of Business and Project Management*, Spring)

much greater risks than those that work in more conservative and well-understood fields. The degree to which an organization needs to approach the fully mature level will thus be governed by the extent that it feels it is necessary. It must be remembered that before the advent of a definable risk management process many businesses and projects were still successful; that does not mean there were no risks involved but their existing processes must have handled them effectively. They must therefore have shown a significant degree of risk maturity in their overall approach even if a separate system was not easily identifiable. When deciding upon the implementation of a risk analysis and management system for projects, any organization would thus be well advised to consider the extent to which it is necessary and the level at which it should be pitched. Factors to consider are:

- the inherent degree of risk and uncertainty in the projects undertaken
- the complexity of the overall project tasks and organization
- the nature of the contractual arrangements
- the adequacy of the existing systems and procedures.

Implementing risk analysis and management processes involves the same basic requirements as are needed for any other management system but there are certain aspects that do need particular attention. Popular techniques such as value engineering or earned value analysis are defined by well-understood procedures and a generally fixed methodology so it is usually easy to identify the organizational, procedural and systems aspects that are needed to implement them. Because risk analysis and management can be implemented on a wide variety of dissimilar projects under very different circumstances this feature is absent, it can all come down to the four issues noted above. Nevertheless there are some key issues that are essential if the process of implementation is to succeed.

APPROPRIATENESS OF THE APPROACH

This has already been alluded to – it means that the degree to which formalized risk analysis and management is implemented should be appropriate to the risks involved and the type of project undertaken. If the approach is little more than lip-service to the process then it will not be effective and soon come to be regarded as worthless and an irritation. If the implementation is too heavy, with excessive reporting requirements that are inappropriate to the nature of the perceived risks, it may be viewed as irksome and deflecting attention away from what people see as their main task. No one wants to be constantly asked to report on unlikely situations or things they can do nothing about.

VALUE FROM THE RESULTS

It is one thing to propose a system and implement it but to maintain it and gain general acceptance it must generate results that are seen to be valuable. This aspect requires considerable thought as whatever system is proposed must address the issues that are seen to pose the greatest risk or help in solving the most pressing problems. This can vary considerably from one project to another and it need not be the risks themselves; the way in which the risk issues are depicted and communicated can be a vital aspect of the success of the system. Variations can mean that in one project, maintenance of the timescale is a vital issue hence simulation methods might be most appropriate to assessing probabilities and criticalities. On another project a complex series of tests may be involved with a number of alternatives to be considered and evaluated, hence an approach that directly aids decision making would be most useful. People engaged on the project must be able to see that whatever approach is implemented generates something of value to the progress and stability of the project even if they as individuals are not directly responsible for the handling of risk issues.

SUITABLE SYSTEMS AND PROCEDURES

The questions of appropriateness and value from the results leads directly to the design of the systems and procedures and the organization that is created for handling risks. The most obvious expression of this will be appointment of staff to be specifically responsible for risk issues and the implementation of software tools. Large complex projects may involve the appointment of a risk manager to handle the process of data gathering and risk analysis; the risk manager will also be expected to be a major contributor to the risk decision-making process, although not likely to be responsible for the final decisions. In smaller and simpler projects, the project manager may act as his own risk manager, with the exception that he may well have the power to take risk decisions. The degree to which formalized risk management is implemented is the most fundamental issue in deciding what procedures to introduce and what software tools will be acquired. In general, new systems should be compatible with existing data-gathering and processing arrangements and interface with current project management methods. This does not mean that no changes will be involved, because that is certainly not the case but risk analysis and management procedures are more likely to gain easy acceptance if they can be seen as an extension of existing practices rather than a revolution. There is probably more choice of software that suits a range of different problem issues than in any other aspect of project management and to some extent the choice of software will govern the overall approach; some of the packages on offer are considered in Chapter 11.

PROPER EDUCATION AND TRAINING

The subject of risk is among the most intellectually challenging in the whole of project management. It can be peppered with terms that seem to have specific meanings in specific cases and, for those who wish to delve more deeply, it can involve mathematical concepts that are beyond secondary school level. Furthermore, it deals in that elusive field – the future – and no one knows for certain what is going to happen. There will be those with a sceptical outlook who might feel that risk analysis is at best a black art or at worst management mumbo-jumbo; some might even feel threatened as their performance could come under scrutiny. The best counter to these difficulties lies in proper education and training. Staff who are going to be directly involved need to understand all the relevant concepts and know exactly what their role will be and what is expected of them. The worst approach would be to suddenly announce that from a given date risk management procedures will be introduced and on that day Mr X, Ms Y and Mr Z will be risk owners and have a new set of responsibilities. A reaction of bafflement is probably the mildest one can expect.

People must recognize and understand the aims and objectives associated with risk management and it must be demonstrated beyond doubt, through a process of education and consultation, that the intended procedures will work and the project will benefit from them. Where people need knowledge they do not currently possess then proper training should be organized. The process also needs monitoring to ensure that procedures, once instigated, are properly adhered to. With anything as subjective and potentially harmful as a risk assessment, it should be the aim of the project manager to ensure that information being fed into the risk analysis process is objective, realistic and not being distorted for political ends.

ACTIVE USE WITHIN THE PROJECT

If a formalized approach to risk analysis is implemented then it must be effectively used. It means that those who are required to report on or be responsible for risk issues must continue to support it, which means receiving some relevant feedback from the analysis process and being involved in the decision making and management that springs from it. Both aspects are important: risk matters should not become something that is always reported upon but rarely discussed, or if it *is* discussed, only among a very small cadre at the top of the project. This does however, raise a question for the project manager, as a fully objective risk analysis might reveal potential situations that could be very damaging, but they might not arise at all. It might not be in the general interests of the project to make too much of this because it could have an unsettling affect on the staff. A balance needs to be struck, people need to be involved where they are asked to contribute and they should see that their contribution is being used, but that does not mean everything must be available to all eyes. Risk is the most difficult of all areas in project management as it deals with the things that could go wrong; staff need to have an input where their expertise could ensure that things go right, but there are often risk issues that are external to the project to which staff have no direct input.

SENIOR MANAGEMENT SUPPORT

No management process will survive for long if it comes to be realized by the staff that the senior management have little real interest in it. This can happen if people start to think that risk management procedures are another management fad that will be all the rage with the top brass for a few months then forgotten in a year when another new fad comes along, or that the procedures have been introduced to satisfy a sponsor requirement but have little real impact on the running of either the business or the project. Of course, senior management must satisfy themselves of the need for risk management procedures as there will be some kind of investment required, but, having done so, they should take personal responsibility for becoming involved in the introduction and ensuring the processes really do meet a defined business need. Support needs to be visible and timely, above all senior management should take an active interest in the outputs of the system and become involved in significant decisions that might be required. If it becomes clear that senior management are paying lip-service to the process and that significant decisions are made through processes that do not involve the formal system (for example, gut reaction, internal politics, gambling instinct, private deals) then people will question its value and, perhaps, rightly so.

IMPLEMENTATION IN A CONTROLLED FASHION

Because of the sophisticated concepts and inherent complexities that can exist in the process of risk analysis and management, its implementation needs to take place in a manner that is suitable to the circumstances and the level of knowledge of the staff. This can take time, particularly if new software is to be acquired and must be integrated with existing systems. The simpler and more straightforward concepts should be implemented first. When everyone is comfortable that they are understood and appreciated, and the systems that support them are working properly, then progress can be made to more sophisticated aspects if it is felt there is a real benefit in doing this. As with any system, the law of diminishing returns applies. The simplest and most basic processes are likely to have most effect; increasing sophistication, generally speaking, does not bring a proportional increase in effectiveness for the cost and effort involved.

A SUITABLE ORGANIZATIONAL FRAMEWORK

This issue has already been covered in Chapter 9 but it is as well to remind ourselves that risk analysis and management systems aim to give a better overall insight into what the future of a project might be so that better decisions can be made at all stages in its life. It does not guarantee that all decisions will be the right ones, but they will at least be well-informed ones. The organization should be one in which a formal chain exists so that risk issues discovered at lower levels are properly reported and reflected upwards where their true impact can be judged. The structure should not allow risk issues to simply get lost between the divisions within the organization as no one will admit responsibility for them. Neither should it allow risk issues to be buried as they are potentially too embarrassing to individuals or departments. Equally important is the way that risks are handled when they are recognized. The management of risks includes recognizing when decisions are necessary and taking actions at appropriate moments; if these two aspects are not supported by the organizational framework, then any risk management process might be much less effective than it could be, even with the most sophisticated of tools.

Problem issues

All the foregoing text has contained a description of the risk analysis and management process and contains an inbuilt argument for using it in a project situation. There can, however, be some drawbacks and problems that should be recognized if the process is to be properly managed.

INVESTMENT COSTS

All systems and processes have a cost – formalized risk management is no different. Data needs to be gathered and analysed, staff need to contribute their time and effort to the identification and monitoring process, output reports have to be generated and staff need to read and take note of them. Special software might have to be acquired and staff will need training in its use and interpretation. As the majority of the personnel working on a project will not be directly involved in risk management, staff and systems costs might actually be comparatively low as a proportion of overall project cost. The direct costs of a risk management process might be seen as cheap insurance when compared to the costs that could be associated with a risk materializing that, with proper analysis, could have been recognized and averted.

DEMANDS ON MANAGEMENT

For some in project management, risk is a dirty word: you don't talk about it unless you really have to and then in the most casual of ways. Risk disturbs a cosy view of the world in which everything goes to plan and all the expectations are fulfilled. To admit that this might not be the case could be seen as damaging to one's prospects. A thorough risk analysis can throw all the potential evils into sharp focus and that in itself can be a shock to the system. However, it does something else: once a risk is identified as being real, it demands that a solution is found. This is often the most difficult part as risks are not certainties – they might not occur – but if they do they could be very damaging; countering strategies may not be obvious and it may take considerable management effort to devise an effective way of dealing with them. Most damagingly, management might have to admit that they really have no way of dealing with some of them, they can only wait and see what happens and hope to think up some means of damage limitation at the time. In some cases money might have to be spent speculatively in order to avert a risk situation but, if at a later point it becomes clear that the risk could not have arisen, then the money will have been wasted. Whereas none of these points are arguments against risk management they can be disincentives.

INCORRECT PERCEPTION

Risk analysis, by its very nature, deals with aspects of the future and is fraught with issues that are subjective judgements. There are risks in this from two angles. First, people may choose to present risks and the judgements that go with them in ways they see as advantageous to themselves; this can arise from fear, politics or ambition. Whatever the reason, if this becomes the recognized but unspoken way of addressing risks, senior management, who have to make the ultimate decisions, might be presented with a distorted view of the real position. Second, risk identification and analysis methods can make use of techniques such as brainstorming aimed at discovering all the risk issues. If not properly assessed for its realism it could lead to the project being viewed as nothing but a large set of risks as the potential benefits become obscured. It can raise spectres in the mind that might otherwise have lain harmlessly dormant and result in a retreat from quite reasonable business risks and a failure to grasp opportunities. Too much emphasis on risks at the expense of a balanced view can raise doubts all round and in the end can be counterproductive.

DECISION-MAKING AUTHORITY

Another issue that can arise relates to staff empowerment where risk decisions are involved. Staff at the lower levels within the organization structure might well be sent on risk management courses at which they will be taught about such things as registers, simulations and decision making. In this author's experience, the issue of decision making can raise certain problems as it often throws into sharp focus where in the organization the risk decisions are made. When staff who are being coached in risk management methods realize that the real decisions are made several levels higher up the organization structure it has led them to question the value of their participation in the whole process. This is not an easy issue to deal with: there is an obvious conflict between the desire to have staff who are well informed and understand the process and raising expectations about the degree of authority people might actually have. Education and training therefore needs to be tailored to the requirements of the individual and pitched at a level that is appropriate to their degree of participation.

A properly conceived risk analysis and management process has a lot to offer the project manager. However, it needs to be implemented in a way that recognizes the level of risk that the project is exposed to, the organizational structure in which it must operate and the expectations and demands placed on those that will operate it.

11 *Software for Risk Analysis and Management*

The systematic analysis of risks and their consequences was born out of the statistical processes associated with the insurance industry and used such measures as expected values and cumulative probability curves. These measures work well in the comparatively limited field of financial losses from misfortunes with a known statistical history, but it is becoming recognized that these measures alone cannot and do not represent the whole description of the risks that may face a project and may only give a limited view of the real situation. In practice, managers face a series of problems in dealing with risks; they may be expressed as how to:

- recognize and identify the risks that exist
- express those risks in terms that those who face them can understand
- make some objective judgement about the seriousness of the perceived risks
- identify what options are open for dealing with the perceived risks
- evaluate the effectiveness of the perceived options
- make the best decision when faced with an uncertain or risky situation
- monitor the state or seriousness of each risk as management actions are taken.

It will be recognized that this listing of risk management problems implies a need for a variety of skills including:

- cognitive – the ability to perceive and recognize
- experiential – the ability to draw on past knowledge
- judgmental – the ability to critically distinguish between alternatives
- analytical – the ability to decompose into fundamental constituents and their relationships
- creative – the ability to generate new ideas and concepts
- perceptive – the ability to cast the mind forward to conceive new situations
- expressive – the ability to describe and communicate
- managerial – the ability to give effective instructions and follow them up.

Effective management of all the issues that arise on projects involves the use of all these skills but few can be embodied in software-based processes at this time. However, software is becoming an important tool for management; it can have a place in both the 'hard', quantifiable, processes as well as in dealing with the 'soft', qualitative, issues, even if it cannot necessarily take a part in the actions that are taken.

Categories of software

Chapter 4 gave a division of risk into categories that derive from the origins of the risk, but this is not the only way in which risks can be viewed. Risks can be seen as springing from a combination of the decisions that are made and the conditions that arise. If either turn out for the worse the project will experience some kind of loss or damage. The decisions can be divided into two broad areas: i) those that are associated with the initial investment, that is, what do we expect as a return on the outlay?, and ii) those that are associated with the project strategy, that is, how do we go about this project? After the decisions have been made, the conditions that arise on the project could turn out to be different from those that were expected and contained in the plan and are thus another area of uncertainty about which further decisions might have to be made as the conditions alter.

No one can doubt that the processes involved with the range of skills indicated above are still very much in the domain of the human brain and a long way from the comparatively primitive processes offered by even the most sophisticated risk management software packages. However, by combining the listing of managerial problems and the list of skills with the decisions and conditions that give rise to risks, it is possible to see how a range of software is evolving that goes some way to addressing a significant part of the total problem. Risk identification, decision making, monitoring and generating a view of an uncertain future are all subjects of software packages.

The range of software products is wide, both in terms of intent and operation, but the packages can be seen to fall into four broad categories, each of which covers a different aspect and has resulted in software specific to that category.

1. **Risk identification aids** – Systems of this type aim to guide the analyst or manager in the process of identifying risk issues and attaching some measure of seriousness to them. Such systems can only function if the basic risk issues and the contributing factors are known to the system in the first place. As they contain cognitive, experiential and analytical elements they can be considered as part of the general class of 'knowledge-based' or 'expert' systems.

2. **Risk status monitors** – Packages that perform this function allow the analyst or manager to record, in a regularized format, the risks that have been identified together with information about them such as the magnitude of the risk effect, its likelihood, who is responsible for taking action and what, if any, action has been taken. The systems may also contain some mathematical or ranking capability so that perceived risks can be presented in the order of the most serious to the least each time the system is updated or interrogated. Systems such as these contain no inherent knowledge of their own, whatever information they contain is entirely at the discretion of the manager; they are basically management databases.

3. **Decision-making aids** – These aim to help the manager in the process of dealing with risks when a choice among alternatives is required. The process of making a decision when there are alternatives, each with a different outcome, can be complex or simple depending on the situation. Often, when the decision has a clear economic determinant such as the lowest cost or most profitable outcome, the best course of action can be established by purely numerical (quantitative) processes providing a reasonable measure of the possible outcomes can be made. However, some decisions

involve more complex issues; for example, when balancing the divergent interests of a variety of project stakeholders. These issues cannot be so easily accommodated using a strictly mathematical approach. Software that can aid the decision-making process has evolved along a series of different lines, each of which is tailored to a specific type of decision problem, and cannot be so simply classified as those in the previous two categories. These systems are essentially analytical in character but one may need cognitive, experiential, judgmental, creative and perceptive skills in order to use them effectively.

4. **Simulation models** – Among the most popular form of risk analysis system for use in project situations is the simulation model. In part, this is due to the fact that most project planning is now done using software-based planning systems and these plans are expressed with precise logic and numerical values for durations, resources and costs; in this form they are particularly suitable for further mathematical processing. Uncertainties are likely to exist about the conditions that will arise on a project because it can be expected that there will be differences between the planned values of the various parts of the project and the actual out-turn values. Simulation modelling of a project aims to give a greater insight into the range of outcomes that can arise. Probabilistically based values are used in simulations of this type but other types of model can be built that do not include probability aspects. These models are used when the specific effects of just one or two parameters on the end-result or the behaviour of a system under specified conditions is being studied. Although these are essentially analytic systems, they contain a perceptive element as situations may be described by the simulation output that could not have been perceived in the same way by a simple consideration of the input situation.

Although these categories may seem mutually exclusive in the way they have been described, practical risk management packages can usually be identified with one primary category but they may also contain elements which allow them to perform tasks associated with other categories.

Software products currently available

Given below are brief descriptions of some contemporary products, all of which address some aspect of the risk analysis problem categorized according to their primary role. This is not intended as an exhaustive listing but rather a series of examples of software packages that exhibit the general characteristics of products in their category.

RISK IDENTIFICATION AIDS

The process of identifying risks is essentially a creative one as it implies casting the mind forward from a known position to a future in which some adverse effect arises. Historically, this has been the preserve of human intellect and, for the most part, the risk identification process has been carried out by such methods as interviews with experts or brainstorming sessions. However, pure creativity is not the only approach that may be useful. There is a powerful argument that history tends to repeat itself and, despite the changes in society and advances in technology, projects of similar types, now and in the future, will tend to exhibit the same kinds of problems as those that occurred on previous projects unless some very specific action is taken. For example, projects with a highly innovative content can be expected to exhibit failures and need rework at various points in their cycle as that has been the experience of earlier projects and nothing has occurred to indicate the future will be any different. If some way can be found to capture that past experience and structure it so that the outcomes can be related to the conditions that brought them about, then, by a process of interrogating the conditions of the actual project, a view may be generated of the risks the project is likely to face. This is the essence of the knowledge-based approach to risk identification and it has been embodied in several packages.

Knowledge *per se* presents a problem: once you start applying knowledge you have to know what you are dealing with, and given that no system can have knowledge of all risks in all projects, any system that emerges is either going to operate with some precision in just one field of expertise or be rather unsophisticated and general. One system that has come on the market that does contain a structured knowledge base is *Project RISK for Windows* from Niku UK Ltd; in its released form it contains a knowledge base that deals with risks in information technology projects and there is also a version that incorporates the PRINCE methodology. However the installed knowledge base can be replaced with one that deals with any particular type of project if one cares to develop it. The risks to which the project can be exposed must be predefined as a set of 'risk conditions' and the knowledge base is used to determine the likelihood of the risk conditions arising.

In operation, *Project RISK* consists of answering a series of questions about a predetermined set of issues that affect the project. These cover ten aspects, from Strategic Issues, Business Issues, Project Size and Scope right through to Operations and Support. Each main issue contains a more detailed set of questions. With each question there is a set of answers and the analyst is required to select one answer from the set. A typical example is:

Question: What is the financial case for the system?
Answers: 1) Benefits repay costs within 12 months, 2) Benefits repay costs within 3 years, 3) Payback period exceeds 3 years, 4) I am unable to answer this question.

When first introduced to the system, the user may have some difficulty in deciding how to answer some of the many questions. Here *Project RISK* is helpful as a complete guide to answering each question is available through a context-sensitive Help screen and is repeated in the manual.

Once the questionnaire has been completed, *Project RISK* will generate a bar chart showing a series of undesirable project features, the risk conditions, such as: 'never be delivered', 'lacking functionality', 'errors in system', etc., set on a vertical axis against a listing of severity levels ranging from 'none' to 'emergency'. The bar chart representation is shown in Figure 11.1 which shows a risk profile for a project using a knowledge base that was not supplied with the software but specially constructed by this author.

The system works by reference to a set of risk levels, scored from 0 to 3, defined against each of the risk conditions for each possible answer. Given that there could be about 90 questions, each with 4 or 5 answers, this is a set of about 400 answers. The set of questions relevant to the particular type of project plus the range of possible answers, the scores awarded to the identified risks and the advice on how to answer form the core of the knowledge base. It cannot be created by any other process than by using expert judgement

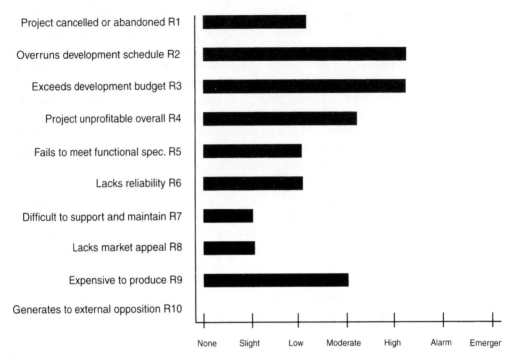

Figure 11.1 Risk conditions bar chart screen from *Project Risk* – in this case the knowledge base relates to risk conditions associated with engineering development projects. Here it is being used to assess a project concerning an airborne system and the project is on the high side of being moderately risky but not unreasonable as a business venture. Other projects assessed using this software have shown much higher levels of risk and experience has proved that they have run into major difficulties.

based on the knowledge and history of previous projects of a broadly similar type. To arrive at the final probability level for the particular risk condition, a suitable algorithm is needed to combine the total scores and generate the answer.

After creating an initial view of the project, and perhaps noting that there are aspects of the proposal that have risk levels that appear excessive, it is natural to look at the issues that give rise to the problems. Here *Project RISK* helps by printing an Action List; this is a listing of all the issues that have some level of risk and how those risks can be viewed. The Action List is prioritized in the order of the issues requiring the most urgent attention and these can be categorized as Unavoidable, Manageable, Avoidable or Not Known. Where issues are either Manageable or Avoidable a note on the course of action can be added and the model modified accordingly.

In practice, users of this system either believe the results or they do not; if they do believe them, the inference is that the knowledge base in *Project RISK* is similar to their own experience. If the results do not look believable then one would suspect that the particular situation is, in some way, different from the generalized conditions contained in the model. If this is the case, users can customize either the knowledge database or the questions and answers to suit their own situation through an additional feature called the 'Customiser'. ICL has made considerable use of *Project RISK*, customized to suit its own requirements, and its use forms an integral part of that organization's project approval and risk management process.

For people in the world of IT projects, this is an immediately useful tool requiring little or no modification in order to get started. The fact that the Customiser gives complete access to modify the knowledge base means that this system need not be restricted to IT projects for it can be reconfigured to model projects of any type. However, considerable investment in time and effort is required to construct the new knowledge base and the set of risk conditions.

This very effective system was developed during the early 1990s by Hoskyns and later ABT Corporation (before being taken over by Niku) based on their own experience of software development projects but, due to a strategic change of direction, no further work has been done to develop it since 1996 although it was marketed for quite some time after that. Anyone interested in acquiring the system should contact Niku, who still own the software (see Appendix II).

TDRM from HVR Consulting Services uses a broadly similar question-and-answer approach to *Project RISK* but in a more limited way. The package is aimed at the initial project evaluation stage and, unlike *Project RISK*, is deemed to be applicable to projects of all types. This generality inevitably restricts both the knowledge and the detail it can contain and only four types of risk condition are considered: Resources, Technical, Management and External. There are eight questions in each category with six predefined answers from which a choice must be made. The principal output is a column graph showing a measure of the risks in the four categories on a scale ranging from zero to very high. Other reports including the answers given for all the questions are available. If required, the knowledge base of questions, answers and weightings can be fully customized to meet the specific requirements of particular project types, but with only four risk categories and a maximum of 32 questions it may not have the sophistication to deal with the range of risk issues that exist in many real situations.

Other packages offering a similar methodology are available and it can be anticipated that more will follow, particularly as companies are increasingly recognizing that the knowledge they possess is one of their most valuable assets.

Risk status monitors

All project managers involved with projects with some clearly identified risks need to keep an eye on the situation and the most popular method is the 'Risk Register'. This is a record of the risks that have been identified in a project together with whatever additional information about the situation may be relevant to the project manager. At its simplest, risk registers can be maintained with software that is no more complex than a standard word processor, spreadsheet or a database system.

However, the requirement to organize and display the information in a series of different ways has led to a number of data-base-style packages configured specifically for the risk management role. Examples of this genre include *REMIS* from HVR, *Predict! Risk Controller* from Risk Decisions and *RisGen* developed jointly by Line International and QinetiQ.

The risk registers in the above mentioned packages tend to be of similar form and contain similar data, typically:

- risk description – statement of the risk issue.
- risk probability – given on some scale, typically V. Low, Low, Medium, High, V. High or a score 0–100.

- risk impact – this may be given as a statement but typically has a cost or duration associated with it; aspects of performance may also be included and it may also have a score.
- risk category – categorization of the risk against some criteria such as manageable, avoidable, acceptable, etc., or other issues such as technical, legal, investment, etc.

Project Report

Project : Power Station Construction   Status : Pre-Construction   Draft Issue : 3

Top Risks

Number	Title	Owner	Time Score	Cost Score	Perf Score
4.02	System integration problems	William Marsh	0.36	0.18	0.05
6.02	Inability to meet all H&S requirements	William Marsh	0.05	0.10	0.20
4.01	Interface complexity of project una	Robert Brown	0.10	0.10	0.03
12.01	Political impacts	John Smith	0.06	0.06	0.00
8.01	Unable to obtain and maintain reso	Alexandra Norton	0.06	0.06	0.00
5.01	Inability to meet reliability requirements	William Marsh	0.06	0.03	0.03
11.01	Poor Communications	Robert Brown	0.06	0.03	0.02
5.02	Unclear demonstration of reliability	John Smith	0.05	0.05	0.05
6.01	Inability to meet safety requirements	William Marsh	0.02	0.02	0.02

Risk Distribution

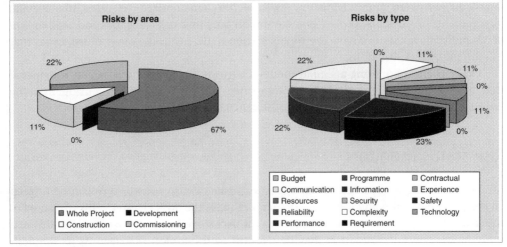

Risk Metric Trends

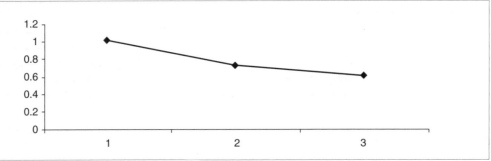

Figure 11.2   Part of a risk register and pie chart of risk types from *REMIS*.

- risk owner – person held responsible for monitoring the status of the risk situation (although a person may be designated as the risk owner, he or she may not be in a sufficiently high position to make a decision that will directly affect the risk, particularly if speculative expenditure is involved).
- mitigating actions – description of the proposed course of action to counter the perceived risk, this could be a two-stage process with an initial action and a fall-back position.
- current status – description of actions outstanding and developments since the last report.

Beyond this basic information additional facts may be added but this will be dependent on the particular package.

A degree of analysis is possible depending upon the package; the severity, calculated from the impact and probability values, can be used to create an ordered list. When combined with the timing at which the risk can be expected to materialize, a 'Top 10' risk issues list can be generated as a management action list. Some packages, such as *RisGen*, allow further numeric processing; if information is entered about the variability of either project costs or activity durations then a spread of end-results can be obtained.

All the packages are able to produce a variety of reports; typically they could include:

- ordered risk registers
- risk summaries
- history of each risk since first recognized
- graphical summaries of risks in each category
- risk trend analyses.

Figure 11.2 shows a risk register and pie-chart from *REMIS* while Figure 11. 3 shows a view of the risk register by risk owner from *Predict! Risk Controller.*

DECISION-MAKING AIDS

The breadth and complexity inherent in decision making has led to a variety of software packages each of which presents the problem in a different light. However, the general process of decision making tends to follow a set pattern which includes identifying the issues involved, structuring the problem, adding some subjective or objective measures of the possible outcomes and identifying the most favourable option. All the software packages contain the elements of this approach but the processes inherent in each package are different. The software can first be divided into those packages that adopt a numerically based set of criteria to determine the best outcome and those that help to present the problem in all its complexity so that the decision maker can go through a more qualitative or subjective process of consideration to find the best solution for himself.

The numerically based packages tend to follow one of two possible processes, the first being the classic decision-tree approach and the second using the multiple criteria decision-making method. The essential difference between these two approaches lies in the number of issues that are involved in the decision and the clarity with which the outcomes can be expressed. Where the number of issues is relatively small, the choice between outcomes can be seen with clarity and they can be defined in purely numerical terms such as anticipated profits arising from one of two or more courses of action, then the decision tree is the appropriate process.

Risk Register by Risk Owner

Risk Number / Risk Description	Organization Category / Review date	Status	Probability	Cost Impacts	Actions	Action owner / Action Status / Action Review Date

Risk Owner   R.E. Jones

Risk Number / Risk Description	Organization Category / Review date	Status	Probability	Cost Impacts			Actions	Action owner / Action Status / Action Review Date
76. Test. 31 Clash of usage with project p. 106 over vibration test rig. Projected timescale indicates that there could be excessive demand on the test rig at the time when the first unit is due for initial testing.	Dept S07 Test 21/11/2003		**208. Test rig availability**				**31. Negotiate with JSC Co. for hire of vibration rig** Potential clash over in-house testing dates, consider using outside facility	R. E. Jones Authorized 26/9/2003
			Pres 20%	£10000	£12000	£16000		
			Hist					
			Post 5%	£2000	£3000	£4000		

Risk Owner   A.J. Smith

Risk Number / Risk Description	Organization Category / Review date	Status	Probability	Cost Impacts		Actions	Action owner / Action Status / Action Review Date
85. Design. 24 Indication from returned vehicle that paint adhesion may be a problem. Peeling paint in exposed area may indicate a different choice of top finish may be needed	Dept S01 Design 21/11/2003		**209. Paint not suitable**			**32. Research into alternative top finishing paint** Detailed examination of peeling paint required, look at alternatives	A. J. Smith Authorized 26/9/2003
			Pres 15%	£8000	£10000		
			Hist				
			Post 5%	£1000	£2000		

Figure 11.3   Example of the risk register in risk owner format from *Predict! Risk Controller*.

One example of a decision-tree system, *DPL* (whose name derives from Decision Policy Language), comes from Standard and Poor's Applied Decision Analysis. It can draw and evaluate decision trees with the same appearance as the conventional hand-drawn version. DPL can also use the influence diagram for formulating the problem by making use of a rule that any conventionally drawn influence diagram can be converted into a decision tree, although the reverse is not true. Three types of nodes are involved: 'decision nodes' shown as rectangles, 'chance nodes' shown as circles, and end conditions shown as triangles. Decision nodes (decision-maker's tree) must have at least two branches as must the chance nodes (nature's tree). A probability value must be entered against each branch from the chance node; the program automatically checks that the probability values add up to one (1). Figure 11.4 shows an example of a decision tree drawn in *DPL* for a decision about a new product following a market survey. Depending on whether the decision maker is looking for a maximum or a minimum value, the optimum set of decisions can be shown in a decision policy view. This is created by evaluating the decision tree using the standard probability calculus to give the resultant combined end-condition plus the paths that lead to it. The decision policy diagram is shown in the lower part of the figure. The heavy lines indicate the best decision for either outcome of the survey based on the assumed probabilities.

DPL can carry out sensitivity analyses if single variables are allowed to change within set limits. When this is done it will show at what particular values of the variable the decision policy will change. It can also create a diagram for any decision which shows the potential range of values that can result from the chosen course of action with the associated cumulative probabilities. Another package that works in a similar way is *Precision Tree* from Palisade Corporation.

Decision trees stemmed from the comparatively ordered world of games of chance and are thus most applicable to the more simply expressed problems. Sometimes however, the problem can involve many different issues, all of which have a bearing on the result but at first sight it may seem difficult to find a best solution with so many competing requirements.

The multiple-criteria decision-making (MCDM) methods have evolved as a way to unravel this problem and *Expert Choice* from Expert Choice Inc. is one package that makes use of it in the form known as the Analytic Hierarchy Process (AHP). This process has already been introduced in Chapter 5 and the principle of model construction and computation is shown in Figure 5.4. Use of the system involves creating a matrix of all the issues that have a bearing on the end-goal or the desired outcome in a situation where there is a choice between clearly defined alternatives. These issues can be defined at a first level that bears directly on the goal while further issues, and these may well be the alternatives, can be defined on a lower level that bears on the first level; more levels can be added if needed. This results in a pyramid-like structure of choices and issues that influence the goal as can be seen in Figure 5.4. To arrive at the most favourable choice, a process of pairwise comparison is employed. Here the decision maker is asked to compare each possible pair of alternatives at the lower level against the issue at the higher level and decide which alternative is either the most preferable, likely or suitable for satisfying the higher issue and give a score to indicate the direction and magnitude of preference. Weighted preferences are calculated from the geometric averages of each of the scores and, as each group of issues is completed, a graph is produced showing the weighted preferences between alternatives based on the choices made. The graph also contains an 'inconsistency index' which, if the value is high enough, could cause the decision maker to reassess his or her answers. When all the issues have been evaluated, a single best choice is indicated. From this position sensitivity analyses can be

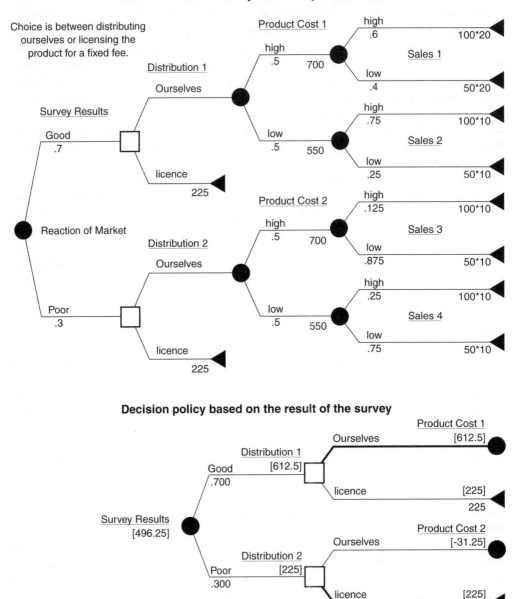

Figure 11.4 Decision tree drawn and evaluated in *DPL*. In this case the choice is between licensing distribution of a product for a fixed fee or doing it in-house (ourselves). The decision is to be based on the result of a test marketing study as shown in the upper diagram. The lower diagram gives the best policies as heavy lines, based on the expected result of the study. The overall expected value of this project is £496.25k before any decisions are taken and based on a 30% expectation of a poor result. If the test reveals a poor market potential it would be better to license the distribution than do it in-house and accept a fixed return of £225k. If the test shows a good potential and the decision is taken to do it in-house, a better expected value of £612.5k is obtained.

carried out and the performance of each alternative can be displayed against each of the decision issues; several formats are available for this. Figure 11.5 shows an output format from *Expert Choice*.

If the problem is unstructured at the start and the decision criteria are not clearly seen, *Expert Choice* offers an alternative way of structuring the problem by considering the advantages and disadvantages of each option. Once this has been done, it should be possible to group these into related issues which can then be converted into the decision criteria and the decision model built directly from that analysis. Software of this type is at its most useful where the decisions involve a complex set of issues whose priorities may not be easily resolved at the outset. Where the decision is largely an economic one such as how much profit is made for a given outlay, other evaluation methods such as discounted cash flow may be more appropriate.

An extension of the multiple criteria method exists in a package called *STRAD* from Stradspan. This has elements of the *Expert Choice* approach but has less reliance on the concept of making a choice between alternatives although alternative strategies will be a feature of the problem. Instead, it aims to facilitate the decision-making process by allowing the problem to be described through a series of screens, each of which can define an aspect of the problem. By using the different screens, the decision maker is invited to work his way logically through the problem to arrive at the solution he or she considers most suitable. It contains more opportunities to express issues involving relative values, and their bearing on the problem as a whole, than the previous two packages and its emphasis is decidedly on the opinion-based process of decision making. The originators of the package envisaged its primary use as being in a group decision-making situation.

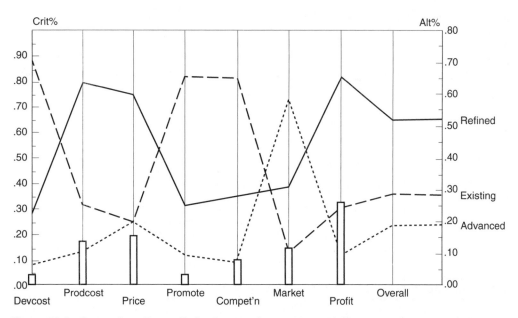

Figure 11.5   Output from *Expert Choice* showing the sensitivity of the various parameters in the problem and the overall result. In this case the choice is between the three options given in Examples 6.1 and 6.2 (Chapter 6). Although this analysis was performed using pairwise comparisons rather than a mathematical approach, it will be seen that an overall ranking, similar to that calculated in Example 6.2, is obtained and the refined product emerges as the best choice.

The basic model contained within *STRAD*, is defined in the 'Overview window' shown in Figure 11.6. Issues of uncertainty are positioned in the UV, UR and UE fields according to their impact on the project and the decisions that have to be taken; issues of uncertainty positioned more closely to the centre are more important than those nearer the edge. Figure 11.6 clearly shows that *STRAD* is more concerned with how the project will be implemented rather than the basic decision to go ahead. It allows the decision maker to insert issues about which there is uncertainty, issues where decisions have to be made and those issues where a comparison between alternative approaches may be made. If the project problem does not easily fit the above model, then *STRAD* will prove awkward to use. However, there are many major issues that face projects where this formulation would be relevant, for example, planning a project for developing a new road scheme. This can have areas of uncertainty concerning routing, traffic levels, environmental effects or community effects, and decision issues such as conducting a traffic census before going ahead or conducting a neighbourhood survey. It is this kind of multidimensional problem that a tool such as *STRAD* can help resolve.

As the principal reason for the exercise is to arrive at a sensible series of decisions, the relationship between all the decision issues can be specified in a 'Focus screen'; this has much the same form as an influence diagram, the layout is shown in Figure 11.7. The relationship between decision issues can be described on this diagram with a differentiation

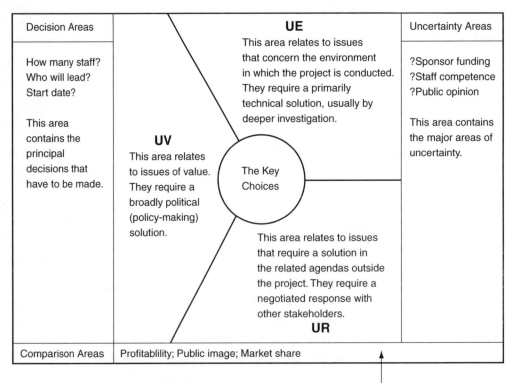

Figure 11.6 The basic problem structure in *STRAD* given in the Overview window shows it to be divided into three broad areas associated with issues of Value, Environment and Related agendas.

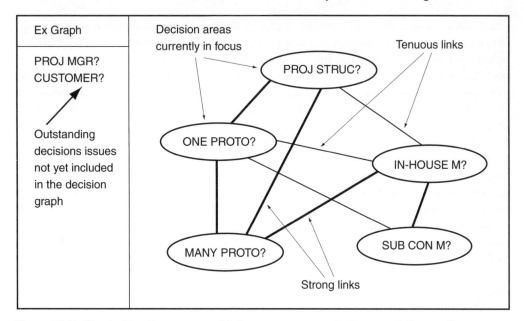

Figure 11.7 The decision Focus screen, this has an appearance similar to an influence diagram.

between those decisions that are strongly linked and those for which there is a more tenuous connection. This diagram can be analysed for all single issues, pairs of issues and these can be ranked in order against the urgency and importance ratings entered against each decision issue, hence the combinations that require the most urgent resolution can be identified.

Using the weightings that have been entered, the decision options can be viewed as a tree diagram ordered according to importance, urgency or a user-defined criteria. Before this however, any non-feasible options, that is, any obviously conflicting pairs of options, can be eliminated. This one process alone can rapidly focus the mind on the feasible solutions.

To make a more reasoned comparison between the decision options, an assessment is required of the effect of each decision option on each comparison area. This is a pairwise comparison process involving the decision maker assessing whether the choice of Options A or B, for any decision, will have a more or less beneficial effect on each of the comparison criteria. This process is done using a graphical screen that allows one to position a marker either towards or away from the beneficial end of a comparative scale; the spread of uncertainty about the assumed benefit can also be defined. When this comparison process is complete, *STRAD* will rank all the possible routes through the tree of options to show them in the order of the most advantageous to the least. That being done, the obviously poor options can be eliminated from the tree. Further exploration of the decision options can be done in the 'Balance window' which allows a pairwise comparison of each possible decision path showing, in each case, which is the more favourable option and the balance in favour or against on the basis of each area of comparison as well as providing an overall weighted score.

Whereas the decision and comparison areas have been related in the model, the third area, that of uncertainty, remains outside. Having made a selection of one or several decisions, one is invited to reconsider which, if any, have a bearing on the issues of uncertainty and what exploratory options one may wish to pursue. There is no formalized link between any area of uncertainty and any decision option, thus the model is not dynamic in the sense that a selection of a particular set of decisions does not automatically reflect itself in a movement of the uncertainty fields in the Overview window. Although operation of the software is relatively straightforward, it will be realized from this brief description that *STRAD* is a complex system in concept as it attempts to encapsulate a complete decision-making process in which many of the issues may be conflicting and can only be expressed in terms of opinions and feelings.

Although the Bayesian approach to decision making was introduced in Chapter 6 and applications are beginning to be found for it, little use has been made of it in the general field of project risk analysis. This may be because it went out of fashion as a statistical process in the 1920s and the advent of games theory in the 1950s displaced it as a technique for decision making. However, it is beginning to be recognized for its value in specialist applications, one system that makes use of it is *WinAward* from Bayesian Systems Inc.; this addresses the problems of how to bid in a competitive situation or which business leads should be pursued and which should be abandoned. In the latter situation, it can be seen as operating on the opposite side of the risk problem: the evaluation of market opportunities. This is an important point: it is just as vital to recognize and take advantage of the opportunities as it is to recognize and avoid the risks. Both, however, require good decision making.

The systems described above indicate the range of products and approaches that are available to resolving the multifaceted and often complex issues that can arise when a decision has to be made. There is no single best approach, each method has its place according to the situation.

SIMULATION MODELS

The process of simulation is one in which the behaviour of some aspect of a situation is replicated without actually achieving reality, thus any form of mathematical modelling contains an element of simulation. In practical terms, for project management problems, simulation models can generally be divided into two: i) those that are an essentially static representation of the problem which, for a single statement of the position, will generate a single result, and ii) those which contain an element of variability and generate a range of results from an initial position.

Providing they are kept to a strictly mathematical statement of the system, static simulations need no special software; general-purpose spreadsheets are well suited to this type of problem. If one can define all the relationships between the various aspects of the problem in numerical terms, then the bearing of one issue upon the outcome can be determined by varying the input in a systematic way. This form of model can be made both complex and sophisticated if sufficient understanding of the issues exists. In terms of risk analysis, the spreadsheet simulation is particularly useful for sensitivity assessment. An example of a model developed for assessing the global market for airliners using a spreadsheet is given in Figure 11.8

From the earliest application of computers to project planning it was recognized that variability could exist in the estimates associated with both activity durations and costs. The PERT method attempted to incorporate variability into the planning process but was soon discredited. However, a more useful solution has evolved over the last 15 years with the advent of Monte Carlo simulation packages. These make use of the random numbers to

Sheet 1, World Airliner Market Projections

Title	Data	1997	1998	1999	2000	2001	2002	2003	2004
Growth in world GDP	3.2								
World Air travel growth	5.19	To the year 2007							
Market Segment	% growth		Assumes fixed 3% growth in air travel plus an element proportional to the world GDP						
N. America	3.96								
Europe	5.02								
Asia/Pacific	6.97								
Rest of World	44.1								
Total 1997 fleet	11500								
	% Share								
	1997 Starting position			Total No of Passenger Aircraft by Region					
N. America	35	4025	4184	4350	4522	4701	4888	5081	5282
Europe	25	2875	3019	3171	3330	3497	3672	3856	4050
Asia/Pacific	25	2875	3075	3290	3519	3764	4026	4307	4607
Rest of World	15	1725	1801	1880	1963	2050	2140	2235	2333
Total	100	11500	12080	12691	13334	14012	14726	15479	16272
% growth	4.64		5.04	5.06	5.07	5.08	5.10	5.11	5.12
Cum.			5.04	10.10	15.17	20.25	25.35	30.46	35.59
% Share									
N. America %									
Europe %									
Asia/Pacific %									
Rest of World %									
Aircraft Productivity	Maximum 20% inc								
Growth load factor	0.0115								
Size changes	assumed constant								
Size change	Annual rise								
N. America	0.0125								
Europe	0.0125								
Asia/Pacific	0.018								

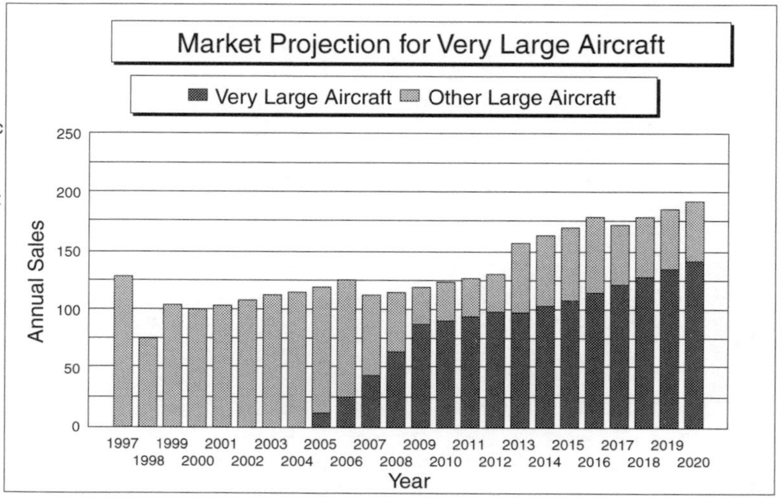

Market Projection for Very Large Aircraft

Legend: ■ Very Large Aircraft ▨ Other Large Aircraft

Y-axis: Annual Sales (0, 50, 100, 150, 200, 250)
X-axis: Year (1997, 1998, 1999, 2000, 2001, 2002, 2003, 2004, 2005, 2006, 2007, 2008, 2009, 2010, 2011, 2012, 2013, 2014, 2015, 2016, 2017, 2018, 2019, 2020)

Figure 11.8 Composite view of a simulation model using a Lotus 1-2-3 spreadsheet. In this case the model describes the composition of the world's airliner fleet until 2020 and can be used to study potential market sizes when subject to changes in various parameters such as projected growth in World Gross Domestic Product.

generate the range of possible outcomes in situations subject to variability. Simulation software products are often marketed as 'risk analysis packages' and, in the minds of some project management practitioners, represent the core of the risk analysis process. The simplest approach to simulation, adopted by several risk analysis packages, is to take a project plan that has been created on some popular project management system such as *Microsoft Project, OpenPlan* or *Primavera Project Planner* and import the durations and logic. Using the risk analysis package, estimates of the durations are added that include a description of the variability by stating, for example, shortest, most likely and longest durations and the shape of the distribution, such as triangular, normal, log-normal, uniform or beta. With this information, the project can be simulated for a sufficient number of runs to give a clear picture of the spread of possible end results. Other aspects such as costs or resources can also be modelled in a similar fashion.

An example of a package of this type is *Risk+*, Version 1.5, from C/S Solutions which is designed specifically to fit with *Microsoft Project* (MSP); once installed it embeds itself in the MSP software and when accessed it will generate a small toolbar of its own on the planning window. Data on the spread of both activity durations and costs can be entered and simulations of the variations in these quantities can be run. Figure 11.9 shows a typical output from *Risk+*, in this case it shows the relative frequency of occurrence of the completion date of a project in histogram form and also the cumulative probability of the project being completed by any given date. Notice that with this approach, the distribution of completion dates is approximately bell-shaped with a single high point (mode). This is typical of simulations that are performed on conventional project networks as they do not contain branches for alternative courses of action that may or may not be pursued and thus contain only a single scenario for the project. It is not impossible that two modes could arise if there are two independent, but not exclusive, parallel paths through the project, either of which could become critical if the conditions are right.

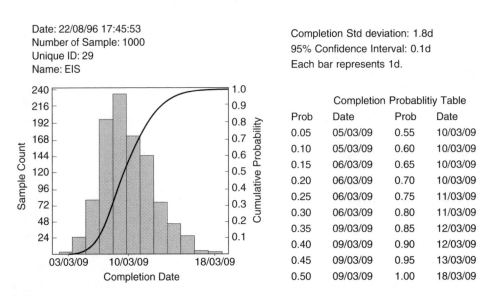

Figure 11.9 Individual completion date and cumulative probability values as calculated by *Risk+*; the single mode distribution is clearly seen.

DIVERGENT PATHS

Occasions may arise where alternative futures due to major areas of uncertainty will be clearly perceived and, if it is wished to simulate these effects, a more sophisticated approach is needed. A number of ways of doing this have been devised and the range of contemporary software reflects this.

For many people familiar with project planning, the most obvious approach to this problem of variability is to devise a plan which has a series of branches within it, each branch leading to a different series of activities, then, using probabilistic rules about the likelihood of going down any particular branch, simulate the whole project by the Monte Carlo method. *Risk+* (version 2) and *Pertmaster Project Risk* (version 7.6) allow branches to be included in the plan built in *MS Project 2000*. For this to happen the plan must contain the alternative groups of tasks that occur at a branching point. Branches can be of two types: probabilistic or conditional. When a probabilistic branch is encountered, the software decides, according to a given level of probability, which group of tasks will be scheduled. Typical examples occur where an important test is encountered; either the test will be passed and the project can proceed or there will be some rework and retesting before more progress can be made. Conditional branches arise in situations when, if a particular condition is met, a specific course of action follows, while an alternative course will ensue if the condition is not met. An example is the laying of oil pipes in the sea, this can only be done during the calm summer months; if completion of pipe-laying is delayed beyond the late autumn, the pipe-laying will not be completed and the oil pumping cannot begin until the next spring. Conditional branches can also arise due to the outcome of earlier probabilistic branches as has been shown in Example 7.1 in Chapter 7. An example of a branched plan is shown in Figure 11.10 using *Pertmaster Project Risk* from Pertmaster Ltd.

In practice, considering variations in the plan results in a major complication for the whole planning process as it leads to a potential series of alternative futures for the project and destroys the concept of a clearly identified critical path. It is probably true to say that in the vast majority of current project plans this complication is ignored and in many cases ignoring it is fully justified on the grounds of expedience and practicality.

ALTERNATIVE APPROACHES

When project plans are very complex with many detailed activities, it may become difficult to perform a risk simulation, particularly if complex branching is involved. In this case, it may be more useful to devise a simplified planning model of the overall project by combining groups of activities into major blocks. This was done in Example 7.1 and it made it suitable for analysis by direct calculation; however, reducing the project plan to a simplified form can also make it amenable to analysis by a number of other methods. The *Predict! Risk Analyser* package from Risk Decisions Ltd. uses a spreadsheet to define the project plan by using the cells as activities into which cost and duration information can be entered and by defining the structure of the project through the logical relationships between the cells. Monte Carlo simulation can be performed on this simplified project plan to produce the resulting distributions of cost and time. Figure 11.11 shows the output of a simulation created in *Predict! Risk Analyser* for the problem formulated in Figure 7.4 in Chapter 7. Because it uses a spreadsheet, the graphical representation of the problem is not visible. It will be seen that the resulting distributions of the dates for all the activities in the

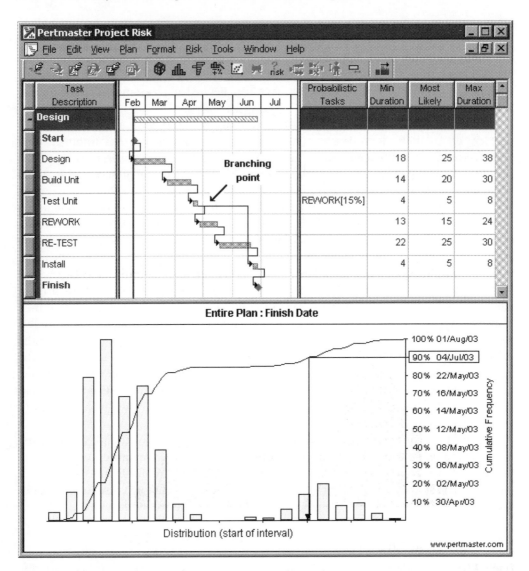

Figure 11.10 *Pertmaster Project Risk* allows probabilistic and conditional branches to be modelled. In this case there is probabilistic branch after the Test Unit activity as the project could proceed directly to the installation activity or there could be a re-work and re-test if there is a problem. The result is the bi-modal distribution of possible end and the division is governed by the probability assigned to a first-time success.

project is identical to that produced by hand calculation using the controlled interval method and shown in Figures 7.5 and 7.6. Besides containing the plan within itself, *Predict! Risk Analyser* can import project plans from standard planning packages such as *MS Project, Primavera Project Planner* and *CA SuperProject,* in which case it runs in a mode similar to *Risk+.* Another package that makes use of the spreadsheet format for problem formulation and Monte Carlo simulation is *@Risk* from Palisade Corporation.

A further and somewhat more radical method of defining the uncertainty in a project is to use an **influence diagram**. The *(I) Decide* package (formerly marketed as *Definitive*

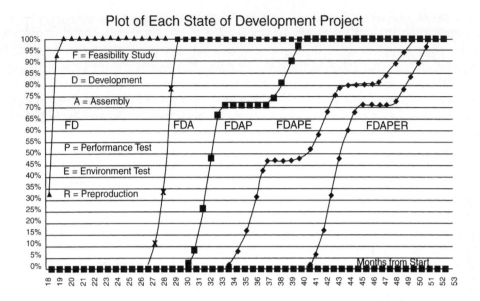

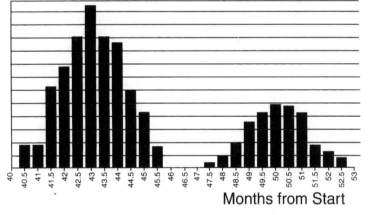

Figure 11.11 Composite view of the cumulative probabilities for completion dates of project activities and the histogram of the final completion date as modelled in *Predict! Risk Analyser*. This is the same problem as shown in Figure 7.4 although some activity titles have been simplified; the bi-modal distribution of the end-date is apparent and reflects the branching in the model. Compare with Figures 7.5 and 7.6.

Scenario and *DynRisk*) from Decisive Tools uses the influence diagram for problem formulation; it too can perform Monte Carlo simulation which makes it rather different from the influence diagrams in systems like *DPL*.

With *(I) Decide*, the basic symbol used to create the model is the Node and there are five types to choose from. Each type has a representative symbol at its centre, the types are: independent, sum, product, maximum and minimum; these terms refer to the 'global' properties of the node and define how the node reacts to the incoming variables. For example, the 'product node', symbol **X**, multiplies together all incoming values. There is also a 'local' operator that defines how the local value of the node (that is, the value generated internally) will react with the global value at the node (that is, the value generated by the process applied to all the inputs). To give an example, if the global operator is a 'product', all the input values at the node are multiplied together; if the local operator is a 'sum', the local value is added to the product of the input values to generate the output. Arcs are drawn to connect the nodes; when two nodes are opened, selecting the appropriate menu item causes an arc dialogue box to open. Through this box, a series of mathematical functions, including probability distributions, can be chosen which will transform the data traversing that arc.

To give an example of its use in a project situation, the problem given in Figure 7.4 has been formulated as an influence diagram in *(I) Decide* and it is shown in Figure 11.12; it looks sufficiently different from Figure 7.4 for it not to be obvious that they both represent the same thing. With the influence diagram, each possible activity, shown as a node circle, is included and this can include mutually exclusive activities. Which activities feature in the simulation run is determined by the logic and probabilities; these influence the activities that are selected and the resulting course of the project. The result for the end of the project is given in the lower part of Figure 11.12. Again there are two distinct possibilities: a more likely optimistic 'future' with a mode at 43 weeks and a less good 'future' with a mode at 51 weeks. Despite the difference in problem formulation this result is basically the same as that obtained with *Predict! Risk Analyser* and, not surprisingly, the same as by hand calculation.

The basic methods of simulating uncertainties in projects have been shown in the examples above together with some current software tools. When it comes to selecting a product for use it is essential to consider: a) the existing planning and management system in use in the organization, b) the type of problem to be evaluated, c) what, if any, linking there will be between the main project plan and the modelling of risks, and d) the scale and demand for risk information. These factors will dictate which method is most appropriate and the choice of software.

Combined approaches

At present the distinctions between the categories can be seen in contemporary software but this distinction may not be so clear in the future as efforts are made to unite some of these functions in common packages. In particular, links have been forged between the planning function, simulation modelling, the maintenance of a risk register and communication of risk data. *ARM* (standing for Active Risk Manager) from Strategic Thought Ltd. is a Web-based tool that aims to integrate these risk analysis functions through interfaces with a variety of systems that have either an input to the risk analysis process or have a role in report generation and dissemination of risk information. Interfaces exist with commonly used tools such as *Artemis Views, Lotus Notes, Microsoft Excel* and *MS Project*. In a similar vein, Risk Decisions have links between *Predict! Risk Controller* and *Predict! Risk Analyser* as well as planning systems such as *MS Project* which means these systems can work as one. Thus quantitative risk information held in *Controller* can be matched with planning data in *MS Project*, exported to *Analyser* for Monte Carlo simulation analysis and, if required, reports can be generated in *Microsoft Office* products.

Whereas the approach adopted by Strategic Thought and Risk Decisions is to link the risk database with simulation and communication tools, Palisade Corporation has linked its

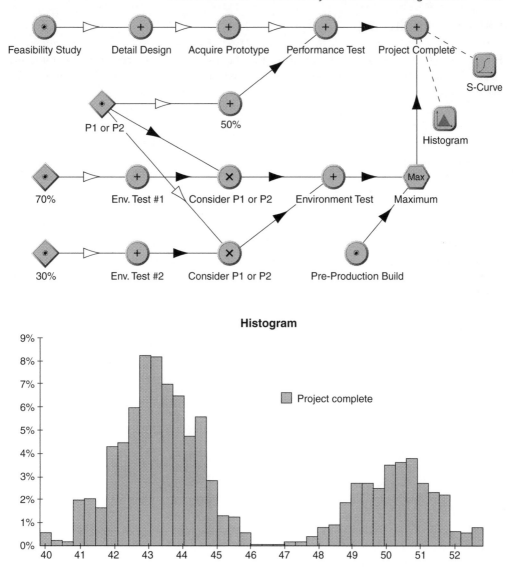

Figure 11.12 Problem formulation using an influence diagram in *(I) Decide*. The problem is exactly the same as that shown in Figure 7.4. Also shown is the result for the end of the project, the bi-modal outcome is generally similar to that derived with *Predict! Risk Analyser* shown in Figure 11.11.

simulation and decision-making products to form an integrated product called *The Decision Tools Suite*. This approach is aimed specifically at the issue of making decisions in uncertain or risk-prone situations such as those involved in major strategic matters like the launch and timing of a new product development project. The intended use of the product is rather different from the risk-tracking, modelling and situation management that is the intent of the suites provided by the two previously mentioned companies.

Contact details for the vendors of all the software mentioned in the book can be found in Appendix II. Examples of some of the software tools are given on the disk accompanying this book.

Overall conclusion

For anyone wishing to purchase software for use in risk analysis and management, the choice is wide although it has been wider as some products that emerged during the last decade have not survived into the new millennium. It must also be said that many of the products were created during the early 1990s and their general operational characteristics and functionality was established by the mid '90s; they have not altered to any great extent during the last five or six years. Where changes have arisen they have tended to be in the field of integration with other systems rather than any significantly new capabilities or methodologies. Other than the use of Bayesian techniques, there is nothing really new in terms of methodology on the horizon so this may well be a subject that is reaching maturity.

Four categories have been identified for classifying packages according to their functionality but that may not be the end of it as other applications may be found and give rise to new categories. One field in which software may have a significant use is training people in the use of risk analysis techniques hence training aids may become a fifth category. At present the distinctions between the categories can be clearly seen in contemporary software; some products can span two categories but none is capable of working in all four. Fundamental differences exist between the types of problem that the software in each of the four categories attempts to solve and this is reflected in the differences of approach that each takes. One may conclude that an all-embracing risk analysis and management software tool is still some distance away, if it ever emerges.

Terms used in the discussion and description of risk analysis and management

Given below are a set of definitions for the terms that are frequently used when risk analysis and management is either described or discussed. These definitions follow the commonly understood meanings of the words rather than attempting to associate any special meaning with them in the context of project risk management except were indicated.

Acceptance (of risk) – 1 choosing an approach that does nothing about a risk other than to note its existence. 2 Choosing an approach in which risks are known to exist.

Action – the process of doing something.

Activity – the state of being in action, alternatively, an action; in the context of a project – a step taken or function performed, either mental or physical, toward achieving some objective of a project.

Assumption – that which is taken to be true without proof.

Attribute – a particular characteristic or property; in the context of a project, its attributes may include functionality, cost, schedule, risk or any other associated characteristic.

Average – common parlance: typical; mathematical: the result obtained by adding a series of values and dividing by the number of values taken, the **Mean**.

Avoidance (of risk) – choosing a course of action in which the risk is not encountered.

Bayes' Theorem – mathematical theorem that gives the resulting probability of an event occurring when an initial belief about the probability of the event occurring is combined with some later observed information.

Benefit – something that gives rise to an advantage or results in something of value.

Brainstorming – a group process designed to produce a large number of ideas in a short space of time.

Cause – something that produces a particular effect or outcome.

Causal chain – the string of causes that leads to a particular outcome.

Central Limit Theorem – mathematical theorem that states that the mean of a sample drawn from any distribution of a variable will always be normally distributed.

Chance – the state of being undesigned or unplanned.

Condition – a circumstance or set of circumstances that lead to a particular result.

Conditional probability – a probability value assigned to a variable that is dependent upon some earlier condition arising.

Consequence – the result of some action, event or set of circumstances.

Context – the surrounding non-physical environment in which something exists.

Contingency – something held in reserve for the unknown.

Contingency plan – a plan which includes a reserve or an alternative to be used when and if a deviation from the original plan occurs.

Control – the act of directing; *v.* to direct towards some objective. (Controlling risks, as with any other act of management, includes analysing the existing situation, deciding how to proceed and executing those decisions.)

Controlled interval and memory method – a mathematical process for deriving the probabilities of completing any activity in a project network, subject to variability, using direct calculation from the rules of probability theory.

Critical path (of a project network) – 1) the longest path through the network; 2) the path that governs the overall duration of the project.

Criticality index – a measure of the frequency with which a particular activity appears on the critical path in a Monte Carlo simulation. (Activities with a high criticality index are likely to determine the overall project duration.)

Cruciality index – a measure of the frequency with which a change in duration of an activity coincides with a change in overall project duration in a Monte Carlo simulation. (Activities with a high cruciality index have a direct bearing on the variability of the overall duration.)

Decision – a choice between alternatives.

Decision theory – the mathematical treatment of the problem of choice between alternatives.

Decision tree – a pictorial (tree-like) representation of the alternatives and outcomes in a decision situation.

Distribution – common parlance: the process of handing out; mathematical: the numerical description of the scattering of the value of a variable. (In some cases the pattern of the scatter can be described in mathematical terms with a formula, for example, the Normal distribution.)

Effectiveness – a measure of how well an action meets its intended requirements.

Expected value – mathematical: the average value of a variable, subject to probabilistic variation, that will arise over the long term, or many repetitions. (In mathematical terms, it is the value of the variable multiplied by the probability of occurrence, the expected value is not what is expected on a particular occasion.)

Fate – 1) that which is ordained to happen; 2) inevitable fortune; 3) destiny.

Game – common parlance: a sporting or amusing activity involving one, two or more players, mathematical: a structured problem involving choices between courses of action, in a competitive situation, leading to a particular objective.

Games theory – the mathematical treatment of the solution to game problems, devised by J. von Neumann and O. Morgenstern.

Hazard – risks to the person, mental or physical, that form a part of life.

Impact – the resulting effect on some entity or system of an action or event; in the context of project risk – the practical effect on the organization, project or operation if a risk materializes.

Influence – *n.* an effect; *v.* to have an effect on some person or thing.

Influence diagram – a pictorial representation of the logic and sequence with which a set of variables have an effect on each other.

Insurance – an arrangement where payments are made in exchange for which an appropriate sum will be paid if a risk materializes.

Insurable risk – risk that can be covered by an insurance policy.

Latin hypercube sampling – a sampling method applied to Monte Carlo simulation in which the values are sampled in quantities that are in relation to their relative frequencies.

Life cycle – the sequence of activities and events that begins when a product or system is conceived and ends when it expires or is no longer available for use.

Likelihood – the scale of opportunity for something to happen.

Luck – 1) the chance of something happening; 2) fortune.

Maturity level – the degree to which a system has achieved its ultimate potential or development.

Mean – mathematical: the average value of a set of variables.

Median – mathematical: the value of a distributed variable that divides the distribution into two groups of equal probability (that is to say half are above the value and half are below).

Method – a way of performing a task to arrive at a desired result.

Methodology – a grouping of methods that defines an overall approach to a particular process or solution to a particular problem.

Metric – a quantitative measure of some aspect of a system, component or process.

Mitigation – the act of reducing the severity of a risk impact (mitigation tends to have an 'after the fact' connotation, that is, in the context of a risk, mitigation can be applied after the risk has materialized).

Mitigation costs – those costs directly associated with mitigating specific risks to the project, that is, the cost of carrying out the mitigation plan.

Mitigation plan – a plan of action for risks that are to be mitigated in the event of the risk materializing.

Mode – mathematical: the value of a distributed variable that occurs with the greatest frequency.

Monte Carlo simulation – a mathematical process for describing the behaviour of a dynamic system subject to variability, using values drawn at random to represent the effect of chance.

Network (project plan) – a pictorial representation using arcs and nodes of the logic and sequence of the activities in a project.

Normal distribution – a mathematically derived set of probabilities that describes the random propagation of an effect, that is centred on a particular value, through a population subject to that effect (sometimes referred to as the **Gaussian** distribution).

Opportunity – 1) a combination of circumstances that favours a particular outcome; 2) a chance, if taken, for gain.

Outcome – the end result of some process.

PERT – acronym for Project Evaluation and Review Technique, a 1950's developed technique for planning and evaluating projects which attempted to replicate the effect of variability by using three estimates of each duration.

Possibility – something that has the potential for turning into a reality.

Preventive action (of risk) – an action aimed at stopping the risk materializing.

Probability – common parlance: an implied expectation that something will occur; mathematical: the ratio of the number of the particular case to the total number of possible cases in a situation of uncertainty, for example, an event which occurs on one occasion in four possible occasions has a probability of occurrence of 0.25 (25%).

Probability theory – mathematical treatment of the way in which uncertain variables interact to produce specific outcomes and their respective probabilities.

Process – a set or sequence of activities that leads to some defined end-result.

Project – an undertaking that is directed towards the accomplishment of a unique end-goal.

Qualitative assessment – the process of considering the characteristics of a situation using only language and without making use of numerical scores.

Quantitative assessment – the process of considering the characteristics of a situation using numerical methods.

Risk – common parlance: an opportunity for exposure to adverse consequences; in the context of a project: a deviation from that which is expected or planned that, should it occur at some future time, will have an adverse effect on the project's operations, objectives, goals or expectations.

Risk assessment – the process of identifying, analysing and prioritizing risks.

Risk control – the process of taking action to limit the effect of a risk, either by reducing the probability of its occurrence or by minimizing the impact.

Risk exposure – the degree to which the risk taker could be affected by an adverse outcome.

Risk identification – a process of establishing the risks to which a project is exposed.

Risk-management (of a project) – the process of acting upon perceived risks in such a way as to preserve the project's objectives.

Risk management plan – 1) a document which sets out the approach required to incorporate the risk management process into a project or organization, 2) a document which sets out the general approach to how risks will be identified and dealt with.

Risk manager (in a project) – one who is put in overall charge of matters connected with risks, or certain aspects, of risks on a project. (A risk manager may not have overall responsibility for risk decision-making).

Risk monitoring – the process of observing the state of the identified risks (also called risk tracking).

Risk owner (in a project) – one who has special responsibility for dealing with a particular risk issue.

Risk planning – the development of strategies and tactics for dealing with risks before or in the event of the risk materializing.

Risk prioritization – the ordering or ranking of risks on some basis, typically severity or urgency.

Sensitivity analysis – the technique of assessing the degree to which small changes in conditions or other parameters affect the final outcome of a process.

Simulation – a process by which some dynamic aspect of a system is replicated but without achieving reality.

Standard deviation – a measure of the range (or spread) and grouping of values of a distributed variable, (Mathematically it is the square root of the Variance).

State of nature – the situation that actually arises, over which we have no control. (It is used in decision theory to depict events due to chance. For example, a test can result in one of two states of nature: either a pass or a failure, but we cannot know which until the test is carried out.)

Strategy – military: 1) the art of disposing ones forces so as to engage the enemy on favourable terms; 2) the long-term, overall plan to defeat the enemy.

Strategy – business, decision theory: the rule for making the best decisions in an uncertain situation; business, general management: 1) the overall approach to the conduct of a project or business; 2) the long-term plan aimed at securing a favourable position or outcome.

Tactics – military: the art of directing one's troops, ships or aircraft on the battlefield; business: 1) the approach to managing day-to-day activities; 2) operations in the short term.

Task – an activity within a project directed at some defined end.

Transfer (of risk) – the process of handing the responsibility for the handling and consequences of a risk to another party.

Treatment (of risk) – the process of dealing with a risk

Uncertainty – a state of incomplete knowledge about a proposition

Variance – common parlance: the difference between the observed value of a variable and the anticipated value; mathematical: the mean square difference between the value of all the observed variables and the mean (average) of the variables. (It is a measure of the spread and grouping of the distribution of a variable.)

▮▮ Software products and vendors

Product title	Vendor	Tel/Fax	Web site/E-mail
ARM (Active Risk Manager)	Strategic Thought Ltd The Old Town Hall 4 Queens Road London SW19 8YA	Tel (44) 020 84104000 Fax (44) 02084104030	www.strategicthought.com Info@strategicthought.com
Artemis Views	Artemis International Solutions Corporation 268 Bath Road Slough Berks SL1 4DX	Tel (44) 01753 727100 Fax (44) 01753 727099	www.aisc.com Greg.jarvis@uk.aisc.com
	Artemis International Solutions Corporation 4041 MacArthur Boulevard Suite 260 Newport Beach CA 92660	Tel (001) 800 477 6648 Fax (001) 949 660 7020	www.aisc.com Greg.jarvis@uk.aisc.com
DPL	Standard and Poor's Applied Decision Analysis 68 Willow Road Menlo Park CA 94025	Tel (001) 650 688 8600 Fax (001) 650 688 8610	www. adainc.com
Expert Choice	Expert Choice Inc. 1501 Lee Highway. Suite 302 Arlington VA 22209	Tel (001) 703 243 5595 Fax (001) 703 243 5587	www.expertchoice.com info@expertchoice.com
(I) Decide	Decisive Tools LLC PO Box 101673 Denver CO 80250–1673	Tel/Fax (001) 800 7329414	www.decisivetools.com sales@decisivetools.com
Microsoft Project Microsoft Office	Microsoft – MSM Microsoft House 10 Great Pulteney Street London W1R 3DG	Tel (44) 0870 6010100 Fax (44) 0207 4346555	www.microsoft.com

Product title	Vendor	Tel/Fax	Web site/E-mail
	Microsoft Camapus Thames Valley Park Reading RD6 1WG		
OpenPlan Professional	Welcom 26/28 Church Road Welwyn Garden City Herts AL8 6PW	Tel (44) 01707 331231 Fax (44) 01707 330187	www.welcom.com uk-sales@welcom.com
	Welcom 15995 N. Barkers Landing Rd. Suite 350 Houston TX 77079	Tel (001) 281 558 0514 Fax (001) 281 584 7828	www.welcom.com sales@ welcom.com
Pertmaster Project Risk	Pertmaster Ltd. Epworth House City Road London EC1Y 1AA	Tel (44) 020 79720514 Fax (44) 020 79720522	www.pertmaster.com software@pertmaster. com
Predict! Risk Analyser Predict! Risk Controller	Risk Decisions Buchan House Parkway Court Oxford Business Park South Oxford OX4 2JY	Tel (44) 01865 718666 Fax (44) 01865 716600	www.riskdecisions.co.uk enquiries@riskdecisions. co.uk
Primavera Project Planner	Primavera Systems Inc. 2nd Floor Commonwealth House 2 Chalkhill Road London W6 8DW	Tel (44) 020 85635500 Fax (44) 020 85635533	www.primavera.com sales@primavera.com
	Primavera Systems Inc. Three Bala Plaza West Bala Cynwyd PA 19004	Tel (001) 610 667 8600 Fax (001) 610 667 7894	www. primavera.com sales@primavera.com
Project Risk for Windows	Niku Ltd. Ziggurat Grosvenor Road St Albans Herts AL1 3DL	Tel (44) 01727 888000 Fax (44) 01727 888100	www.uk.niku.com

Product title	Vendor	Tel/Fax	Web site/E-mail
REMIS TDRM	HVR Consulting Services Ltd. Selborne House Mill Lane Alton Hants GU34 2QJ	Tel (44) 01420 87977 Fax (44) 01420 89819	www.hvr-csl.co.uk www.RiskTools.co.uk www.HVRGroup.com productinfo@hvr-csl. co.uk
@Risk @Risk for Project Precision Tree Decision Tools Suite	Palisade Europe The Blue House Unit 1 30 Calvin St. London E1 6NW	Tel (44) 0207 4269950 Fax (44) 0375 1229	www.palisade.com info@palisade.com
	Palisade Corporation 31 Decker Road Newfield NY 14867	Tel (001) 607 277 8000 Fax (001) 697 277 8001	www.palisade.com info@palisade.com
Risk+	C/S Solutions 2180 S Loudoun St. No 290, Winchester VA 22601-3615	Tel (001) 540 877 2900	www.cs-solutions.com info@cs-solutions.com
RisGen	Line International Ltd. Avon House Avon Mill Lane Keynsham Bristol BS31 2UG	Tel (44) 0117 9862194 Fax (44) 0117 9862204	www.lineint.com www.ris3.com Info@ris3.com
STRAD	Stradspan Ltd. 17 Birks Wood Drive Oughtibridge Sheffield S35 0HY	Tel/Fax (44) 0114 2863662	www.stradspan.com jfreind@btinternet.com
WinAward	Bayesian Systems Inc. 8310 Montgomery Village Avenue, Suite 615 Gaithersburg MD 20879	Tel (001) 301 987 5400 Fax (001) 301 987 9387	www.bayes.com helpdesk@bayes.com

Note

This listing was up-to-date at the time of writing, September 2003. Both product names and vendors' details can and do change from time to time hence this information may no longer be correct by the time you read this.

■ ■ ■ *Software products on the CD-ROM*

Listed below are the products on the disc that accompanies this book. Inserting the disc will reveal a page showing the products on the disc; selecting a product will reveal a page with more details and buttons that will either allow the demonstration to run or start a product installation process onto the hard drive. Once installed, the products can be run in the normal way. Note that some products are fully functional but time-limited, others are unlimited in time but reduced-capability demonstration and evaluation versions while others are 'walk-through' demonstrations with no functional capability. For help and information with any of these products contact the vendors through the details given in Appendix 2 or shown on the appropriate page on the disc.

Expert Choice 2000 from Expert Choice Inc.

Based on the Analytic Hierarchy Process, EC 2000 2nd Edition for Groups provides an easy-to-use approach to guide a decision maker through the process of: i) Structuring the decision into objectives and alternatives, ii) Assessing the objectives and alternatives using pairwise comparisons, iii) Synthesizing objective and subjective inputs to arrive at a prioritized list of alternatives, and iv) Managing the final decision with documentation, reporting and sensitivity analysis capability.

For installation the serial number is:-

I0001-90700-001B0-29B0F-0AA18-35323

The demonstration version is fully functional but limited to 15 days use from installation; this may be extended on application to the vendor. The program contains tutorials if you wish to build a decision model. To see some problems evaluated using Expert Choice do the following: from the initial Welcom screen select Open Existing Models and Samples then select from a range of decision models displayed. The model behind the result shown in Chapter 11, Figure 11.5 can be located on the CD under the directory labeled Expert Choice.

(I) Decide 2000 from Decisive Tools, LLC

(I) Decide is a decision/risk analysis program that allows the user to build influence diagrams in a straightforward way to represent a particular situation then run a Monte Carlo analysis. Many charts and graphs are generated to help with interpreting the results. It can work with Excel but is primarily a stand-alone application.

The demonstration version includes online help, tutorial and samples. It includes a viewer application which allows users to modify data items but not change the structure of the model. The problem given in Chapter 7, Figure 7.4 and shown in Chapter 11, Figure 11.12 is included in the file named 'product development project.mcr'.

After program selection install the Demo License version. It is fully functional but limited to 30 days use from installation, this may be extended on application to the vendor.

Pertmaster from Pertmaster Ltd.

Pertmaster Project Risk is a modelling tool used to identify project risks and quantify the chance of completing a project on time and budget. It uses Monte Carlo simulation and includes calculation of criticality indices, probabilistic and conditional branching, task existence risk and sensitivity analysis to help model and identify key activities that are likely to delay the project. Pertmaster can run as a stand-alone risk system or as a risk 'add-on' to all versions of Primavera scheduling software and all versions of Microsoft Project. An example of an integrated time and cost simulation of a product development project with similar characteristics to that shown in Chapter 7 Figure 7.4 is given in the file named 'product Development.pln' in the Samples folder.

The evaluation version supplied is fully functional but is limited to analysing networks of 25 or less activities. Tutorials are included in the help system.

Predict! Risk Analyser from Risk Decisions Ltd.

Predict! Risk Analyser, is a quantitative schedule and cost risk analysis tool that uses the Monte Carlo simulation method. It applies 3-point estimates and uncertainty data to produce the aggregate confidence levels for both cost and delivery dates and to indicate key drivers of the project milestones and budgets, thus improving overall project decision making. When integrated into an Earned Value Management (EVM) process, Risk Analyser helps deliver a broader and more robust picture of a programme than EVM alone. It is fully integrated with Predict! Risk Controller.

The problem given in Chapter 7, Figure 7.4 and shown in Chapter 11, Figure 11.11 is included in the Examples section. In addition to the time relationships, a costing of all the activities in this simulated project is given in a separate but associated sheet. To view the Risk Analyser solution to this problem go to File, Open, Examples and select DEVPROJ3; to ensure you can see all the sheets and reports select Window, Cascade then open the spreadsheets and report views as required. As this is a functional version you can create more reports and analyses. However, functionality is limited as it cannot save or print files but it contains all the features hence it can be used for experimentation, demonstration and evaluation.

REMIS from HVR Consulting Services Ltd.

HVR's REMIS risk management database software is a packaged solution to the identification, assessment and management of risks. Using the power of a relational database, risk information can be recorded and tracked in a register at every stage of the project or business lifecycle. Clear outputs provide detailed analysis of risk exposure allowing users to actively manage risk through informed decision making.

The version on the disc is not a working copy of REMIS but a flash demonstration product that shows all its features. It can be run directly from the disc or be installed in a directory of your own choice.

RisGen from Line International Ltd.

RisGen is an enterprise risk management solution using a risk register that organizes and communicates all risks aligned to the project or enterprise objectives. It has evolved from the 6-phase approach implemented in the original Ris3 tool (which supported risk management in a single project), into a web based corporate system, which meets all current risk and compliance management requirements. It is applicable through the complete range from the smallest project to a full enterprise wide corporate governance solution.

The software provided on the disc is a flash demonstration of Line International and RisGen's capabilities, there is a spoken commentary for those with audio capability. It can be run directly from the disc.

STRAD from Stradspan Ltd

STRAD is a software package that offers flexible decision making support to managers and informal planning groups. Its unique capability is to enable users to chart a more confident course through a tangle of tough decisions, while contending with fast-moving events and daunting uncertainties, whether technical, political or managerial.

The disc copy is a restricted use version that includes an introductory section responding to frequently asked questions, a tour of the principles behind the software and a 'try STRAD' option that enables the user to gain hands-on experience in applying STRAD to any one of eight demonstration project files. The projects relate to a variety of realistic problem situations drawn from experience in business, consulting and the public sector.

TDRM from HVR Consulting Services

TDRM is a high-level risk evaluation tool using a knowledge base that provides management with information during the bidding and conceptual stages of projects when little detail is known. It involves a question and answer approach that builds a risk assessment of the project in four key areas. This assessment can be used to assist in the bid/no bid decision and to identify if further investigation and analysis is desirable for those bids or projects which show a significant level of overall risk.

The version on the disc is not a working copy of TDRM but a flash demonstration product that shows all its features. It can be run directly from the disc or installed in a directory of your own choice.

Whereas every effort has been made to ensure that the software contained on this disc is compatible with Windows equipped machines, we cannot guarantee that all the above packages will work satisfactorily under all machine configurations. In the event of problems with a particular product it is suggested that the reader should contact the software vendor.

Index

Purchasing Scams and How to Avoid Them
Trevor Kitching
0 566 08281 0

Credit Management Handbook 4ed
Burt Edwards
0 566 07904 6

Handbook of Financial Planning and Control 3ed
edited by Robert P. Greenwood
0 566 08372 8

Handbook of International Credit Management 3ed
Brian W. Clarke
0 566 08376 0

**Activity Based Management:
Improving Processes and Profitability**
Brian Plowman
0 566 08145 8

The Gower Handbook of Management 4ed
edited by Dennis Lock
0 566 07938 0

Statistical Sampling and Risk Analysis in Auditing
Peter Jones
0 566 08080 X

For further information on these and all our titles visit
our website – **www.gowerpub.com**
All online orders receive a discount

GOWER

**Presentation Planning and Media Relations for the
Pharmaceutical Industry**
John Lidstone
0 566 08536 4

Using the PC to Boost Executive Performance
Monica Seeley
0 566 08110 5

The 'How To' Guide for Managers
John Payne and Shirley Payne
0 566 07726 4

**Managerial Consulting Skills
A Practical Guide 2ed**
Charles J. Margerison
0 566 08292 6

**Creating a Thinking Organization
Groundrules for Success**
Rikki Hunt with Tony Buzan
0 566 08230 6

Guide to Internal Communication Methods
Eileen Scholes on behalf of ITEM
0 566 08217 9

Gower Handbook of Management Skills 3ed
Ed by Dorothy M. Stewart
0 566 07889 9

Proven Management Models
Sue Harding and Trevor Long
0 566 07674 8

GOWER

John Clare's Guide to Media Handling
John Clare
0 566 08298 5

Making the Connections
Using Internal Communication to Turn Strategy into
Action
Bill Quirke
0 566 08175 X

How to Measure Customer Satisfaction 2ed
Nigel Hill, John Brierley and Rob MacDougall
0 566 08595 X

The Goal
A Process of Ongoing Improvement 2ed
Eliyahu M. Goldratt and Jeff Cox
0 566 07418 4

Benchmarking
Sylvia Codling
0 566 07926 7

The New Guide to Identity
How to Create and Sustain Change Through Managing
Identity
Wolff Olins
0 566 07737 X

It's Not Luck
Eliyahu M. Goldratt
0 566 07627 6

GOWER

Design for Six Sigma:
Launching New Products and Services Without Failure
Geoff Tennant
0 566 08434 1

Gower Handbook of Quality Management 3ed
edited by Matt Seaver
0 566 08149 0

Six Sigma: SPC and TQM in Manufacturing and Services
Geoff Tennant
0 566 08374 4

Design for Six Sigma:
Launching New Products and Services Without Failure
Geoff Tennant
0 566 08434 1

Implementing ISO 9000:2000
Matt Seaver
0 566 08373 6

The Quality Audit for ISO 9001:2000:
A Practical Guide
David Wealleans
0 566 08245 4

eCommerce: A Practical Guide to the Law
Susan Singleton
0 566 08515 1

Quality Costing 3ed
Barrie G. Dale and J.J. Plunkett
0 566 08260 8

GOWER

Security Manual 7ed
John Wilson and David Brooksbank
0 566 08174 1

Corporate Fraud 3ed
Michael J. Comer
0 566 07810 4

Investigating Corporate Fraud
Michael J. Comer
0 566 08531 3

Statistical Sampling and Risk Analysis in Auditing
Peter Jones
0 566 08080 X

Managing Communications in a Crisis
Peter Ruff and Khalid Aziz
0 566 08294 2

**How to Keep Operating in a Crisis:
Managing a Business in a Major Catastrophe**
James Callan
0 566 08523 2

Fire Precautions: A Guide for Management
Colin S. Todd
0 566 08182 2

For further information on these and all our titles visit
our website – **www.gowerpub.com**
All online orders receive a discount

GOWER

Join our email newsletter

Gower is widely recognized as one of the world's leading publishers on management and business practice. Its programmes range from 1000-page handbooks through practical manuals to popular paperbacks. These cover all the main functions of management: human resource development, sales and marketing, project management, finance, etc. Gower also produces training videos and activities manuals on a wide range of management skills.

As our list is constantly developing you may find it difficult to keep abreast of new titles. With this in mind we offer a free email news service, approximately once every two months, which provides a brief overview of the most recent titles and links into our catalogue, should you wish to read more or see sample pages.

To sign up to this service, send your request via email to **info@gowerpub.com**. Please put your email address in the body of the email as confirmation of your agreement to receive information in this way.

GOWER